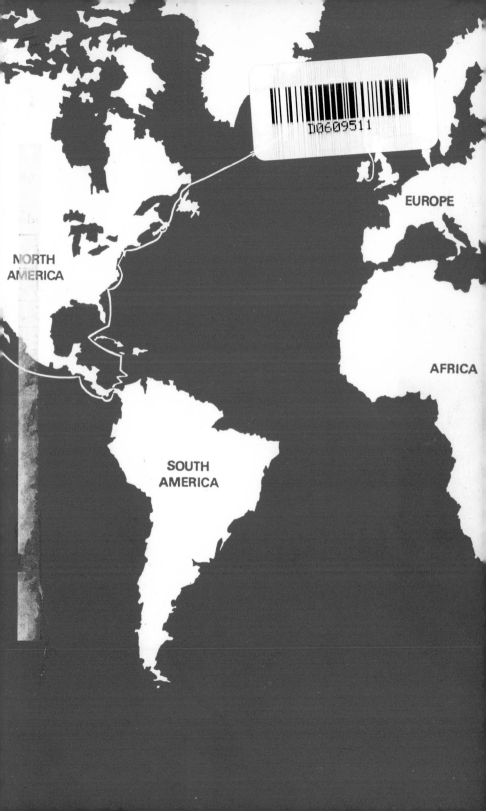

NORTH
AMERICA

EUROPE

AFRICA

SOUTH
AMERICA

D0609511

MILES SMEETON

The
Misty Islands

*'From the lone shieling of the misty island
Mountains divide us and the waste of seas'*

NAUTICAL PUBLISHING COMPANY

K. ADLARD COLES   COMMANDER ERROLL BRUCE RN (RTD)

Captain's Row · Lymington · Hants

in association with

GEORGE G. HARRAP & COMPANY LTD

London · Toronto · Wellington · Sydney

© MILES SMEETON

SBN 245 5 96437

First published 1969 by
NAUTICAL PUBLISHING COMPANY
Captain's Row, Lymington, Hampshire

Composed in 11 on 12 pt Monotype Baskerville
and made and printed in Great Britain by
THE CAMELOT PRESS LIMITED
LONDON AND SOUTHAMPTON

To all Tzu Hang's friends
in many parts of the world

Contents

Contents

Maps and Illustrations

1 *Tzu Hang* arrives in Japan

When *Tzu Hang* anchored outside the breakwater at Kago-shima, at the southern end of Japan, it was like being suspended in space between two worlds. Behind us was the long restless passage from South Africa; ahead was Japan, with whatever pleasures or frustrations it might have in store for us. For me all would be new, but Beryl had been there before, years ago, before the war, before we were married, an unshared experience.

The sun went down and the shrill bird calls of bos'n's pipes twittered across the water from the three Japanese frigates that shared our anchorage. For a few moments the smoke from Sakurai Jima, the volcano above us, glowed redly. Then lights began to shine from the ports and galley doors of the small ships anchored round us.

'What about a drink?' Beryl asked.

Every night at sea, at about the time of sunset, we have a drink, and it would have to be bad weather or an empty locker before we would forgo it. I find myself looking forward to that drink as if I were an alcoholic. We have one drink only, a vermouth for Beryl, a gin for me, or if rum is in the locker our favourite tipple is a rum sour, made with fresh limes or lemons. This, and a glass of wine for lunch and another for supper, helps to compensate for the discomfort of a small ship at sea. Tonight, however, was a night to be celebrated with an extra drink before dinner, for we were at anchor; we had arrived.

Our dinner was out of a tin, both meat and fruit, helped by a Californian Burgundy from a case that we had bought in Okinawa, and during it we talked about the future.

'I think we should spend a year in Japan, and not hurry on to Canada,' said Beryl, 'then we could really see something of the

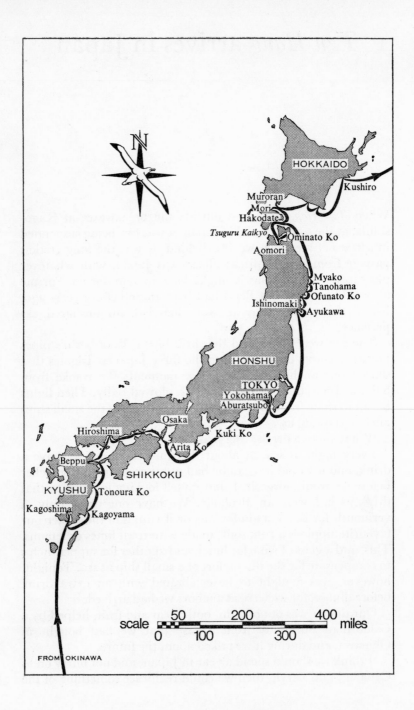

country. Perhaps we could get a house somewhere for the winter.'

It was March now. One of the difficulties about visiting Japan in a small ship is that there is only a limited period free from the danger of typhoons. In the south the best months for arriving are January to March; in the north, where winter conditions prevail till the end of March, the best time for leaving is May and June. We could therefore have gone straight on up the coast of Japan, but it would only have given us time for one or two short stops before we set out on the long crossing to Attu, the westernmost of the Aleutian Islands. We had talked about all this on our crossing from the Philippines, but now on this first night of our arrival nebulous plans for the future began to take a positive and immediate shape.

'If we are going to spend the winter here, let's go and spend it in Hokkaido,' I said. 'I long to see some snow again.'

'Yes,' Beryl agreed, 'then we could really see something of Japan.' Her thoughts turned to our daughter in London. 'Then we could get Clio out. If we're going to spend so long in Japan, she ought to see something of it too—besides, we are going to need an extra hand for the Aleutian journey.'

'Perhaps if I find my General and give him back his sword, he will help us to find a house,' I said. 'He might even have a house in Hokkaido, but I don't expect that he'd stay there for the winter.'

The sword was one that had been surrendered to me at the end of the Burma campaign. We had brought it out in *Tzu Hang* with the intention of restoring it to its owner. Perhaps the second cocktail and the wine were having effect on me. I imagined myself returning the treasured sword to the General, living in his baronial hall. Of course he would have a house in Hokkaido. Perhaps there would be horses there. An old comfortable farmhouse with dark wooden walls hung with Japanese paintings and a charcoal fire glowing in the *hibachi* in a well in the middle of the floor. Beryl had described the *hibachi* to me. Then there would be silent and attentive servants longing for work to do to pass the monotonous winter months until the General's return in the spring. Only a hint and he would offer the house to us. *Tzu Hang* no doubt could be safely hauled ashore in some nearby port, and Beryl would find herself a pet carpenter so that all kinds of wonderful work might be done on *Tzu Hang*. My thoughts leapt ahead until I was brought back to earth by her suggestion that it was time to wash up.

While we did this the planning continued, but on a less exalted plane. We decided that we would spend only a day or two in Kagoshima, in order to get our mail and buy some stores, and that then we'd take *Tzu Hang* off to some small place nearby where we could relax and enjoy ourselves. It had been a hard thrash to windward coming up from the Philippines and both Beryl and I, and *Tzu Hang*, were ready for a rest. We turned in early, short of sleep since we had both been up almost the whole of the night before, beating up through the Kagoshima Kaiwan in cold squalls of rain. For the time being, Pwe, the Siamese cat, remained on deck listening to the sounds from the shore. She wasn't short of sleep at all.

Three hours later—the time for my watch if I had been at sea—I was wide awake again. Beryl was lying in the other bunk, curled up, because it was still cold, with the cat behind her knees. I heard her move.

'Are you awake?' I asked.

'Yes,' she said, 'I was thinking.'

I wondered what she was thinking about. Was she building her castles? Was she thinking about a house in Canada, or was she thinking that if we got there we might as well go on to England in order to complete an east-about passage round the world? I didn't ask her. We had to get back to Canada first.

'I was thinking that we'd get a bath tomorrow,' she said sleepily.

Tzu Hang stirred comfortably in the light swell. The wavelets slapped against her side and the chain gave a rumble as the tide shifted her. Often she reminds me of a horse. A horse asking to be allowed to gallop on; a horse gathering himself for a jump, and now a horse in stable after a long day. These were stable noises; like the munching of hay, and the rustle of clean bony legs in deep straw.

'Well, here you are,' she seemed to say, 'I carried you all right, didn't I?'

From where I lay I could look aft through the main cabin, to where the galley light was burning. At sea we always kept the galley light burning although not usually in port. It is an old-fashioned oil lamp in gimbals, shedding a dim light on pots and pans and the odds and ends that go to make a home ashore or at sea. The water was squelching along the breakwater wall, and from time to time I looked through the port at my side to see that we were not swinging too close to the anchored ships. Presently I fell asleep again.

Soon after breakfast next morning a harbour launch laid alongside, manned by sailors in grey fatigues and wearing white peaked caps, which did not fit close to the head but were perched on top, as if they had arrived there by chance. They were the coastguard, the *Kaijōhowancho*. They had brought a doctor and a Customs officer, and with the minimum of difficulty and, to our relief, no mention of quarantine for cats, we were cleared for entry. They told us to tie up to a small passenger steamer at the wharf below the Customs Office. I left Beryl on board and climbed up a steep iron ladder to the top of the wharf. A crowd had gathered.

'Immigration Office?' I asked brightly, and then, surrounded by looks of absolute incomprehension, set out to find it by myself.

When I returned and looked down from the quay on to *Tzu Hang*'s deck it seemed as if all the passengers from the steamer to which we were tied were now on board. The coastguards were keeping a ring around Beryl, their white caps showing like daisy petals with Beryl's fair head as the centre. The petals withdrew and advanced in response to her gestures, and although she then spoke hardly a word of Japanese, she seemed to be carrying on a conversation with her usual talent.

'The coastguards say that we had better move up alongside their ship farther up the harbour, Number 136,' she called up to me, as I climbed down.

'Let's go then,' I said, 'we're all clear with Immigration.' The visitors were hustled off, and with several of the coast-guards still on board, all of whom took turns to steer, we moved up the harbour. Number 136 was a white cutter mounting a small gun forward and very smart. An electric light connection and a water hose were passed down to us.

'We will look after you,' they said, and thereafter in any major port this is exactly what they did. They were hospitable, efficient, and friendly. When I am asked what made the biggest impression on me in Japan, I reply that it was the *Kaijōhowancho*.

In the afternoon we were taken to the Fuji Bank by a surprised passer-by who was shanghaied by a Customs officer for this task. The Fuji Bank is in a new building—new like most buildings of any importance in Japan, for the majority of the old ones were destroyed during the war. They stand like islands in a dreary sea of mediocre housing, which looks as if it had been rebuilt from rubble to provide temporary shelter, and yet has an ominous menace of permanence. There is something unbelievably dull about most Japanese cities.

Behind the long counter a number of girls were sitting at their regimented desks, their heads lowered over the various machines that do a bank's business. Their strong little hands and busy short fingers slipped up and down the typewriter keys. Bright eyes, demure, inquisitive or mischievous, glanced towards us from under tall headdresses of black hair. At first glance they looked like a classroom of guardsmen.

'Can I help you?' asked Mr Myake, holding in his hand a Japanese–English phrase-book for bank employees when dealing with English-speaking customers. He shone with cleanliness and hair cream as he sorted out some mail for us with well-manicured hands. Beryl and I became conscious of our own rope-worn fingers and broken nails.

'Can you tell us where we can have a bath? We must have a bath,' she ended on a note of desperation, afflicted now that she was onshore by a sudden compunction for cleanliness.

Mr Myake looked anxiously round the bank as if seeking a bathroom door. This was something that the phrase-book had not dealt with.

'I'm afraid there is nothing suitable here,' he replied.

'But there must be some public baths,' said Beryl. 'An *Ofuru*?' she asked, delving into the memory of her first visit.

'Do you mind?' he asked, because the Japanese are often reluctant to recommend the public bath to foreigners. 'But I think not very suitable,' he added. 'Please come later to my house. Japanese-style bath. Very small house and later we have dinner. I fetch you after work finished, say five o'clock.'

In this case the very small house was not mere modesty on

the part of Mr Myake. It was in fact the smallest of small houses, a little wooden shack in a stony street of wooden shacks on the outskirts of the town. I felt as if I was in a dolls' house, but not the usual dolls' house which looks rather roomy in relation to the size of the dolls. In this house the accessories of living had taken over most of the available space. We sat on the *tatami*, the grass mats, so sweet-smelling, that make the floor of most Japanese rooms. In the centre of the room there was a hole, where the charcoal stove—the *hibachi*—usually stands, but where there now glowed an electric heater. Attached to its wiring there were a number of plug-in connections, so that it was impossible to stretch a cramped leg without putting out the television set, a standing lamp, or the electric kettle.

We took it in turns to have our bath in a small wooden tub in a screened alcove shrouded in baby linen. This was just across the passage and it was almost impossible to dress without obtruding some part of one's anatomy into the living-room. Those seated there almost shared the bath, the scrubbing and splashing as the occupant washed, sitting on a little stool beside the tub, the puffs and groans as he inserted himself knees-to-chin in the boiling water, and the lobster-like silence as he stewed.

While we were having dinner Mrs Myake flitted like a butterfly through the foliage of electric wires, coat-hangers, and the baby's cot, to alight for a moment, wings a-quiver, between us, to press us to more food, her little face shining at the pleasure of entertaining.

Back on board we had just got into our bunks when we heard a tapping on the deck and an anxious voice calling.

'Hallo, hallo. Are you still awake please?' It was Mr Myake, who had just dropped us an hour before. As we pulled on our clothes we wondered what on earth could have brought him back again.

'Have you heard the radio?' he asked breathlessly. 'There has been a great earthquake in Alaska and they are expecting the tidal wave to reach Japan in an hour's time.'

'We'd better get out,' I said to Beryl. 'No point in getting caught against the wharf like this.'

By the time we were ready to move Mr Myake, who had been talking to the coastguards, was back again.

B

'It's all right now,' he told us. 'The tidal wave has already reached Hokkaido and it is only a foot high. Very sorry.'

Mr Myake went off home in the taxi that he had hired in order to warn us. It had probably cost him a day's pay that he could not very well afford.

Just behind the harbour at Kagoshima there is a hill on which there is a temple. Beryl and I climbed up the hill to see it, following the road. Then, rather than take the same route back, we cut directly down the hill towards the town, down the steep tree-covered hillside, over slippery dead leaves and brambles. The slope grew steeper until it fell away completely in a rocky gorge and watercourse. As we looked doubtfully over this precipice we saw two teenage girls on the road just across from us, behind the railing which guarded the gorge. Their hands were at their mouths in alarm.

'Stay, stay!' one of them cried to us in English, and they both made off up the road and disappeared round the curve, as hard as they could run.

'I think they are coming to rescue us,' said Beryl, laughing. 'Now you've got to let them do something.' We started climbing up the slope but soon there was such a noise of puffing and sliding above us that we stopped and called to let our rescuers know where we were. They slithered down through the dead leaves, both stocky in build. The more articulate one was of pale complexion, her dark hair shining, her cheeks flushed with the excitement; her friend was larger and of coarser features, red-cheeked and with untidy hair.

'Come, come,' cried the pale-faced girl, reaching for Beryl's hand and whisking her away, while her companion slid down towards me. She caught hold of a sapling and reached down to me with the other hand. I took it and she heaved me up the hill; her legs as strong as a pony's, clad in black stockings, and working like pistons as she stomped up through the underbush towards the road. I thought of a cavewoman snatching her man, and found it a pleasurable sensation.

We arrived breathless at the top and they told us that they were schoolgirls on holiday and that they thought we were going to jump over the cliff. As this way of ending troubles is not exceptionally uncommon in Japan we understood their dismay.

'When I see you,' said Beryl's rescuer, 'I thought strange, strange. Dead dead.'

They took us first to the temple, where we clapped our hands and bowed and threw some coins into a table like a letter-box, and then down the hill. They were gay with their adventure and as we went they called to friends whom they passed to tell them that we were Canadian or English and that we were from a boat, and that they had found us on the hill. When I got back to *Tzu Hang* I too thought 'Strange, strange'. So few years ago— only yesterday for me—these people were our enemies.

Sakurai Jima, the big volcano at the head of Kagoshima Kaiwan, sent its rolling smoke clouds over us during our stay, covering *Tzu Hang* and all Kagoshima in a thin layer of grey volcanic dust and mixing with the early morning dew on decks and doghouse, where it made sooty smudges on the white paint. We began to think of leaving and talked to the *Kaijōhowancho* about suitable harbours. At first they protested that we should stay longer, but when we pointed to *Tzu Hang*'s decks they shook their heads sorrowfully and apologized for the dust. We were talking to a group rather than to an individual. They clustered round us in their grey fatigues and white caps, like pigeons round a few grains of corn, their faces changing from intent concentration to sudden comprehension and laughter, as they turned towards one another to discuss their next move. They soon understood that Beryl and I were in need of a few days' peace and seclusion, for this is the aim and the prerogative of the aged in Japan, and they went off in search of charts. When they returned they gave us blueprints of a new survey of two typhoon shelters in the neck of land that connects Sakurai Jima to the north-western shore of the Kaiwan, and a beautiful little chart, drawn on rice paper, of the fishing port of Yamakawa at the entrance to the Kaiwan.

'Will you please give us your itinerary, so that we may keep a lookout for you?' asked their captain. We pleaded that this was too difficult, as weather or fog might make it impossible for us to visit some place that we had intended. He compromised by telling us to report to the nearest harbourmaster should we put in anywhere. Then they cast off our lines and we headed down the harbour and out between the moles.

Sakurai Jima was once an island at the head of Kagoshima

Kaiwan. In one of its major eruptions it had sent such a volume of lava pouring down its eastern slopes that it had bridged the gap between the shores. It was in this isthmus of lava that there were two typhoon shelters, deep natural harbours with narrow rock-bound entrances. We decided to go into the second one, called Tai Sho Wan. *Tzu Hang* followed the hazy shore until we found the entrance, and then crept diffidently between the rocks which guarded the pool and between jagged lava points so close that I could have swung the lead on to either shore.

Inside was a small lagoon, but a lagoon so desolate that we might have been in one of the craters of the moon. There was no vegetation of any sort. Masses of lava and rubble hemmed us in, and at one point a small sulphur stream trickled steaming out of the rocks, and over greasy black stones to the sea. It was possible to get a hot wash there, but the water smelled so strongly of sulphur that it wasn't a pleasant one. Round the shore at regular intervals concrete bollards had been placed to which ships seeking refuge in a typhoon might secure, and above the beach there were a large number of rectangular baskets, as big as *Tzu Hang*'s main cabin.

We had just got our anchor down when there came the stentorian thumping of a single-cylinder diesel engine at the entrance, and a fishing boat came swirling in with the assurance of long practice. It was buried completely in these huge baskets. It ran its bow ashore, off-loaded the baskets on to the beach, reloaded with those that were already there, and then thumped away through the narrow channel. It had not been gone long before we had another visitor. A heavily built boat, that looked as if it had once been a fishing vessel, a large seiner, came ponderously in and anchored in the centre of the lagoon. A diver, wearing his red woollen hat, was sitting in the bow. Soon he was screwed into his helmet and disappeared over the side. A derrick was swung outboard and a wire strop lowered, and presently a large rock was hoisted up and lowered into the hold.

'Now what on earth are they doing that for?' I asked Beryl.

'I suppose they are deepening the anchorage,' she replied.

'And what are the baskets for? I feel like a man from Mars. Everyone seems to be doing things that I haven't seen before and I cannot ask them what they are doing.'

Above us a road ran along the isthmus. We took the dinghy ashore in the evening, scrambled up the lava to the road, and then followed it towards the mainland. On our right was a bay sheltered from all but southerly winds, and in this a long row of baskets were floating, moored and buoyed. As soon as we saw them we understood. They were fish storage baskets. The ones that had been brought in to our lagoon were for repair and had been replaced by the ones that the boat took out, and the diver had been collecting rocks to use as mooring anchors.

Two days later we left for Yamakawa, steering a compass course for all the surrounding hills were shrouded in a blue-grey haze; a thick haze compounded of smoke from Sakurai Jima, of dust from country roads, of the industrial smog that is thickening over Japan, and perhaps a little morning mist—that silver morning mist that cuts out detail and incongruous backgrounds, and brings a special beauty to Japanese paintings, as it did once to their countryside. As we motored across the bay we found ourselves travelling through a thick pink scum on the surface of the water, which smelt strongly of fish oil, and what with the fog and the smell and the pink scum, we began to think that we might as well have been sailing in a tin of herring and tomato sauce, until the fog came and blew all these imaginings away.

Yamakawa is a fishing port and there was a busy coming and going of fishing boats, and an unloading of fish, particularly of tuna, at the fish market. The boats using Yamakawa were generally the larger sea-going types, some of which we had seen as far afield as in the Moçambique Channel. They had a long platform like a bowsprit, used both in fishing and as a means of getting on and off the ship, when moored bow-on to the quay. There were racks of bamboo fishing poles beside the deckhouse, and buoys and marker flags were stacked about the decks. The harbourmaster welcomed us, having been warned of our arrival by the coastguard in Kagoshima. He was a very enthusiastic man, who wore a London police whistle round his neck, a souvenir of a visit to London on a Japanese merchant ship before the war. He would not allow us to leave Yamakawa until we had visited Ibusuki and made a tour by bus of the Nagasaki Promontory, the south-western end of Kyushu. The Harbour Authority, he said, would stand us the cost of the tour.

We must be their guests and he would send one of his men to conduct us.

We started next morning, and while we waited for the bus four girls approached us. They were at college and on holiday, eager, diffident and gay, longing to practise their English on us.

'Where are you going now?' they asked, and when we told them that we were on our way to Ibusuki they quickly decided to accompany us. After a crowded bus ride to the station and even more crowded train journey we arrived there. Our guide led us to the bus station from where the tour was to start. The Japanese are the most dedicated tourists in the world. Every beauty spot, every ancient monument, and every mineral bath receives its daily pilgrimage from students, holiday-makers, and those in search of relief from aches and pains. Great silver buses thunder up to turning areas and disgorge their chattering cargo, nobbly with cameras, lenses, binoculars, and small radios. As they disperse to photograph themselves and their surroundings, the little blue-clad hostesses, with whistles in their lips, help the driver to park his vehicle.

'Peep, peep,' go the whistles, as he reverses, 'Peep, peep.' It has become one of the nostalgic sounds of Japan. Sometimes they stand on the rear step calling to the driver instead.

'Alri, alri, alri,' they call, from the English word that has found its way into the Japanese bus-driver's language.

As we waited for our bus to arrive Beryl and our guide were busy in conversation. Beryl had a book called *Japanese in 36 hours* and our guide had a similar volume called *English in 36 hours*. No doubt there was soon going to be a breakthough, but at the moment they seemed to have a long way to go. The four girls were a great help.

'First we must all assemble for the group photograph,' they told us, and we were soon arrayed with a hundred other adventurers for the official bus photograph, which would be ready for us when we returned.

Then we set off. As we drove through hilly country, where every patch of earth that could be persuaded to stick to a slope was carefully cultivated, our little hostess sang the local songs; a song for the stony shores of Lake Ikeda, a song as we drove round Mount Kaimon, and a song for the lighthouse at Kaimon Saki. She was so eager to entertain us and worked so hard towards that end that we could not help loving her in spite of the squalling loudspeaker. The four girls, who were travelling in another bus, came up to us at each halt, but by now we had met a young university student, who was studying engineering and spoke English well, so that we had no longer to depend on *Japanese in 36 hours* until they arrived.

We got back to Yamakawa in the evening and set off next morning for the Inland Sea.

2 To the Inland Sea

As we sailed out of Yamakawa harbour we heard a series of whistle blasts from the quay and distinguished the harbour-master at its end, blowing on his London police whistle and waving his handkerchief. The red lighthouse that marked the entrance to the harbour soon faded and for the rest of the day and all night we were in fog.

The small lighthouses that usually mark the ends of the breakwaters protecting Japanese harbours are painted red and white, the red being on the starboard hand when entering, and in fog the red one can always be seen first. On the headlands the great lighthouses are usually painted white, or white with a red or a black band or cupola, and are well equipped with directional radio, which sends out a series of long and short dashes that may be picked up on an ordinary radio. By counting the number of short and long dashes, and referring to the appropriate tables, the bearing of the ship from the light is found. They are fine when sailing offshore, but no great help when entering ports on the coast between them.

It was a long time since Beryl and I had sailed in fog, and the watches passed quickly as we listened to the rumble of engines inside and outside, but never exactly on our course. At times the fog receded so that we could not distinguish the limit of our visibility, and at times it hung round us like a shower curtain. By morning it had gone, and we sailed into Tonoura Ko, a fishing harbour half-way up the coast of Kyushu, guarded by islands, reefs, and rocky islets, on which grew twisted pines.

The bay was sheltered enough to allow oyster rigs to be moored there, and it is something to remember that where there are oyster rigs it will usually be safe to leave a yacht at anchor. These were big, bamboo rafts, to which lines were attached, each hung with half a large shell at every foot. The pearl oysters had attached themselves to these shells, and men and women were hauling up the lines and selecting suitable oysters for the insertion of the pearl base. Presently they rowed over to *Tzu Hang* and sat on the deck; while one of them, who was in charge of the operation and spoke English, explained what they were doing. The women wore white cotton towels over their heads, and an apron over a blouse and trousers of a blue cotton pattern; the working dress of all peasant women in Japan. Their fingers were stubby and work-hardened, and the shapeless dress left their figures entirely to the imagination; but their eyes were dark and bright and their cheeks, in spite of their outdoor life, round and smooth. The Japanese working-class women, especially the younger ones, often reminded me of a bundled parcel with an attractive head sticking out, and I wanted to undo it to find out what was inside.

There was no harbourmaster at Tonoura Ko, so we decided to take the bus to Aburatsu, a few miles farther north. We wanted also to do some shopping and were in need of charts. The road followed the coast to Aburatsu, where we found the harbourmaster installed in a fine office, well dressed and affable in a business suit. As soon as we told him who and where we were his look changed to one of anxiety. He spoke English slowly, explaining that he was out of practice.

'It is forbidden for foreign ships to enter anything but Specified Ports,' he said.

Beryl and I knew all about this. It is written as large as life in the Japanese Pilot. 'The position with regard to liberty of anchorage in the ports and territorial waters of Japan, even on account of stress of weather or "force majeure", is different from that obtaining in any other part of the world. The only waters that are freely open to anchorage are the Specified Ports . . .' it says. Aburatsu was not a Specified Port, nor certainly was Tonoura Ko. Never mind. It was only a difficulty to be overcome like a head wind. Now it had occurred.

'But we can't sail only to Specified Ports,' I complained. 'They are big commercial ports like Nagasaki, and there is no place for a yacht to go. Besides we've come ten thousand miles to see Japan, we can't just go to the commercial ports.'

'We don't go very fast,' Beryl added, 'and we have to put in somewhere for a rest. There are only two of us, you see. It would be really dangerous in coastal waters if we could not put into a port when necessary.' Beryl can go for days and nights without a rest when necessary, but dismay grew on the harbourmaster's face. He did not know. There was the advantage that we were talking to an ex-merchant navy captain, and he appreciated the difficulties of handling a yacht in coastal waters with such a short crew.

'It is in the regulations,' he said, 'you should have known all about it. Did they not explain it all to you at Kagoshima?'

'Oh no.' Beryl replied. 'They were so nice to us. They said that we were the first foreign yacht to come to Kagoshima. Perhaps the regulations do not apply to private yachts. You see, we are not commercial in any way. And we've been to over forty other countries and never had any restrictions put on our movement after the initial entry.'

The harbourmaster wavered under the assault. 'Very well, then,' he said. 'I shall ring up the head office in Hiroshima.' There followed an explosive conversation on the telephone which stuttered backwards and forwards like machine-gun fire, until the harbourmaster hung up the receiver, pushed the telephone away and buried his head in his hands.

Presently he looked up. 'They have told me to refer to the regulations and to instruct you accordingly.' He looked as if he wanted to add, 'Bloody typical'; but he did not say so.

'I cannot believe that the regulations refer to a privately owned foreign yacht that has come all this way to visit Japan,' I said.

'You know,' he said, 'it hasn't happened before and they don't want to take the responsibility and have handed it back to me.' He buried his head in his hands again, the picture of despair. Beryl and I knew that he wanted to help us, but that the shadow of the head office loomed above him. Suddenly he flushed, as if he found difficulty in saying something. Then his mouth opened. 'Decision,' he roared. 'You may go anywhere that you like.'

Then he sank back in his chair, relaxed and smiling, and no one made any other attempt to put a restriction on our sailing. We asked him about the charts and he told us where to get them. 'Come back then,' he said. 'I should like you to meet the Press, and we must have a drink.' We got back to a regular Press meeting, with representatives of the local morning and evening papers—and to some excellent *saki*, the Japanese wine distilled from rice. We were already beginning to get a taste for it.

Next morning we left in a dank mist and sailed up the coast for Hososima, a commercial port. We passed many fishing boats, with riding sails set, trolling in the swift currents; but, as evening approached and the fog came down they disappeared. Once more we could see nothing, but heard the constant dull throb of big ships' engines as they passed up and down the coast; and once we saw a haze of lights pass by.

As the sky began to lighten a steady murmur of fishing boats' engines came towards us from the shore, growing and swelling to a chorus all round us, as the hardy and tireless fishermen set out once more for the grounds that they had left the night before. We never saw them because the fog hid them all, but when we thought we had run our distance we headed in for Biro Shima, a small island from which we could lay our course for the harbour entrance. We were in a null point between lighthouse signals, so had to rely almost entirely on dead reckoning, but we were in luck, for presently a hazy little island took grey shape ahead of us. It would have been the worst kind of arrogance, on a coast littered with islets, to assume that this was Biro Shima, but a cable beyond we could make out the dim outline of a rocky islet. I aligned both southern faces and took a bearing, then checked the bearing on the chart between the southern side of Biro Shima and a rock beyond. They corresponded exactly, so, without further doubt, we laid a course for the harbour entrance, which we discovered only when we were almost between the heads of the moles.

The fog was still thick inside when we anchored; but, as it cleared, a small, grey patrol boat came in through the entrance. They hailed us and then went on to the quay, from where they soon returned with a shaven-headed Japanese of about our own age, wearing a grey kimono. 'The coastguards heard that you were coming from Aburatsu, and they have been out looking for you since early this morning,' he said. 'Will you now please follow us and they will show you where to tie up. I am not coastguard,' he explained, 'but they have taken me as interpreter.'

Once we were safely tied up we asked him on board. 'I am

very small business man,' he explained. If he was talking about
his stature he was correct; but if he was talking of his business
it was an understatement of the worst kind, for we later discovered that he had the salt monopoly for all the Hososima
district. 'Would you like to come to my house for a bath?' he
asked. 'I find a bath every day is indispensable to my health.
That is why I have such a pretty face,' he added, looking at our
weather-worn features.

The house was a rambling affair, so that we never knew
whether we were in the living-room, the kitchen, the bathroom,
or a bedroom, as they all ran into each other. In the room in
which we sat and drank *saki* with him, we were shown a large,
lacquer cabinet, where the ashes of his ancestors rested in
boxes on the shelves, amidst paper prayers and flowers. Beryl
and I were unsure whether we should bow to them, express
sympathy, or examine the containers.

'I find a glass of *saki* is indispensable to my health,' he said,
and when he came on board he brought a bottle with him.
'Of very first rank, but incomparable, of course, with your
excellent English wines.' We were almost certain that he was
having a little fun at our expense. We made a note of the *saki*
of 'the very first rank', and used to buy it for special occasions.
In the evening he came shining from the bath. 'I have had my
bath and drunk some wine, and now I am a little intoxicated,'
he told us with relish.

We made two more anchorages before entering the Inland
Sea by the Bungo Suido, the narrow strait between Kyushu and
Shikkoku. The coast is lovely and looks as wild as the west
coast of Scotland, and in calm weather there are many delightful anchorages. Since the weather was calm we chose the
more deserted places, but there were safe little fishing harbours
if we had wished to enter them. The visibility was constantly
poor and if there was no fog there was still a smoky haze that
limited our view to about three miles. The fishing harbours,
usually well protected by moles, are crowded and busy, and
every small industry connected with the sea goes on there. It is
almost impossible to tear oneself away from the ships' chandlers'
stores, with their hooks and cordage, their nylon and polyester
ropes, their shackles and chains and charts, and an old-fashioned
smell of tarred twine.

We entered the Inland Sea through the Hayasui Seto, where the tide races round the corner of Sagonoseki Hanto. As we approached the channel the fishing boats all left and throbbed off to Shita Ura, a fishing cove on the southern side of the peninsular. It was the sign that the tide was changing, and by the time we were entering the Inland Sea, at the top end of the strait, it was already running strongly against us. A small cargo ship came swirling round, going at what seemed to us a tremendous pace. We were soon out of the current and went into Uwa Ura, a cove on the north side, from where we walked to the southern cove. There Beryl bought a large hunk of fish. It looked like an elegant bonito, with a yellow tail. The merchant measured off half an inch and looked at Beryl inquiringly.

'Oh, no,' she said, showing the span of her hand.

Every other shopper had crowded round, and there was a gasp of either admiration or dismay as the man sliced the fish and wrapped it for us. There was a gasp of dismay from Beryl when she heard the price. It was an excellent fish when we came to eat it, and apparently a great delicacy only to bought in shavings; but Beryl and I felt as if we were eating gold.

Behind us, on Sagonoseki Hanto, a huge chimney towered up into the clouds. We never saw its top, and we wondered how much it moved when the typhoons blew. During our stay in Japan, Shikkoku was the island most regularly hit by typhoons, and yet there is quite a timber industry on the island, and Sagonoseki Hanto itself was well wooded. The trees must have tough roots, or they are skilfully planted. The latter certainly, because the forestry in Japan seemed to be of a very high order.

Beppu is only a short sail from Uwa Ura, and there is a small basin there. It is mentioned in the Pilot and a correction in the Notices to Mariners said that it had a depth of from seven to twelve feet, otherwise I should never have attempted to go in. The notices did not mention that at the sill in the entrance there was a depth of only six feet, where we ran firmly aground. By good fortune there was a large ferry ship moored to the quay which formed one wall of the basin, whose stern almost overlapped the entrance where we were aground. We passed a line to her, and she pulled us off with an electric winch in her stern. We shot out like a cork from a bottle, and made off for the International Port, about four miles to the north and then

still being built. We anchored there between the quay and a
detached breakwater that was under construction.

The submerged portions of the breakwater were marked
with red flags, and in the afternoon a number of sturdy boats
arrived, so loaded with a deck cargo of stones that their decks
were almost awash, and they looked like piles of stones ad-
vancing across the placid waters of the Naikai. The first to
arrive positioned itself carefully between the red flags. Then a
heavy stone was hoisted on the derrick and swung outboard.
To our horror the boat heeled suddenly and virtually capsized,
as the captain and mate scrambled on to the upper rail. With
the thunder of an avalanche the top-heavy cargo cascaded off
the deck, and the boat leapt upright again, shaking itself like
a bronco that has just got rid of its rider. Captain and mate,
having survived as it seemed to us one of the worst disasters
possible at sea, nonchalantly lit cigarettes, hauled in their
lines and chugged off again for another load and another sudden off-loading.

At the International Port there was a small police station,
standing by itself in the centre of the approach to the harbour
offices and wharves. It was occupied by an English-speaking
policeman, whom we found in his shirt-sleeves, watering the
flowers round the office. In the window there hung a little wind
bell that tinkled pleasantly. It was a Utopian police station, full
of charm and helpfulness, tinkling bells, flowers, and cups of tea.
We asked the policeman if many visitors came to Beppu.

'Oh yes,' he replied. 'Many Americans come in the afterlife
for the hot baths.'

In this life too, and almost immediately, for many Americans
were expected as a warship was about to visit the harbour.
The policeman's office was full of beautiful and well-dressed
girls, all of whom spoke a little English, who were relying on
him to provide them with suitable dates. The town, too, was
aboil with excitement. As I passed down the street, a neatly
dressed, middle-aged woman with a gentle face thrust a pink
card into my hand. On it was printed.

Nude Models		*Beautiful Girls*
	BAR TWO	
Models available	500 yen	
Observers	200 yen	

I wasn't sure whether this was the price bar two, or whether Bar Two was the name of the joint.

While we were in the International Port a newspaperman who called on us asked if he might bring his children on board the next morning. I embarked the two children first in our tippy dinghy. The newsman then stepped straight off the stone steps on to the side of the dinghy, and consequently straight into the sea. As soon as he reappeared from his submersion he floundered towards us, and I knew that if he got a hand on the dinghy he'd have us all in the sea. I took to the oars, trying to keep out of his way and at the same time to direct him to the steps. The children, who had been dumb with horror, now raised their voices in the most penetrating screams of 'Oh Dadda, Oh Dadda', but Dadda made his waterlogged way safely to the steps and I was able to return the children intact. He was very distressed, and would not try again. As he sat and emptied his shoes, he kept repeating miserably, 'I did my best, I did my best.' I knew that he was suffering from an acute loss of face, but it was a pain that I did not know how to assuage.

The Inland Sea, or Naikai, apart from the charm of sheltered waters, provides some fascinating anchorages. At Izui we anchored on clean sand and just outside a well-protected little harbour, too shallow for us to enter. A cement path ran along the shore from the harbour to the village, and the sturdy, dark little pines leaned over it. The village was bright in sunshine, with a sparkling stream running under plank bridges to the sea. The roofs were tiled with grey tiles, the houses small, but well made. Everything seemed to be on a miniature scale. Little stables and small cows; little pathways and bridges; little hen houses built on to the sides of the houses and hordes of little children who escorted us. Behind the village the fields were small, with barley growing thick and level. We were overtaken by a student in his black uniform and peaked cap, who carried a tape recorder and asked us to say something into it.

On the whole the Inland Sea was disappointing. Its still waters were always shrouded in haze. Fishing boats seemed to float suspended in air as the calm, grey water and the grey haze mingled. We sailed with the sound of ships' engines always in our ears, but we rarely saw them. As I stood in the bow searching the smog for a landfall I was never out of sight of plastic. A plastic bag to starboard, a plastic bottle to port, a plastic sandal ahead. Sometimes we thought that we had found a nice beach. We anchored and rowed in, only to find that our white sand was a frill of plastic containers. Nothing seems to destroy plastic, and if the Japanese go on making containers and throwing them away at the present rate it will not be long before the islands vanish under them. Fuji has almost gone under with empty tins as it is, and may ultimately vanish under plastic. The Japanese are the worst litter-bugs.

At other times, when we thought that we had selected a secluded anchorage from the chart, we found, as we approached it, that the stern of some huge tanker under construction was projecting from it. No chart can keep pace with the ever-growing industry of Japan. We went to no small fishing harbour where there was not construction going on. It was usually by some form of communal effort, with perhaps a student driving a small bulldozer, having just got home from school.

When we talked to young people we found that they were all proud that their country had renounced war, but they were equally assured that they would eventually dominate Asia, if not the world, by their economic power. This is the whole basis of their drive towards Western methods and Western customs: that they may excel in the skills that brought them to defeat—that is to say, the skill of production rather than the skill of arms. Yet, in a country so given to discipline, where every smallest shack boasts a television set, they could be swayed in any direction, and I should never be surprised to hear that, in the name of national defence and national pride, they are busy arming again. Today the generals and admirals are discredited, but tomorrow is another story.

After Beppu we sailed to Itsuku Shima, and anchored in a lovely bay amongst pine woods. There was a holiday camp ashore, but fortunately this was deserted. We walked round the island to see the famous shrine on the other side. As we approached the temple we came upon stone and bronze lanterns along the edge of the sea. The temple itself is built over the sea at high water, on many pilings. There are some great rooms and long, red-pillared corridors and galleries looking out on to the famous Torii, the lovely Water Arch, built of camphor wood over a hundred years ago, and erected in the sea. The

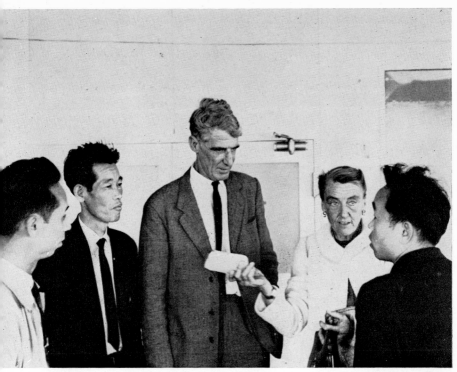

Miles Smeeton, in the centre, with Beryl on his left, having language problems in Japan

The Water Arch of Itsuku shima

3. Kannon Sama

4. Fishing boat suspended in the Inla
Sea

temple and the little town behind it were full of organized groups of students, or holidaying Japanese and a sprinkling of American tourists and sailors. On our side of the island all was peace. We took the cat for a long walk in the woods.

From Itsuku Shima we sailed to Hiroshima, and carried a good breeze right past the quays and into the long arm of the Kaidawan. We sailed under high-tension cables feet above our masts, but still looking as if they would catch in them. At the end of the Kaidawan there were so many oyster rigs that there was no room to swing. We shifted to another bay and no sooner had we anchored than the *Kaijōhowancho* arrived and took us away to moor alongside their ship.

We went ashore to look for Dr Reynolds, who sailed round the world in his ship *Phoenix*, and later became involved in various exploits in the cause of Peace. Hiroshima is a dreary place and one could not help thinking of Betjeman's poem:

> Come, friendly bombs, and fall on Slough
> It isn't fit for humans now.

The huge, empty area which lay beneath the centre of the bomb is naked, with only a twisted building and single Japanese tomb in the centre as a monument. The museum welters in the horror of the bomb, and to walk through it is as shocking as finding an old, mutilated corpse upon a beach. It did not affect my outlook, nor enlighten me, nor turn me to work actively for Peace, although I may have thought that whoever dropped the bomb, it was not the Americans who started the war. I found only that I was angered that I had been afflicted by a promenade through its gruesome halls, when I should have known better.

It was before all this, however, that, searching for Earl Reynolds, we went into an American institute that corresponded to the British Council, but was disguised under some name inoffensive to the Japanese. Inside its spacious halls everyone was busy, solemn, hurrying, typing, dictating, or just looking important. A tall Japanese came up to me. 'I understand that you are interested in Peace,' he said.

Of course I am interested in Peace; but if we have too much of it we are going to have other problems on our hands, and after all I am, or was, a soldier. My reply was one of shock.

c

'Good heavens, no,' I said. 'I'm a soldier. I'm interested in war.' Perhaps I imagined it, but I thought that silence fell, and that the whole room stood still.

We left the Inland Sea on May 8th, just a month after we had sailed from Kagoshima Kaiwan, having spent every night at anchor. We avoided the main passage between Awaji Island and Honshu which leads to Osaka, and went through a narrow pass between the islands of Okina Shima and Jino Shima. There were fast tides here, so we had to hit it at slack water. As we approached the pass a large number of fishing boats that had been lying to the tide got up their anchors and moved away. This is one of the signs which we were always looking for in Japan, where we were so conscious of strong tides. Everywhere round the coasts of Japan, but particularly in the Inland Sea and in the more sheltered waters, hosts of small boats are lying to the tide. As the time for the change approaches, first one boat then two will take up their anchors and move away. Then suddenly all will go, off to harbour or to another place to fish in. They are like terns all fishing in one place, who suddenly cease their diving and then flit quietly away.

We anchored under the shelter of a rocky cape, Myazaki No Hana, since the tide was running against us. In the evening seiner after seiner came hammering past us from seaward; fifty of them at least, coming home to Arita Ko, a fishing port a few miles behind. As they passed us they cheered and jeered, waving their arms frantically and signalling us to follow them into the port. They were much more subdued when, at five in the morning, they all came hammering out again. Their single-cylinder diesel engines were firing like anti-aircraft guns in action, but sending them along at a great pace.

We left as usual in visibility of about a mile, with the big steelworks across the strait sending a mass of orange smoke out of its four chimneys to mingle with the mist lying low on the surface of the sea. We decided to make only one more stop at Kuki Ko, and then to push on for Yokohama.

That evening we were sailing up the coast with a following wind, when the haze lifted and showed us a long wall of cliffs and headlands. They were so high that we thought we were closer in than we were, until we saw a cargo ship like a toy beneath them. It began to look as if we would have a race with darkness if we wanted to get in to port. The wind began to freshen and a dark cloud came up astern. Soon we could see the white horses showing bright against the darkness and here and there a white fishing boat heading in for home. One or two came close past us, powerful and buoyant, driving across the sea, their motion infinitely more violent than *Tzu Hang*'s. Far ahead we could see one flying a big black 'success' flag, going the same way as we were; but there was no sign of any entrance ahead, and we began to think of a night at sea. Then suddenly the boat was gone, as if it had ducked into a cave.

'There,' said Beryl. 'That must be the entrance, but we're going to be late.'

It was an hour before we got to the same point and found the sound, with darkness really closing in. The cliffs on each side were so tall and black that it felt as if we were steering up an alley, but there was still enough light in the sky to show us a channel between lines of buoys supporting fish trap nets, which almost closed the entrance. A dim light blinked ahead of us, marking an angle in the sound, and as we turned to starboard round the light we saw the lights of Kuki Ko, another mile up the sound. As we came up we could see, on the starboard side, a row of fishing boats with their bow platforms towards a wharf, and on the port side we could make out long booms of logs. The wharf lights were bright, and we came in slowly, sounding to see if we could anchor; but finding only deep water.

Presently we could hear men calling, and saw them signalling us to come alongside the fishing boat that we had seen enter the sound. She was still flying a huge black flag to show that she had a big catch. They were ready to take our lines and we were soon secured alongside. We asked them on board and they scrambled on deck, laughing at the size of our crew and that one of them was a woman. A woman at the helm—I always do the sounding and throwing of lines—is a thing unheard of in Japan. They would not come below, knowing that we wanted to cook and turn in, but they gave us a fish for the cat and a fish for ourselves, and said good-night. They left early again in the morning, giving us a shout so that we might secure alongside the wharf as they moved away.

Kuki Ko is a busy fishing harbour and a timber port surrounded by hills, and a safe refuge. We wandered about the village, watching all its various activities. Here a net was being repaired on the shore, there nets on racks were being picked clean by women who were removing crab claws, starfish, seaweed, and other debris. In a shed a row of women were sitting making a long net, in another an old man was covering a large glass float with rope netting, under another a boat was being built, with the carpenters' umbrellas leaning against its side. Everywhere there were smiles and friendliness.

We walked up to the point where the little light had flashed and found a temple there. Farther on, looking out over the bay, there was a single uncut stone. It had the names, so many names, of those who had lost their lives during the war. Most of them had been lost at sea, and most of them had once sailed out below this stone to go fishing. We had just seen their sisters and their brothers at work in the village, and I suppose none of them doubted that they had not lost their lives in a good cause.

'It just makes me think how bloody crazy war is,' I said to Beryl.

'Oh, I don't know,' she replied. 'I think we just have to have it sometimes. Anyway, I think people are rather nicer in wartime than they are in peace.'

3 The General gets his Sword

The yacht harbour at Yokohama was small and some way out from the shops, bank, and post office, which we reached by bus. There wasn't much water in the harbour, it was dirty, and there was little room to swing at our anchor, so it had few attractions for *Tzu Hang* and her crew, although it attracted plenty of small-boat sailors. We saw no other suitable place for us in the Tokyo Wan.

Yachting has been taken up in Japan with typical Japanese enthusiasm, and there were a number of small yachts available in the yacht harbour for the instruction of High School and University students. They were used by classes of thirty or more who slept in bunkhouse and boatshed and were up at break of day doing physical training on the breakwater wall. As soon as the wind got up they were on the water and very soon in it. They collided, upset, and dragged each other out of the wreckage with the greatest gusto and enjoyment. Their instructors ran up and down the wall, shouting orders through a megaphone. At night there were campfires and songs amongst the boats which had been put on shore and repaired, and after three days' hard work one lot of apprentice yachtsmen left and another arrived. Never were small boats harder worked, nor so often capsized.

Cruising in Japan was only just beginning, except in the waters about Yokohama and Aburatsubo, and we saw only one yacht outside. Kenichi Horie had made his single-handed trip to America and became something of a national hero, but Beryl and I thought that the most remarkable thing about his trip was not that he had arrived, but that he had started at all. The Japanese love to do everything in a crowd, and individuality is restricted by conformity, rules, and regulations. Horie knew that he was unlikely to get official sanction for his journey and left without permission and without a passport, which must have taken more courage than was needed for the journey itself.

Our main object in coming to Yokohama was to give the General back his sword, but it was complicated by my having forgotten his name. He had been, as far as I remembered, the Chief of Staff of the Japanese 33rd Corps and later of the Japanese Army in Burma. As my Infantry Brigade was still in contact with them when they surrendered, I was ordered to give them certain preliminary instructions, which were handed over to this General, whose sword I now had but whose name I had forgotten. Later, when there were a large number of Japanese prisoners in the area that I was in charge of, I saw a lot of him, and when the generals officially surrendered their swords I was given his.

I met him under circumstances when I felt I had to put on a stern and uncompromising look, although I felt a liking for him. When I left Burma he came to say good-bye to me, and I remember wondering what he would think if he knew that his sword was rolled up in my bedding roll, which was just being loaded into the station wagon. I took it to my sisters' house in Yorkshire, where it remained in a drawer in the hall for the next eighteen years. My daughter brought it out to South Africa, and from there it travelled in *Tzu Hang*; our only weapon.

I had been told that the best way to find out the name of the owner was to get in touch with a colonel who was writing the history of the war in Burma. We found him in his office at Defence Force Headquarters in Tokyo. He was a small, precise, and well-dressed man.

'Oho,' he said, when I told him of my mission, 'that will be General Sawamoto. He is at the officers' club now. What good fortune. He has only come up to Tokyo today. I will tell him that you are bringing his sword.'

He rang the telephone and spoke in Japanese. More talk and then a long silence followed by a few more words.

'He will be here in a moment,' he said.

General Sawamoto. Of course. That was the name. Silly to have forgotten; and when he arrived, although I knew at once that I had met him before, he was quite unlike the General Sawamoto that I remembered. My Sawamoto was lean and twenty years younger. This Sawamoto was square and looked like a prosperous business man, but he sat down, after shaking hands, and began to remind me of the days that we spent together in Burma.

'I am garden man now,' he said, 'and do you remember that you gave us permission to fish in the river?' Yes. I remembered that, but somehow I could not absolutely assure myself that this square, gold-toothed, and Hawaiian-shirted man was the same as my lean and conquered General.

'Tell me,' he asked, the colonel translating, 'this sword that you have so kindly brought me, had it the old Samurai hilt, or had it the general's hilt, like this?' and he drew on a piece of office paper the curved gilt hilt and sword knot of a Japanese general's sword.

'That is the hilt, the general's hilt,' I said, thinking that he might be disappointed that it was not the Samurai sword. He sat back in his chair, dropping his hands to his thighs, and beamed at me over his spectacles.

'It is the sword of honour, given to me by the Emperor, when I passed out of the Military Academy,' he said.

'How can I return it to you?' I asked. 'Shall I bring it to you somewhere, or would you like to come to the boat, and may I give it to you there? Whichever you find convenient.'

'I should like very much that my wife and I should come to your yacht,' he said, 'and I will bring a friend as an interpreter.' I wondered whether he thought that I was on some big motor yacht, and whether I could ever get them out in the dinghy. He looked active enough still, but what of the wife and the interpreter? We could have a shot at it. I arranged to meet them all next day at the Hong Kong and Shanghai Bank in Yokohama.

When I met them his wife was wearing Japanese dress, complete with obi and gaetas, not exactly suitable for climbing on board *Tzu Hang*, but the interpreter was a tall, rangy, and rather untidily dressed man with a merry, roguish face. He had been a senior officer in the Japanese Intelligence Service and spoke English well.

'You people were always after me,' he said, 'but you couldn't catch me. I was the man in charge of Subhas Chandra Bhose.'

He looked as if he was well able to get in and out of trouble. Subhas Chandra Bhose was the Indian politician who defected to the Japanese at the beginning of the war with Japan, and was the nominal head of the Japanese Indian Forces, that poor little army of prisoners who were persuaded to bear ineffectual arms against us. Subhas Chandra Bhose died in an air accident before the end of the war.

We got hold of the yacht club boat and were soon all on board *Tzu Hang*, and had even accomplished the more difficult feat—until you know the way—of getting down to the cabin. We had some talk and tea. Then General Sawamoto cleared his throat, put on a serious and official look, and spoke to me in Japanese. 'The Rogue', as I had already christened him in my mind, translated.

'The General wishes me to read you a letter,' he said. We sat solemnly attentive and listened to the address. This is what he read:

MR AND MRS SMEETON,

When I learned from the Japanese Safety Board of your visit to Japan, the news brought back memories of the days that I spent in Burma after the war ended. The meeting in Japan this time with you and Mrs Smeeton after such long years was a very happy one. I must say that I was quite impressed with your happy countenance. You seemed so much more cheerful than the time in Burma.

It envies me to learn that you are now on a thrilling world tour with Mrs Smeeton, as a member of the Royal Cruising Club. Of course your such position is quite deserving for the parts you have played in the last war to bring victory to your country. [*Here I began to wonder why the Royal Yacht Squadron had not offered me honorary membership.*] However, it touched me deeply to learn that you had brought your pet cat on this trip. It shows the human touch in the act of a soldier, who had braved the horrors of war.

After my return to Japan I was asked by the Burmese Government to help in gathering of data for the last war in Burma. Since then my days are spent in the nursery, in growing flowers and plants to console myself.

When the war ended in August 1945, I was the Chief of Staff of the Japanese Army, and was stationed in Thaton. I was then assigned to contact you, and at that time I had to surrender myself and the arms that I had on me. But the only weapon that I carried then was my sword. It never occurred to me that for nineteen long years you would be the very person who would be keeping that sword and that you would take the trouble to bring it back to me all the way from London. I am simply overwhelmed and words failed me to express to you the feeling I now have for the kind thoughts behind your such action.

In gratitude I wish to say thank you to you and to your great nation.

May I also extend my sincere 'Bon Voyage' and best wishes to you and Mrs Smeeton and to your pet cat for a happy and pleasant journey blessed with good health. Please remember me to other friends in your country.

(Signed) R. SAWAMOTO
Ex Chief of Staff of the Japanese Army in Burma

When it was over I went into the fore-cabin and brought the General his sword. He took it in both hands, holding it in front of him across his chest, and then gave a great shout of 'Oh', as if he had been grievously wounded. Beryl and I were appalled. I turned to 'The Rogue'.

'For heaven's sake, it's not the wrong sword, is it?' I asked him.

'No, no,' 'The Rogue' replied, 'it's only emotion, only emotion.'

The General, quite oblivious of these remarks, and under the anxious gaze of his wife, slowly turned the sword in his hands, and then as slowly half unsheathed the blade. Then he turned to me.

'But why is it not rusty?' he asked.

'Well, being a soldier, I like to keep swords clean,' I said, but didn't add that I'd spent about an hour cleaning it the evening before.

'I thought it would be all rusty,' he said. It was obvious that he was deeply moved. Presently he took out of his pocket a small piece of pink tissue paper.

'When the time came for us to hand in our swords,' he said, 'I thought that I would bury this one and only hand in the other. Then perhaps I would return one day to Burma to recover it. Then I thought that you had dealt honourably with me and that this would be a dishonourable action. I therefore surrendered both swords, but this I could not give you.' He unwrapped the tissue paper and produced a small gold-inscribed washer to fit over the blade against the hilt.

'This is the seal,' he said, 'that shows it was given to me by the Emperor.' He drew the blade, slipped the seal over its point and up to the hilt, and then with a contented sigh, sheathed the sword again. He then wrapped the whole thing in some blue silk cloth that he was carrying so that it was suitably disguised. They were ready to go, but before leaving he gave me a silver cigarette case. I am sure he was not well off. I thought then, as I had thought long ago, that he was a good man. I was glad that I had brought him back his sword that he valued so much.

When I got back to Canada I had a letter to tell me that the General was dead.

We sailed from Yokohama back to Aburatsubo, which is only a day's sail from Yokohama, through the Uraga Straits and westward round the Miura Peninsula. The coast was withdrawn in haze. To starboard, coastal towns and villages, storage tanks and chimneys revealed themselves reluctantly, but to port the hills stood higher and cleaner and a tall statue of Kannon Sama, the Goddess of Mercy, specially revered by sailors, looked across the traffic in the busy Straits to the teeming peninsula beyond. She looked down on her wooden ship, for '*Tzu Hang*' is said to mean 'The wooden ship of Kwan Yin', or rather 'under the special protection of Kwan Yin', and Kwan Yin and Kannon Sama are the Chinese and Japanese names for the same goddess. We have a little porcelain figure of Kwan Yin in the slot in the samson post, where the butt of the bowsprit used to fit, when *Tzu Hang* carried the taller rig that she lost in the Southern Ocean. Japanese fishermen always used to make obeisance to it when they discovered it there.

Aburatsubo was then the only good yacht harbour, a safe typhoon refuge, which is crammed with fishing boats during a typhoon warning. It is sheltered from every direction and would have been a safe place to spend the winter in, but we felt it was an unenterprising thing to do. There were numerous American-owned yachts and we felt that we would not see much of the Japanese there. We hadn't come all the way to Japan to live on *Tzu Hang* amongst Westerners, which we might have done equally well in San Francisco. Also we wanted to take a house, and to take one in this area would be much more expensive than in a less-frequented place. We decided to go ahead with our plans for wintering in Hokkaido.

Mr Fukatome was running the yacht harbour. He owned the moorings, the store, and a small ship. He was a man of good family and, being keen on boats, had started this yacht harbour —Japan's first yacht harbour of any importance, excluding the one at Yokohama. He was a good sailor himself, and was at that time being tested as a 'Dragon' helmsman for the Olympics. He was young, tall for a Japanese, with an attractive smile and the preoccupied manner that is a characteristic of most people in charge of boatyards. We decided to ask his advice about where to spend the winter.

'Come up to the office,' he said, when I had explained what we wanted. We followed him up a rickety stair to a room above the store. It was crowded with all sorts of yachting equipment. Mr Fukatome pushed his way round some gaily coloured sail-bags, moved a half-unpacked compass from his chair, sat down and looked for a moment of despair at the papers on his desk. Then he wiped his hand over his short black hair and said:

'I know exactly what you want. You must go to Mori. It is a small fishing harbour and they could haul you out there. There are no other suitable harbours in Hokkaido for you to spend the winter.'

He called for his wife and she came from a little room adjoining the office. She had a small athletic figure and a hard peasant face, not unattractive by any means, but she was wearing a toque to cover a temporary disaster with a 'home permanent', which didn't suit her. Fukatome, who had been shuffling some papers, spoke to her in Japanese. She answered him with a nod to the corner of the room where some charts were lying. It was said in the yacht harbour that she ran the office and kept the accounts and did it very efficiently—almost too efficiently, the yachtsmen said.

Under the charts Fukatome found what he was looking for. It was an outline chart of Hokkaido, showing the aids to navigation.

'There you are,' he said. 'There's Mori. I have a friend there called Takahashi. I will write to him. He will look after you and perhaps he will find you a house.'

Hokkaido is the northern island of Japan, 300 miles north of Yokohama. Its bottom end curves like a fish's tail round the bay of Uchiura. In the fork of the tail, in the straits between Honshu

and Hokkaido, called the Tsuguru Kaikyo, is Hakodate. Just
across the fork of the tail, on its northern side, lies Mori. Right
across Uchiura Bay, twenty miles to the north, is Muroran.
Hakodate and Muroran are big commercial ports, but Mori is
only a small fishing harbour. It was shown as a little dot on
Fukutome's chart. The Japanese characters, which I was able
to recognize later, represented three hills, three peaks of the
volcano, Komagatake, which stands behind the port. The very
smallness of the dot attracted us and from then on it became our
goal, the place where we and *Tzu Hang* were going to spend the
winter.

Before leaving Aburatsubo we hauled *Tzu Hang* out and
painted her bottom in a little yard a mile below the yacht
harbour. As we stood below her and admired our handiwork,
the setting sun outlined Fujiyama below her stern. It was
already July. The first typhoon, Agnes, had threatened Okinawa. From Nojima Saki, the eastern entrance point of the Uraga
Suedo, northward to Matsu Shima, there is a long stretch of
coast with no suitable typhoon refuge. Farther north from
Ishinomaki to Myako there was a wild indented coast with all
kinds of refuge within easy reach. The farther north we went
the less likely we were to be caught in a typhoon, because they
are prone to start their recurve as they go northward and to
leave the coast. This is a generalization that should not be
relied on, but it is safe at least to say that there are more
typhoons in Kyushu than there are in Hokkaido.

We started off on July 2nd and arrived in Ishinomaki on
July 6th after deciding not to visit Matsushima on account of the
shallow water and fog. Typhoon Betty was reported south of
Okinawa, but she had not made up her mind which way to go.
Still, we were glad to get into Ishinomaki.

We motored up a long channel like a river, with fishing boats
both going and coming and lining the quays. We went right up
to a bridge in order to avoid the wash of passing boats and tied
up to a ferry which was temporarily in disuse. When we went
ashore to do some shopping we found a shoe shop called 'The
London Shoe Factory' where Beryl found some shoes that she
has worn ever since and where I had some shoes made that I
have never been able to wear since.

We waited in Ishinomaki for a few days for friends from

Tokyo to join us for the weekend. David had been in the British Navy and Bruce in the American Navy. As soon as they arrived we left for Tsukinoura in the poor visibility which we had had almost every day since we had sailed. Tsukinoura is an almost land-locked little port, hidden from the road, and dedicated to the oyster business. It is wrapped in black barrels and cordage, beneath piles of old shell waiting to be threaded on lines, for new shell in the making.

It was also the port from which, in 1613, Date Masamune, the one-eyed dragon of Sendai, sent a ship to Mexico, bearing a delegation to the Pope in Rome. She was named the *San Juan Baptista*, and Hasakura Rokuemon was her pilot. She was 108 feet long, with 36 feet beam, and returned from a successful mission two years later. It was a few years after the dispatch to America of the ship built by the British seaman, John Adams, who was working for the Daimyo, Iyeyasu. Date Masamune probably wanted to keep the construction of his ship as secret as possible, lest the Daimyo might consider that he was poaching on imperial preserves. If so he could not have chosen a better place than Tsukinoura, the Half Moon bay, which is screened from the sea by islands and tucked so closely under the hill that it cannot be seen from the road.

We sailed that afternoon to Ohara and all went ashore to a dinner in the hotel where David and Bruce were staying. It was served in their bedroom where we sat on the floor. During the meal we were joined by a Japanese and his girl from the bedroom next door. He was very drunk, pressed his whisky on us, and insisted on kissing everyone in the party except me. When he staggered away it was obvious that his girl would have no great joy from him on that night anyway. Drunken Japanese are one of the hazards to a foreigner in upcountry hotels, and when they are drunk their good manners vanish and they become intolerable bores.

Beryl and I walked down the road to the harbour. A dank fog had drifted in from the sea. We followed the curving eight-foot wall built round the head of the bay to control the tidal waves that do so much damage after an earthquake, until we found the watertight doors. They were open and are only closed in the event of a tidal wave warning. Then we picked our way in black darkness along a wooden pier, regretting that we

had forgotten to bring the flashlight with us, for there were large
gaps in the planking. At the end of the pier several fishboats
were tied, and after scrambling over these we found the dinghy
tied to the outside boat. We set off in the direction that we had
last seen *Tzu Hang* and soon her white masts loomed close
ahead and another hazardous after-dinner journey was safely
completed. Before I went below I looked around. We could see
neither the harbour light nor the lights of the village, and
could barely make out the bow from the cockpit.

'I'm sure it's going to be like this tomorrow,' I said.

'Well, you don't have to go, you know,' Beryl said.

'Of course we've got to go. We can't hang about in harbour
when they've come all the way from Tokyo.'

'Well, you could find your way to Ayukawa, couldn't you?'

Ayukawa is about twelve miles down the coast, and I supposed I could.

Next morning the fog was just as thick as fog can be. After
getting David and Bruce on board it eased sufficiently for us to
grope our way out of the harbour, between the long rows of
oyster barrels. We took a compass course until I thought I was
in the mile-wide channel between the shore and an off-lying
island, then we turned down the coast. Almost immediately
some black rocks appeared ahead, the swell licking at their feet.
We withdrew back on to our old course for a few minutes and
then turned down the coast again. This time no rocks confronted us, so I knew that I was in the channel; but we still had
the tides and currents to contend with, and we could find no
useful beacon on the direction-finder.

From time to time we stopped the engine in order to listen. A
ship was coming up from astern. The throb of its engine grew
steadily louder, and presently I could hear its bow wave
soughing. It overtook us on the port side, but we saw nothing.
Beryl was at the helm with David and Bruce in the cockpit,
talking and laughing as if they had no care in the world, while
I peered into the fog from the bow or felt my ears growing out
like asses' ears as I tried to interpret the faint sounds about
me.

After three hours, with the fog as thick as ever, we altered
course for what I hoped was the entrance to Ayukawa.
Presently a white bow wave appeared from dead ahead and

turned to pass us so closely that we were able to make out a ferry boat, which I hoped had just left the harbour. Then some dark objects loomed largely close to starboard, which turned out to be oyster barrels. I altered course and soon saw breakers on a beach. I altered course again and saw a factory chimney on a large warehouse which changed to a small red lighthouse on a pier. I was beginning to feel boxed in and let the anchor go in five fathoms. We stood on the deck listening to the shore sounds. A bus drove up close to us and stopped unseen. The conductress spoke to her passengers on the loudspeaker, her voice as clear as if we were standing beside her.

'It's all right,' said Bruce, who spoke Japanese, 'we're there. She has just told them that they have arrived in Ayukawa, but that she is sorry that they cannot see it, because of the fog.'

When the fog lifted we found that we were inside the harbour and were able to put Bruce and David ashore to catch a bus back to Tokyo.

For a month we cruised in and out of many lovely sounds and rock-bound anchorages, meeting with much friendliness and endless curiosity. At one little fishing harbour we ran into a German who was teaching at Sendai University. He and his tall and attractive wife were on a holiday. We met them in a store, and she seemed, after the stocky Japanese, to have the longest and most elegant legs that I had ever seen. Beryl asked the pair to come on board if they had nothing else to do, but they were just off on some small expedition, and we parted, although we had just met them, as if they had been old and dear friends. Late in the evening we heard a shout from the shore and were delighted to see them again. They too had run into trouble in their hotel with an over-friendly Japanese and had come to see us until he was safely asleep. The girl wrote in our book when she signed her name, 'We met in a department store'. It has bothered me ever since, the first line of a short poem which I have never been able to complete.

When we came into Ofunato Ko, farther up the coast, we saw a large commercial port filling the head of the bay, but on our right there were numerous little inlets, almost closed by oyster rigs. We motored into one of these, finding barely room to anchor. A village surrounded the head of the bay, and at its centre there was a large steep-roofed farmhouse, probably the oldest building there. We had not been anchored long, before a little old lady was rowed out to us. She came in a tarred rowing boat, with one tattered oarsman and one follower to sustain her, but she had all the dignity of a queen in her royal barge. She stepped on board with more agility than either Beryl or I can show, and installed herself below as if she would never leave. We gave her tea and presently she invited us, or rather ordered us, to the farm.

We sat in a large outer room, the floor raised about three feet off the ground and made of polished black wood. The walls also were of wood, but one wall was missing, so that the whole room opened into the barn. It was as if we were on a stage; as if we were actors, playing to an audience of two or three hens, some ducks, farm machinery, and a pile of hay. At the far end, behind a screen, was the bath already being heated for Beryl and me to enjoy. Above us arched the blackened and cobwebby rafters. In the centre of the floor there was a large sandpit, round which ten or twelve people could sit in comfort, and in the centre of the pit there glowed a wood fire. A large kettle was suspended on a blackened bamboo pole, which slid up and down inside a larger bamboo pole, attached to the rafters, and controlled by some ingenious counterweight.

'Down periscope,' said the old lady, or some such order, and one of her minions slid the kettle down to the fire, where it was soon hissing. Tea was passed round, then *saki*, and beer was brought from the village. Fresh mackerel arrived on wooden skewers which were stuck in the sand close to the fire, turned until they were nicely cooked, and then handed to a guest. Nothing could have been more dignified, or more medieval, than the way the old lady held her court, half in and half out of her barnyard. She must have carried considerable weight in the surrounding country, because soon we had the Press and photographers from Ofunatu Ko, and next morning she brought out the mayor and a councillor to visit us before we left.

The Japanese are the most enthusiastic eaters of squid, and at this time of year all the squid boats were out every night. They drift sideways, trolling from a row of hand-operated reels which are spaced at about every four feet along the side of the ship. A hook with a red plastic lure is fastened at about every fathom down the long lines. Between their short masts are

5. The curiosity of Japanese students

. Packing seaweed in Japan

7. Squid boats in Hokkaido

8. At Omatsuri

strung a row of high-wattage electric bulbs and you can see the glow in the sky from the squid boats, fleets of them fishing together, from miles away. Like almost every edible thing in Japan, squids are hung in racks to dry, along the seashore and amongst the cottages of the fishermen.

One of the places we liked most was the village of Tanohama, where *Tzu Hang* was well protected and where we could go for walks in farming countryside behind the village. Tanohama also has a tall stone wall with watertight doors all round the head of the bay, to protect the village from a tidal wave. At Tanohama the fishing boats were all getting ready for an Omatsuri, a religious procession to a Shinto shrine on a near island, to offer prayers or thanksgivings for a good fishing season.

Every boat was covered in the large flags that the Japanese fishermen love so much, and on the day of the festival many of the fishermen and children were in old Japanese dress. With drums beating and flags flying a procession was formed and all ships were beached in a row beneath the shrine, all with stern anchors out so that they could pull off again. Flags and pennants fluttered brilliantly in the sunshine, so that they looked as Duke William's ships must have looked on the beach below Hastings.

We watched the service at the shrine. There was a great deal of bowing, consecrating, and offering of food to the gods. The chief priest had a black hat with a plume like a Californian quail, and minor priests in smaller hats, in the way of all priests, managed to get a word in here and there, while the chief priest paused for breath. The real sport started when about twenty fishermen dressed in white picked up a heavy portable shrine, and reeled backwards and forwards with it in mock struggle. They weaved down the path to the boats and then first towards one boat and then towards another while the captains, in real or feigned alarm, tried to get their boats away. Eventually one was selected and the shrine was heaved on board, followed and preceded by its bearers, so that the boat heeled. As soon as they were all on board the boat was pulled off, and then with flutes and cymbals playing, with drums beating and flags and pennants flying, it led the procession round the bay.

Myako was our last port on this coast and we sailed from

D

there for the Mutsu Wan, the inland sea that fills the top end of
Honshu. The approach to the entrance of the Mutsu Wan is
through the Tsuguru Kaikyo, the strait between Honshu and
Hokkaido, where the tides run up to seven knots. There was a
short stretch between Myako and the Tsuguru Kaikyo where
there was no typhoon refuge, and as we were now down to
'Jenny' and well into the typhoon season we had to keep our
ears open for their progress. 'Jenny' was still down in the south,
so we had plenty of time. We sailed into the Tsuguru Kaikyo in
the afternoon and as we arrived saw the tide rips slacken, and
knew that we had just caught the change. By evening we were
round Oma Saki, a green point with sandy beaches and a white
lighthouse, and turned up for the Mutsu Wan, but then, seeing
the snug little port of Oma Ko behind the lighthouse, we
decided to go in. It was a good port to seek refuge in, if it had
been necessary, with a narrow artificial entrance.

We left next morning, thinking that we were well out of the
main run of the tide, but there was a fresh head wind blowing
and we had to tack to avoid the reefs. In doing this I inadver-
tently got into the current and was carried ignominiously back
round the point. We flogged *Tzu Hang* backwards and forwards
through the tide rips, and she was going like an ocean racer,
but she could not make it, and eventually we anchored on the
wrong side of Oma Saki, but well sheltered with a weather
shore. The bottom was rocky, there was a wreck close ahead of
us, and it was a horrible place to anchor if the wind had not
been offshore. We intended to wait only until the tide changed,
but once the anchor was down we decided that we had had
enough hard sailing for that day and that we'd sleep instead.

We turned in after supper, intending to get going early in the
morning, but I hadn't been asleep for long before I awoke to
find *Tzu Hang* pitching to her cable.

'Beryl,' I called softly.

'Yes?' she replied immediately, for she was awake too.

'I think that bloody wind's changed.'

'Yes,' she said, 'I was thinking so too.'

I waited for her to get up and have a look, but as there was
no further sound from her bunk I got up and put my head out.
The wind was blowing from the north and we were on a dead
lee shore. I went back to the cabin.

'Wind's from the north,' I said. 'We ought to get out really, but the tide's dead wrong.'

'How much longer will it be against us?' she asked.

'Three hours.' I waited expectantly for some cheerful note of encouragement from my beloved.

'Well, don't you think the hook will hold?' she asked.

'I don't know. Rotten ground. I'll let out more chain. We'll be in trouble if it doesn't.'

She came up to help me. We let a lot of chain rattle out and then went below, but not to sleep. *Tzu Hang*'s motion became even more violent. Suddenly there was a loud twang which seemed to run through the boat, then a rumble of chain dragging over rock.

'I'll start the engine,' I called to Beryl as she scrambled up on deck ahead of me. It started immediately with a healthy roar, but as I reached the deck I saw that we were already broadside to the sea.

'Keep her head to wind,' I shouted, as if Beryl didn't know what had to be done, and then fell like a maniac on the winch. *Tzu Hang*'s head began to come up. I spun the winch first with one hand and then the other. The chain was so light that I knew we were already in shallow water. I was getting more and more out of breath. The winch handle came off and hit me on the shin with a crack that would normally have sent me dancing and cursing round the deck, but in a moment it was back on and the chain rattling in again. Presently I felt some weight on the chain and wondered if we were overrunning the anchor, but almost at once the winch came to a stop, and I realized the anchor was at the hawse hole.

'Aweigh, aweigh,' I shouted back into the darkness, and heard the note of the engine change and felt the bow begin to punch into the sea. I thought what a good thing it was that Beryl had judged it right. I got the anchor in, found the shaft bent in a hook, and went aft to sit beside Beryl in the cockpit to tell her about it.

'I know what my epitaph is going to be,' I told her at the end.

'What?' she asked.

'Found dead on the anchor winch.'

'You steer,' she said. 'We'll want the jib soon, won't we?' She went for'ard to get it ready.

Oma Saki light drew abeam and soon was flashing on our quarter. As soon as I judged that we were past the rock that lies close off it, we turned to the west and Beryl hoisted the jib. With the wind now abeam and the tide with us, we quickly left the lighthouse behind, and then turned south for the entrance into the Mutsu Wan. With the wind astern we let *Tzu Hang* sail under her jib until we picked up the light at the entrance, and by then day was coming and it was time to get up all sail.

One day, while in the Mutsu Wan, we sailed into Ominato Ko and found that it was a base for the Japanese Defence Force. There were several frigates and the flotilla leader, *Akezuki*, moored in line, three of them up from Yokosuka. All their ensigns were at half mast.

'I wonder why they are all flying their ensigns at half mast?' I said to Beryl.

'Oh, I suppose someone has died,' she said.

The last time we had met a ship with its ensign at half mast had been in a river in Borneo. It was the day of President Kennedy's assassination.

'I wonder who's dead now?' I asked. 'I suppose that we had better put ours at half mast too.' I went aft and carefully fastened the ensign at half mast.

We anchored a little beyond the *Akezuki*, and presently a smart boat came over and a young sub-lieutenant saluted, and asked if he might come alongside.

'Commander Morohashi,' he said, 'presents his compliments and would very much like to pay you a visit, if it is convenient.'

'Ask him to come along now. We would be delighted to see him.'

Presently we heard the boat alongside again and the Commander came on board. He was tall, and except for his features might well have been in the British Navy. He spoke idiomatic English, or rather Navy-English, as it had a distinct nautical panache about it. He was cheerful and confident. We offered him a drink.

'You wouldn't have a gin, would you?' he asked. 'Welcome to Ominato Ko. What brought you here?—anyway, it's nice to see you. We're just up from Yokosuka on a cruise.'

'So are we,' said Beryl. 'We thought of spending the winter in Mori.'

'What on earth would you want to do that for?' he asked, laughing. 'Have you got a fur coat?'

After we had had a drink I asked him why all the ensigns were at half mast.

'It's the Japanese day of humiliation,' he replied. 'V.J. Day to you.' He leant forward to look at my own ensign. 'Now you've got yourself a problem, haven't you?'

I let it fly there for the Japanese who didn't come back to such places as Izue, and Kuki Ko, and Tanohama, and all the little ports and villages along the indented coast.

When we left the Mutsu Wan we had gale force winds from yet another typhoon, Kathie, that had hit Kyusu, but by now had spent most of its strength, and had been down-graded to a storm. I did not like to take *Tzu Hang* into the tide rips of the Tsuguru Kaikyo under these conditions nor to go into Oma Ko in the dark. We spent the night tacking backwards and forwards under the protection of the high cliffs north-east of the entrance. Although the sea was calm the gusts were violent, and at times *Tzu Hang* was quite hove down under them. The water was whipped off the surface of the sea in silver moonlit sheets. No sooner had one of us gone down than there was a call from the deck to tack again. We did not want to get too far out into the tide, and rougher water quickly warned us when it was time to go about.

By daylight the wind had veered and was easing. We sailed up to a fishing boat which came out of Oma Ko and asked them about the state of the sound. The captain made a porpoising motion with his hand and said that we should go into Oma Ko and wait for a west wind. As it was already in the south-west we decided to have a go at it. *Tzu Hang* seemed to revel in it. The passage was as exciting as canoeing down rapids, but she always seemed to have a foot to spare, and had barely wet her decks by the time we were out of the toppling rips and into calmer water. The morning should see us in Mori. Another typhoon was already brewing away out in the Pacific, but if it came our way it looked as if *Tzu Hang* would be in winter quarters and ready to meet it.

4 In search of Winter Quarters

A smell of sulphur from Mount Esan came drifting across the dark sea as we rounded the cape. About thirty miles to go to the southern entrance point of Uchiura bay and another ten miles on to Mori. We were about ten miles offshore with a south-westerly wind. *Tzu Hang* was sailing quietly by herself as if she knew that she was coming in to her winter home. From time to time a bamboo pole with a rag attached to its top slid close past us, just visible in the moonlight, marking a fish trap or net, and whoever was on watch listened anxiously for the scrape of rope along the keel. Whatever the poles were attached to led down steeply and we touched nothing. The lights of successive fishing villages showed ahead, came abeam, and fell astern, until at last the daylight came and the anticipation of coffee and eggs for breakfast. The shore was a long time in emerging from the half-light, a low dim shore with the mountains behind still hidden in haze.

By the time that it was full light we were closing Suna Saki, a long sandspit sticking well out into the sea. The grey swell slid lazily up the beach, carrying with it long rolls of seaweed, which turned with the ripples and rolled seaward again. Along the beach, by the point of the spit, there were hurrying little figures running to catch the seaweed with rakes and to load it on to a horse and cart on the beach behind. On this cold early morning they seemed to us symbolic of constant eager striving, in fair weather and foul, all along the enormous coastlines of the Japanese islands, to win food and livelihood from the sea. Never was there a nation more closely allied to the sea, as if the islands had most recently emerged from it and their inhabitants were still living half in and half out of the water. There must be comparatively few who live far enough inland to be out of touch with its threat and its benediction.

We altered course now for the south-west corner of the bay. All about us was the puff and pant of small fishing-boat engines, the white hulls lifting and then disappearing behind the swell. We were continually avoiding the bamboo poles and wondered how *Tzu Hang* had managed to thread her way during the night through so many underwater obstacles.

As we approached the red lighthouse on the breakwater at Mori we found ourselves hemmed in by a minefield of black net floats, supporting coarsely woven nets that guided the fish into traps. We stowed our sails and motored along outside the minefield until a mile or so from the lighthouse we found a clear passage in. Fishermen hauling in the fine-mesh net, which formed one of the traps, spared a hand to wave, and two students, in their black uniforms and peaked caps, leaning against the base of the lighthouse, whistled to us as we passed. We cleared the narrow entrance between the breakwaters and turned sharp to port, then anchored in five fathoms towards the head of the harbour where fishing boats were moored, well clear of the quay.

We looked about us, like dogs who sniff around before settling down. We were gathering impressions of the place where we expected to spend the winter. The village of Mori was hidden behind the fish market and wharf sheds, but we could see ramshackle wooden huts along the beach beyond the breakwater. Behind them the road ran to Mori town, right in the corner of the bay, a little over a mile beyond the port. East and west of us the breakwaters stretched for a short distance straight out from the shore and then turned at right angles to form the entrance and the long northern wall. It was snug enough for the time being, but I could imagine the north wind in winter sending the spray flying over the wall, and plucking savagely at the boats on their moorings. From the empty moorings I could see that there were plenty of boats to come in and there was not much room to swing at anchor if the harbour was crowded.

Along the parapet of the sea wall holiday fishermen were casting with rod and reel far out to sea. They had creels and bait boxes, wore windproof jackets and peaked caps, and looked as if they had stepped out of the advertisement pages of some American fishing magazine. During all our stay in Mori there was always someone so dressed and so employed, except when the seas broke too heavily over the wall. They were graceful against the sky as they cast eagerly seaward, busy as they tended sometimes as many as four rods, speaking only an occasional word to each other. A watched pot never boils, and though I sometimes saw a little fish on the stones beside them I never saw a fish brought in. Beyond the sea wall, away across the bay, we could see the mountains, and behind the village of Mori the ground rose slowly to the base of the volcanoes, green and cultivated, until it suddenly leapt upward in coarse bush and stones.

We went ashore to look at the village. It consisted of three streets about a mile long, with intersecting dirt roads. There were rows of shabby little wooden houses, and numerous factories and warehouses, most of them in a tumbledown condition, but all dedicated to the storing or processing of fish. From the largest fish factory in the centre of the village there rose a huge chimney, like the minaret of a mosque above an Arab village, a symbol of the cult of fish. There was a fish-meal factory, a fertilizer factory, long smokehouses, drying tables and drying racks, wooden boxes and barrels by the hundred, and pestilential smells. On every bit of waste ground there were fish backbones, crab shells and fish heads, which a multitude of curly-tailed dogs for ever sorted and resorted, interred and disinterred.

Beyond the village there was the railway line which ran to Hakodate, and beyond the railway the open country. At one end of the village there was a river, which cut a deep groove through the soft volcanic soil of the hinterland, and over gravel beds by many alternative courses, to the sea. It was the river, and the country and mountain so close behind, that saved Mori from being a slum on the edge of the sea.

We found a good slip in the area of the harbour offices, but two concrete caissons were being built on it. Mori, like every other fishing port in Japan, was busily engaged in enlarging and improving its harbour, and it looked as if the caissons would not be completed for several months, making the slip unavailable for us. We rowed back to *Tzu Hang*.

'Well, I don't know,' said Beryl. 'Fukutome said that we could haul out here, but I don't see how we can when they are

using the slip like that, and I don't see any of the summer
country houses that people were going to be just too ready to
let for the winter.'

'Nothing but hovels,' I said gloomily, but still there was a
crisp feeling in the air that spoke of autumn, the sun was
shining, and we could not feel gloomy for long. Presently there
came a bang on the side of the ship and a knocking on the deck
—a messenger in a heavy rowing boat to say that Mr Takahashi
would like to visit us.

'Thank goodness,' said Beryl. 'Now perhaps we'll be able to
get something arranged.'

Mr Takahashi, Mr Osanai, and Yasuko, Takahashi's
daughter, who acted as interpreter, came on board, carrying a
bottle of whisky and various supplies from the refrigeration
plant as gifts. With much bowing and smiling and 'thank-you's'
we were soon all seated round the cabin table.

Takahashi San was short and sturdy with wavy well-brushed
hair, with a brownish tint which is most unusual in a Japanese.
He had a quick and merry smile and an open face which showed
every passing emotion. He reminded me of my brother-in-law,
who is a J.P. in Yorkshire, and Takahashi San filled much the
same role in Mori. At the moment he looked polite and rather
anxious, an anxiety induced by the responsibility with which he
had been saddled by his friend Fukutome for looking after us. He
only spoke about ten words of English, and these only after a
drink or two, but he understood more. During all the time of our
stay he felt responsible for our welfare and never failed to help
us in every possible way. He had been badly wounded in the
Philippines and had no inhibitions about talking of the war,
unlike the post-war generation whom we spoke to, who always
looked unhappy and awkward if the war was mentioned.

His daughter, Yasuko, the only English speaker in Mori, had
the same open features. She was twenty-three and wore her
hair neck-length, tied with a ribbon over the top of the head.
Doubt and enjoyment, anger and affection passed like cloud
and sunshine over her face and her eyes would sparkle with
gaiety or as suddenly grow dark and mysterious with private
thoughts. She was as strong as a little horse and, if you touched
her, as firm. Her figure was not suited to the Western trousers
and jersey or jacket that she usually wore, but she looked lovely

in Japanese dress. Her thoughts came out in speech as they were formed with a refreshing candour.

'All Japan,' she said once to Beryl, who in warm weather always wore Japanese sandals over bare feet, 'all Japan thinking about the dirty soles of your feet.'

Osanai San, the engineer of the refrigerating plant, was uninhibited and insular. He had a narrow, oval face, a small aquiline nose, and the look of an American Indian about him. He was unreserved and extrovert, and unlike the average untravelled Japanese, quite sure that all difficulties of communication could be overcome by vigorous acting and a Japanese-English dictionary. He never spoke the English word, but indicated it with his thumbnail as he could only read the Japanese script. He was Takahashi's executive officer in all his dealings with us, and with him we were involved in an endless charade.

Takahashi San spoke to his daughter and she translated.

'My father says,' she said, 'that we are very honoured to have you in Mori and that he hopes you will stay for the winter.'

'It is our honour and pleasure to come to Mori.'

'My father says,' she went on after this return had been translated, 'that he will do all he can to make your stay a happy one.'

'Please thank your father very much.'

'My father says,' she went on, 'you like whisky.'

I am not a whisky drinker, but as the bottle was there and Takahashi San's eyes brightened, I said that I liked it very much. The bottle was opened and we settled down to questions of a house for ourselves and a haul out for *Tzu Hang*, interrupted by Takahashi San's first two words of English, 'You like, you like,' as he poured himself another peg. Fortunately the session, which looked as if it might go on until the bottle was finished, was interrupted first by Osanai and then by Yasuko, both of whom began to feel the slight motion below, and had to go on deck.

When they left we felt that a start had been made. Takahashi San had confirmed that the big slip would not be available, but there was a shipwright who had a shed a little down the shore, who hauled out heavy fishing boats for repair by a powerful electric winch. There was also a 'stone house' that was believed to be available, in which there was a desk. It had been arranged that Osanai would take us on a tour of inspection the following afternoon. The morning, however, was to be devoted to a bath in the public bath in Mori, as the bath in the fishing village was not considered to be up to the standards of visiting foreigners.

Next morning the sun was shining and the sea sparkling, the mountain behind the port clear and waiting to be climbed. Even the dreary village didn't seem so bad. We set off to walk to Mori town along the road that leads beside the shore. It runs between little wooden shacks, those on the right of the road being built over the dirty grey sand above the tide line. On the left of the road we passed a large wooden shed where a small fishing boat was being built. Great wide planks, rough sawn with bark on the edges, were stacked in the yard and a number of big logs lay higgledy-piggledy about it. Wide planking is a characteristic of Japanese fishing boats, the smaller ones having usually only two planks from bilge to deck level. From inside the dark shed came the whine of a saw and the clean smell of fresh sawdust.

Between the huts and almost on the road there were wooden capstans, with capstan bars lying beside them, used for pulling the fishing boats up on to the beach. At one point there was an electric winch, which served several houses, the winch cable being led over a snatch block fastened to the old capstans. Through a gap between the houses we saw a white fishing boat coming in and walked down to watch it.

There were several women, white towels tied round their heads, waiting to receive it. The boat headed in towards them, then dropped a bow anchor and turned quickly on the edge of the breakers, while one of the crew hurled a line to the women standing in the ripples. One of them splashed in to retrieve it and they then hauled a wire rope attached to a bridle on the boat's stern. This was quickly made fast to the capstan cable, the capstan manned with the help of any boy or bystander who happened to be near, and the boat winched ashore. The catch was then unloaded into boxes, the boxes reloaded on to a bicycle-trailer, and within a few minutes the fisherman was on his bicycle, pedalling down the road towards the fishmarket on the quay where the bigger boats unloaded directly.

The boat that we had just seen come in was typical of many all round the coast of Japan. It was about 30 feet long with fore and aft sheer both above and below water, with a very hard turn to the bilge and a shallow keel. It was decked in, with a fish hold for'ard and a high bulwark which extended beyond the side of the boat so that it gave a wide working platform all round the ship and wheelhouse. The wheelhouse was small and gave inadequate shelter to the crew, but covered the engine hatch. The propeller shaft was jointed and pulled up into a housing under the stern, so that the boat could be winched up stern first. On this day the sea was calm, but often in winter, when sudden snow flurries whipped the sea into long white ridges, we saw them beach their boats like this, and marvelled at their seamanship and their hardiness.

During the winter that we spent in Mori we heard that nearly forty fishermen were drowned from the villages along the coast of Uchiura Bay. Nearly all of them were lost from small boats within a quarter of a mile of the shore.

We continued our walk to the bath. The road was being widened and women, again wearing white cotton towels tied over their heads and under their chins, trousers, short rubber boots, and white gloves, were shovelling gravel for the tar-spreaders. One of them was a tall attractive girl, with a bold glance which indicated that she only needed a sign, and she would not be wasting her looks and her time spreading gravel.

The Ofuru at Mori was recognizable, like most Ofuru, by the smoke coming out of a tall chimney. It was open but, as everyone was at work, it was also empty. We went up some steps to an inner door, which gave access to two dressing-rooms, the one on the left for men, the one on the right for women. Between these two entrances there was a high cashier's desk, presided over by a bored and unattractive woman. Here we could buy combs, soap, and the small cotton towels that every working man and woman wears about their head, in different styles according to their occupation. In the bath, however, they are carried modestly in front of you like a fig leaf when walking naked, and are used for both washing and drying. We paid our modest dues—Beryl paid extra because she wished to wash her hair—and separated, I to the left and Beryl to the right.

I took a basket from a pile of baskets, selected a corner not immediately overlooked by the woman at the desk, undressed, put my clothes in the basket, and then with soap in one hand and little towel held daintily in front of me, stepped through glazed glass doors into the bath itself. It was like a swimming bath with a wide white tiled floor round it, and numerous pairs of taps all round the walls. The bath itself was steaming, but in one corner of the room there was a much smaller bath— for salamanders, I suppose—which appeared to be almost boiling. It was all very clean, without even a yellowing cigarette stub in the gutter that ran round the wall under the taps. I took a small wooden bucket and a short-legged wooden stool facing a pair of taps. I mixed the water to the right temperature in the bucket and then emptied it over my head, repeating the process again and again with much splashing, soaping, and rubbing with the damp towel and occasional gasps as I carelessly poured the wrong mixture over my head. Then I lowered myself slowly into the central bath, sat on the step which runs all round inside with only my head out of the water, and stewed. After this there was more washing under the taps, then I rubbed myself as dry as is possible with a little damp rag, dried off in the warm room for a minute or so, then back through the doors to my clothes. There is nothing nicer than the Ofuru when it is empty, but I do not care for it in the rush hours.

When Osanai took us in the afternoon to see the shipwright with the powerful winch, we were horrified to find that, as we had already begun to suspect, they intended to haul us out on the beach in the same way as they had beached the boat in the morning. All the fishing boats, big and small, are built with a hard turn to the bilge, almost flat-bottomed, so that they hardly heel at all when beached. We drew *Tzu Hang*'s underwater shape in the sand, but Osanai and the shipwright were very conservative in their ideas of underwater shape, and obviously considered us to be poor draughtsmen. With the help of Osanai's acting and Beryl's dictionary we found that she was to be propped up with sandbags.

'But how are you going to pull us when she is propped up with sandbags?'

We couldn't ask this question, of course, but we got it over by vigorous acting. Osanai, now sweating heavily, ran busily up and down the beach, laying imaginary skids, moving imaginary sandbags, and making a noise like an electric winch. Even if the winch was strong enough to move us like this there was nothing on *Tzu Hang* that would stand up to it. Eventually the shipwright, who had been taking off his cap and rubbing his head for some time, asked if the keel was made of iron. We told him it was made of lead, and this put an end to the argument. The shipwright thought that the keel would be damaged. So did we—and not only the keel. Perhaps there would be some other way.

The 'stone house' was almost equally disappointing. It was a square stone house opposite a large stone-crushing mill, dusty within and without, standing in untidy waste ground. It was locked, but as we peered through the dirty windows we saw a desk and a table, and although my spirits fell Beryl was undaunted and she was soon planning how best she could make it into a happy home. In Osanai's eyes it had particular merit because of the desk, the table, and two chairs. Just the thing for foreigners, although it had only two rooms, and a passage which acted as kitchen, bathroom, and other utilities. On that afternoon the stone-crushing plant was silent, but as it worked on every afternoon all through the winter, with clouds of dust and thunderous noise, it was just as well that in the end the house turned out to be unavailable.

We returned to the boat for a gloomy tea—until we decided to sail over to Muroran and explore the possibilities of wintering there. Before we left we took the train to Komagatake station and a bus round Lake Onomu, which dropped us at a path leading to the mountain. The guide-book said 'the ascent is found easy even by women climbers', and as we climbed up the steep straight path to the lip of the old crater, which got steeper and stonier as we climbed, we passed a Japanese girl striding down. She was wearing climbing boots, black ski trousers, and black quilted coat over a red pullover, a red ribbon over her glossy black hair. She looked as free as the hills, a spirit of new Japan, but the young man hobbling down some way behind her did not live up to this impression. Perhaps he had the heavier load.

Komagatake must once have burst asunder, hurling lava and ash in all directions, and forming the rich sloping plain between the stony slopes and the sea. There is still, in the centre of the old crater, a small active crater, which last erupted fifty years ago. It is a small raw wound now, in an old scar. Beryl and I, however, were not particularly interested in craters. If we were going to live under a mountain for the winter, we wanted to be sure that we had climbed it first. For the time being the summit was hidden in mist, but we followed round the easy slopes of the inside of the old rim, until we found signs of a track leading upwards, marked as always in Japan by the plastic bags and tins of previous climbers. It led through a notch in the old crater wall and then traversed backwards and upward until we reached the highest point, when the cloud lifted and we could look right down to the sea.

We got down to find that we had missed the bus, and had to walk to the station. I was at least as footsore as the Japanese girl's companion and even Beryl had lost some of the resiliency of her step.

Back at the quay we found Osanai and his son from High School waiting to take us to the refrigeration plant to collect ice and a lobster, but we pleaded that we were too weary. They brought other news, however.

'Tomorrow,' translated young Osanai, 'tomorrow there is a meeting about you. There is another slip which takes big boats which you will be able to use.'

Perhaps it is the volcanic nature of Japan's soil that keeps the spirit bubbling over, or deep at its lowest level, that makes one joyous or suicidal. We rowed out, greatly cheered by this news and by our happy day in the country, to tea and eggs. We put our feet up and opened our books, when there was a resounding crash against the side of the boat, a hammering on the deck, and a voice saying ' 'Allo'. It was the local middle-school English teacher and two of his pupils. He carried a packet of potato chips in his hand and made a prepared speech, but when we replied to him he could not understand a word as he had never heard English spoken by an Englishman. We were able to re-establish his prestige by talking very slowly.

It took only a few hours to sail over to Muroran, and as we tacked up the long harbour we brought a frightened hoot from a big freighter to say that she was overtaking and turning to port. All this was already obvious and it made us feel like a white mouse in the stable of a nervous elephant. Presently the *Kaijōhowancho* arrived, and we were so pleased to see their grey fatigues and white caps that we waved to them as if they were old friends.

'Please follow,' they called, and we followed them as usual to the most secure berth in the whole harbour, and were soon tied alongside the coastguard cutter. It wasn't a comfortable harbour and had little to recommend it. There were no safe anchorages out of the way of traffic, and the southerly wind sent in an unpleasant lop. It was a big commercial harbour which didn't cater in any way for yachts, bitterly cold in winter, with apparently no small slips other than those in big yards. In fact it had nothing to recommend it to yachtsmen, yet we enjoyed our stay there as much as in any other port.

First there were a horde of reporters to be dealt with, then a late lunch on *Tzu Hang* with the coastguard captain. Then the Mayor sent us a car so that we might drive round the town. No sooner were we back than a young American couple riding round Japan on a motor-cycle arrived on the wharf and came down to drinks. After dinner two Customs officers arrived, one of whom had built his own fifteen-foot sailing boat and brought us Eric Hiscock's book *Cruising under Sail* for a 'sign please'. 'I hope to your happy. Mururan Customs', he wrote in our Visitors' Book.

Next morning the Mayor himself arrived with two photographers and a gift of Ainu carvings. He was obviously a great public relations man, and his photographers were anxious to get suitable photos of the Mayor visiting the Canadian yacht that had arrived in the harbour. He came down below for coffee, but they had barely decided on the best angle for their pictures when he began to look uneasy. Although *Tzu Hang* was lying at the quay, there was a lop in the harbour which made her move. He stuck the slight motion, mopping his face with his handkerchief for as long as he considered good manners demanded, then made a rush for the deck and the shore, but not before he had arranged to send his car to take us on a grand tour of the country.

In various ports in Japan we were given this V.I.P. treatment and wondered what on earth had qualified us for it. Perhaps it was because we were the first foreign yacht cruising in these waters, almost the first yacht to cruise there at all. We were certainly an enigma to the Japanese, who associate yachts with wealth and wordly success, and consequently could not understand why we had decided to live in Mori. Perhaps they hadn't heard that a yacht is a well into which you continue to pour your wordly wealth without hope of any return. Maybe there is no return in money, but there are other dividends.

Next day to Noboribetsu, the famous hot springs, a narrow street on a steep hillside. It was full of holidaying Japanese, pink from the baths, wandering under the flags and banners that decorated the curio shops, dressed in sandals and their hotel kimonos, and recognizing each other by their uniform like soldiers in a garrison town. *Onsens* are mineral baths, usually part of a big hotel, and there are several of them in Noboribetsu. Everywhere steam was ascending, from windows and gutters, chimneys and waste pipes, and particularly from the origin of all this heat—a wasteland of sulphurous pools, cones, and craters, a mile beyond the town.

Beryl and I went to one of these Onsens. We separated to different changing-rooms for, though bathing is mixed, dressing is segregated. It was all on a much greater scale than anything that I had experienced before, and as I entered the baths, under one huge roof, I felt correspondingly more naked. There were several large baths, all at different temperatures, and places to wash at before entering them. In one corner jets of hot water fell about twenty feet to the floor, a hot shower that beat on heads and shoulders with thought-numbing force. There were naked bodies all over the place, male and female, and at my first frightened glance I thought that they were all unattractive ones. When I became more at home, from the security of the bath itself, I was able to see that there was an occasional young woman of attractive form blooming like a violet in a vegetable garden.

One has to take the rough with the smooth, and in the Onsen it is mostly rough, but the few pretty girls were charming in their simplicity, unaware, or so it seemed, of the contrast that they made with those less fortunately favoured.

There was a more secluded bath for shyer women, shielded by potted palms, but still accessible to men. Beryl bathed here, but word went round that there was a foreign woman in the bath, and one elderly man, pushing his stomach like a wheelbarrow in front of him, was off like a shot to investigate. His

E

anxious wife pursued him, carrying her load behind. Beryl didn't enjoy the Onsen, but she said that she didn't really mind even the curious Japanese, but had a horror of meeting some-one of her own race whom she knew.

Perhaps the most interesting and the most disappointing thing that we did was to visit the Ainu village at Shiraoi, about twenty-seven miles from Noboribetsu. At the railway station, while trying to decipher the timetable, we met three young American naval officers who were doing the same thing. They were all lawyers, working at the U.S.N. legal office, at their headquarters at Yokosuku. In the crowd of Japanese in the station they stood out in their western clothes and tall good looks, like the three peaks of Komagatake above the foothills and the plain. We rushed together like old friends and were soon exchanging bathing experiences. Fortunately a type of Japanese confidence man who had attached himself to Beryl and I as an unwanted guide, was also exchanged, like a camel fly between dogs, as he recognized more lucrative prey. The three lawyers—Lewis, Addison, and Steel as Beryl called them —were too smart for him, and gave him the slip in Shiraoi. They were members of an Anglophile society, drank the Queen's health on important occasions and sometimes carried tightly rolled umbrellas.

Shiraoi was an example of the degradation of becoming a tourist attraction. I sometimes wonder if the Household Brigade may not suffer in the same way. There were a few miserable Ainu, pale-faced and bearded, dressed up to attract the tourists, and looking as helpless, confined, and bored as a cheetah in a cage. Their principal art, that of carving wooden animals, has been standardized to manual mass production, so that there is no longer any originality in their work. The soul has gone out of them and they are dying fast. The Japanese will say that there are perhaps 16,000 Ainu, but the pure Ainu are very few and far between. Soon there will be none at all. Even the narrow boats that used to be drawn up on the beach at Shiraoi were no longer there, as if they had given up their last manly occupation in favour of the parasitical tourist trade.

The next day was dedicated to the grand tour in the Mayor's car, to visiting the smoking new cone at Usu, to steaming round Nakajima Island in Lake Yoya, and to a session with the English

Speaking Society in Muroran. This is a society organized by the students, and it was touching to see how excited and happy they were to meet Westerners, to speak English and to ask questions about our way of life. For all the terrible annoyance that we were continually subjected to by the curious and ill-mannered, there was always this counterbalance of eager young people, desperately keen to learn, finding happiness in the simplest things, and appreciative of the least kindness.

The Customs officer who had built his own sailing boat, asked if he could 'play at yachting' with us, so we took him for the sail back to Muroran. When we arrived there we heard that there was to be another meeting at the offices of the Harbour Board to discuss the slipping of *Tzu Hang*, but before this Osanai took us to look at the proposed slip. It was in the Harbour Board area where two small quays enclosed a gently sloping beach. It consisted of two 50-foot built-up beams of timber, 12 by 12 inches, grooved on the upper surface, and fastened together about the distance of railway lines apart. Two similar beams similarly fastened, with a ridge on the under side, slid on these rails, and were pulled up or down by the donkey of the floating steam crane anchored in the harbour. The rails could be extended into the water to the required depth by numbers of eight-foot grooved baulks of timber of similar size held down in position by sandbags until they took the weight of the carriage. It all looked very old and shaky, but it also looked as if it might work. Osanai told us that not only did the crane pull a big scow up for the winter, but that it also wound itself up, so it had plenty of strength to pull us. Big boats were sometimes hauled out, he said, but they rested on their bilges. We would need a cradle resting on the carriage, and he insisted again that sandbags were the thing for this. As long as her keel was supported, I didn't mind what she was propped up with.

Oshii San, a retired ship's engineer who ran a machine shop in Mori, presided over the meeting. He represented the local Chamber of Commerce, the Rotary Club, and the Harbour Board, and today was very much the Board Chairman. Everything had obviously already been decided in private session, and after asking us one or two questions, which Yasuko interpreted, sitting straight on a bench with her hands primly in her lap, he told us that they would do it in October and that they would charge us nothing, but would be pleased if we would give the men working on it food and *saki*, and that when she was finally safely up we should give a party for everyone.

Oshii San was a great man. When I went into his shop he was always hard at work in clean overalls and white gloves, looking like a chief engineer on a tour of a ship's engine room. His various engineers worked just as hard and as efficiently. There was no loafing and talking. Oshii San rarely smiled but when he did you felt that you had made a huge success. As soon as he understood the problems that we continually brought him, he seized a bit of chalk, and dashed off the solution with a few bold strokes on some old piece of steel plating. Then he chalked the date on which it would be ready, and if you agreed, gave the smallest indication of a smile to close the interview, as he turned back to his lathe.

Now that he had said we would be hauled out, although I had only just met him, I knew that we would be hauled out, even if Mori sank in the process. It had become a question of prestige. Oshii San was a little out in his dates and in his estimate of difficulties. He, too, like everyone else that we dealt with, had difficulty in appreciating *Tzu Hang*'s underwater shape, until they saw her in winter, towering above the scow and above the deck of the crane that pulled us out, and spent the winter beside us.

5 Winter in Mori

Every day now the wind brought a colder message and the leaves began to show their red warning. Rack after rack of turnips and long, white radishes, which would soon be pickled, began to appear about the houses. We were almost walled in by them. The corn was gathered and hung on similar racks to harden and dry. The long, leafy stalks were collected for silage, fed into a chopping machine and carried through a feed pipe to the tops of the small silos. This was man's work; but in the rice fields the women were as busy as the men. The rice was cut by hand with sickles, then either stacked or hung on post and wire racks to dry. It was then stacked in the fields on tripods, so that each rice stack looked like a round, straw house with an open door. Here they waited, each wearing by day a cap of crows, until the carts came to take them off to threshing machine or barn. All was gone before the snow came, silently drawing its blanket over the empty fields.

Osanai came with a message to say that we should be ready to take the masts out as soon as the crane was available. We set to work to strip *Tzu Hang* of her rigging. At the same time he told us that the lease of the stone house had fallen through, but that there was another house that we could rent, if we did not mind—and here he fell into a perfect paroxysm of grunting and squeaking—the noise of pigs.

We went to look at it. It was a small Japanese house, a little less shabby than the average in the village, with the *tatami* matting in good repair. With sliding screens it could be made into a house of four rooms or a house of two, with a separate dining-room or office, and a kitchen. There was no furniture, but Takahashi had promised us a table and a chair, and a Roman Catholic priest, whom we had met by chance in Mori, sent us another table, two chairs, and a double-burner butane stove. With these we equipped the dining-room and the kitchen leaving the rest of the house in Japanese style, but using cushions from the boat to sit on and as mattresses at night. Beryl set to work to make Japanese *futons*, a kind of eiderdown, out of blue and red spinnaker cloth and nylon fibre padding. These were splendid for the boat, and are still in use.

The advantage of the new house over the stone house was that it was attached to a long smokehouse, and had once been the manager's living quarters. The kitchen door opened into the smokehouse, which was fifty-three feet long, with ten smoke rooms whose doors we kept shut, fronted by a wide, concrete passage. It was an ideal place for stowing our sails, masts, and spars, if we could get the masts inside. There was a foot to spare, and we found that we could pass the masts through a window to the living-room, through the kitchen and into the smokehouse. The factory had been intended for the herring trade, but the herring had gone from these waters and it had fallen into disuse. The disadvantage to this house was that it fronted the back end of a long pigsty. It would have been uninhabitable in summer; but in winter the cold looked after both the flies and the manure, which was shovelled out from time to time, almost into our yard.

We seemed to be progressing slowly towards our goal of a house and a haul out, when suddenly there was drama. A typhoon was heading our way. Osanai arrived to tell us that we had to go alongside the crane, the engine of which was already smoking at the wharf, and that the masts would be taken out immediately. So much the better. We started the motor and went alongside the crane. As soon as we were secured a block was fitted to the slings that we had already prepared and, after a little huffing and puffing from the old steam engine, the masts were picked up and laid gently on the wharf, where all work had stopped as men came to watch or lend a hand. Beryl and I had soon lost control of the proceedings, but Takahashi San seemed to have taken over, with most of his staff from the refrigeration plant, the *Kaisha*, as it was called, under his command. Numerous willing, but unco-ordinated hands picked up the masts and laid them on bicycle trailers, turning them into lethal weapons as they hurried them round corners and across the streets, regardless of traffic, gate-posts, or the small, wooden houses that might be in their way.

By the time that the storm drogue flew stiffly at the mast-head above the harbour offices, and fishermen anxiously tended their lines on the wharf, *Tzu Hang* was riding safely to three anchors, with all her windage gone, and well below the level of the sea wall. We had strong winds and drenching rain; but the typhoon, after killing thirty people and sinking sixty-four boats in Southern Honshu, swung away and left Hokkaido in peace.

Now that we had a house Beryl, with Osanai as her hench-man, set about getting it fit to live in. A carpenter was called to put up a bathroom of sorts in the smokehouse, and a wood-fired water heater and a concrete bath were installed. The bath was the shape of a barrel, into which I could just force myself in a sitting position, and was filled by a cold tap, while the water circulated directly from the bath to the heater and back to the bath. It did not take long to heat, but the difficulty was to stop it heating, once inside. Crouching like a foetus in a concrete womb, we would suddenly become aware that near-boiling water, in inexorable circulation, was coming into the bath. It was too late then to control it by turning on the cold tap, and there was a frantic scramble out of the bath to the cold floor where, later in the year, the sponge was already frozen, if it had been dropped outside.

Beryl and Osanai between them discovered a round, iron stove, and yards and yards of tin stove pipe was bought in Mori. The pipe led straight up from the stove to the ceiling, across and through the wall, then well up above the height of the roof. From time to time it had to be taken to pieces and then pushed through like a cannon, with a brush tied to a bamboo pole. Black soot showered all over the place, staining the snow, in spite of the plastic bag we used to tie over the end of the pipe. The soft coal of Hokkaido must produce its own weight in soot. Trains can be seen fifty miles away, like volcanoes in eruption. 'Hokkaido coal best coal,' the insular Osanai loved to tell me. 'And makes the blackest smoke,' I'd add. 'Yes, Smeeton San, the blackest and best.'

They also found an automatic pump which was installed in the kitchen in place of the hand pump that the sink was fitted with. The pump operated like those in every other house, from a water level about twenty feet below the houses. We always hoped that there was good gravel there as well as clay above, which might act as a filter, for every house in Mori had an outside privy—a *benjo*. And, of course, there were the pigs next door.

'No water like Mori water,' said Osanai, and in this he was probably correct.

October came in with fine weather and men started on the slip, greasing the rails and strengthening the ties between them. The carriage was placed on top, the baulks of timber arrayed upon the shore, and just as we thought all was ready, everything was covered with sacking and old bits of brown paper from cement bags. We had to wait for a suitable tide. Every day we went to the Harbour Board offices and interviewed the two engineers whom we knew as 'Fat San' and 'Thin San'. When I pointed out that the beams on which *Tzu Hang*'s keel was going to rest looked rotten, 'Fat San' smiled and 'Thin San' shook his head. When pressed for a date they replied, 'Soon, soon.'

Then there came high winds and rain, with the storm drogue humming again above the harbour offices. October 12th was a perfect day, and suddenly they agreed to start that very afternoon. The crane was moved into position, the rails and carriage pulled down to tide level, and the extension laid. The outer baulks in deep water were laid by two helmeted divers operating from two diving boats with hand-operated pumps. When all was ready and the carriage pulled down to the required depth it came off the rail, and *Tzu Hang* was sent back to her anchors.

Next day we tried again. This time we got *Tzu Hang* on to her cradle and she started in, moving in alarming dashes, while the crane engine clanked and puffed at its seaward mooring. It was a slow process, as each eight-foot baulk of timber had to be realigned under water as the carriage came in. With the receding tide and her inward progress *Tzu Hang* began to rise out of the water, balanced on her keel, with only a 'V' of sandbags holding her upright at the bow. She wobbled at each inward dash. Soon there were cries for more sandbags to build up a support on the centre beam of her cradle. These were handed down to the divers, bubbling away on each side. Night fell and bonfires were lit on the wharf. Men tore themselves away from their television sets and the Olympic Games to come and watch the work. At midnight 'Fat San' came and asked us to go to bed. We felt that they were embarrassed by our being there, and as we had no control anyway, we left them. At two in the morning we heard a knock at our door, and found a worried 'Fat San' outside. The cradle had broken, but *Tzu Hang* was all right. We went down before breakfast to see her, and found the front beam on which her bow rested had broken in two. She was tipped at a steep angle, resting on the sandbags, but obviously unharmed. There was another foot of tide that afternoon and, in spite of all their work, she had advanced so little shoreward that we were able to pull her off and to put her once more on her anchors.

The whole of Mori town and the *Minato*, the port, were now nearly as deeply involved in the slipping of *Tzu Hang* as they were in the Olympic Games. Wherever we went we met with sympathetic faces and anxious expressions of concern: one from the Mayor and one from the old man who mixes birdseed. 'Fat San' told us that it might be a month before the tides were suitable again, and that meanwhile they would have to send to the woods to get better timber beams for *Tzu Hang* to rest on. Yasuko, who had taken on the job of general help in order that she might study English and the English, in exchange for teaching Beryl Japanese, did not appear one afternoon.

'I couldn't come,' she explained, 'because my eyes were so red with crying because the Dutchman beat the Japanese in the Judo.' She was almost as equally upset at the failure to get *Tzu Hang* out of the water as we were. We felt that now they knew much more of her weight and underwater shape they would get her up all right next time.

One day Yasuko, blushing down to her pretty neckline, told me that she wouldn't be able to come in the afternoon, because she was going to 'a salmon with our father'.

'Yasuko can't come this afternoon,' I told Beryl, 'she's going to the *Kaisha* with her father to get a salmon.' That seemed a good enough interpretation, but she actually was of an inquiring mind and had gone to listen to a sermon by the Catholic priest, to whom she always referred as 'our father'. She brought him back—he who had sent us the table and stove —to see us.

After that he often came, bringing a bottle of sweet red wine for lunch, which we suspected might have been intended originally for other uses. He was a sturdy Basque, who wore a beret, and had a brother running the family farm in France. He spoke to us in English and French, but he had been so long in Japan that he thought in Japanese. He used to take us for drives in the country, and sometimes hunched his head down between his shoulders and mumbled what sounded like curses in Japanese.

'What on earth are you doing, Father?' I asked him once.

'A policeman,' he replied, 'didn't you see him? Spawn of the Devil. They took my licence away for six months once.'

Our father had a well-trained tenor voice and he and Yasuko, with her clear treble, used to sit on the floor and sing Japanese songs in harmony together. He would also sing us Basque songs. He was a good and dedicated man, full of fun, always ready to help with our problems, and we became very fond of him. I saw him laughing one day and asked him why.

'I was thinking,' he replied, 'that now you have a Chinese boat, a Siamese cat, a Pakistani daughter' (Clio was born in Pakistan), 'an Afghan hound, and a Basque father.'

The first snow fell and, though it soon disappeared, Komagatake remained covered for the rest of the winter. By the first week in November the new cradle was ready and this time strong eyebolts were put through the end of the beams, to which long rigging screws were fastened. These were to be attached to iron rods, fastened to angle irons across *Tzu Hang*'s deck, so that she could be screwed firmly to her cradle. I was satisfied that this would be sufficient to hold her steady, but they proposed to make doubly sure by shoring her up with sandbags again. It was a much more efficient arrangement than before.

As the high tides approached the weather changed to snow and strong, cold winds; but by November 10th it was clear again. At the appointed time we went down, but found that they had already brought her in and she was in position over the cradle. The work went on all day and most of the night. First the shore anchor, to which the block was attached, pulled out. Then the hawser broke. This was spliced up again and *Tzu Hang* began to inch shoreward. Bonfires were lit and the light of the flames reflected from her white hull, while above her the moonlight lit the snows on Komagatake. It was freezing hard, but the men continued to splash about her in cheerful but disorganized activity. So it seemed, but *Tzu Hang* came in little by little. 'Fat San' was there, his face glowing in the light of the flames. We bought bread and cigarettes for the men, but 'Fat San' would not allow us to give them *saki* until she was up. By one o'clock she was high and dry and safe for the winter. She looked enormous, towering up above the low-roofed huts and cottages. We went to bed, knowing that we need worry no longer, when the storm warnings flew, when the spray froze on the harbour wall, and the snow flurries hissed down the deserted streets.

If we had had to pay for our haul out in time and in labour it would have been the most expensive haul out in the world; but we paid for it by buying timber for the new cradle, by *saki* for the workmen when the job was finished, and by a party which we gave in our house for Takahashi, Osanai, Oshii, 'Fat' and 'Thin' San, and various of the village dignitaries. Everyone knew the English word 'party', and it has been adopted by the Japanese. Soon Beryl, Yasuko, and the inevitable and ubiquitous Osanai were planning it. Meanwhile, another event in our lives provided interest and speculation for the villagers of the *Minato*.

We felt very far away from Clio in London, and her letters, often written but rarely posted, were few and far between. We wrote suggesting that she should join us and now we got a reply. 'May I come for Christmas and bring Kochi?' it said, Kochi is a Powinda dog that Clio had picked up in Afghanistan when returning overland from her last visit to *Tzu Hang* in Singapore. Coming for Christmas did not mean coming for a weekend visit. It meant a complete evacuation of London and sailing with us back to Canada, and I had offered her an irresistible bait of sea otters and Kodiak bears to be seen on our way back.

'Oh dear,' said Beryl. 'What on earth are we going to do with that ghastly dog?'

'We'd better have it, because if we don't she'll never leave it,' I replied. It is no good expecting the daughter to be very different from the mother. 'I think it's lucky that she isn't bringing the cat and the rabbit as well.'

'She couldn't do that because of Pwe. I wonder what Pwe will think of the dog?' The cat had taken up permanent residence under the lowest part of the stove pipe, where she was gradually burning the hair off her back. She was bored with life, since it was too cold and there were too many dogs about outside for hunting expeditions. It was a life to be endured in as great comfort as possible until it should change, and even Pwe must now be assured that life changes rapidly in her household.

'If only it could have been a dachshund,' said Beryl. 'I can't think of anything more inappropriate than a dog like a Powinda on a yacht.'

When we went shopping now we were always asked about the latest news of our daughter, as telegrams flew back and forth. Everyone seemed to share in our excitement, and all the girls over fourteen were agog to meet her. None of them had ever seen a foreign girl; their experiences of foreigners being limited to priests, missionaries, and elderly tourists, whom they passed occasionally in the streets of Hakodate. There were inquiries from two schools about the possibility of her teaching English during her stay in Japan. One cold morning Beryl and I set off for Hakodate to meet her.

Mori was deep in the snow which would help to hide some of its untidyness until the beginning of March. The sides of the road to the station were banked with it, the road itself snow-packed and slippery. The passengers for Hakodate by the early morning train were huddled in a small waiting-room where a coal stove glowed and moisture ran down the window-panes. Two peasant women were sitting on a bench with baskets of eggs on their laps. They wore the same blue, patterned cotton trousers and jumpers as they did in summer; but now they were so stuffed with underwear and other wrappings that they looked like bundles of old clothes. There was an immobility about their hands and about their bodies, but eyes and tongues were vigorously alive. Beside them sat a silent farmer, wearing a fur cap and a single fox fur, complete with yellow glass eyes, buttoned round his neck. There was the usual sprinkling of students in black, windproof or quilted jackets, with either running noses or white gauze patches tied over nose and mouth. Japan may be the land of the cherry blossom, or at least of the paper cherry blossom; but it is certainly the land of the streaming nose.

A cold wind from Siberia blew down the track, whisking snow along the platform and stirring the loose ends of an old newspaper, frozen to the ground. No one stirred from the waiting-room until a bell rang in the office to tell us that the train had left Mori town station a mile away. Then the door to the platform opened, and a railwayman in a heavy overcoat, with his cap balanced on a black scarf tied round his ears and head, punched our tickets. From the direction of Mori town a tall column of black smoke announced the imminent arrival of the Hakodate train, but on this by-line the trains make a great deal of smoke for little speed, for they take longer to do the thirty-five kilometres to Hakodate than it had taken Adebe to run the fifty kilometres in the Olympic games. Presently we were all inside a fusty-smelling and dirty carriage, jerking along through the countryside that we were beginning to know well from our afternoon walks. The heat was full on, and those who had room took off their boots and curled themselves up on the seats.

When Clio's aircraft arrived at Hakodate we waited anxiously as passenger after passenger disembarked. We had just about decided that she wasn't on the aircraft when she appeared and, since she had come from London and was fashionably dressed and tall, her appearance attracted a considerable amount of attention. From then on, to her annoyance, she became the focal point of the curiosity to which Beryl and I had so long been subjected. In this respect the Japanese, particularly those of student age, are an ill-mannered race. Clio got to know the journey between Hakodate and Mori well, for she took a job teaching English in one of the schools there, and made the journey several times a week; but she never became inured to their curiosity.

When Kochi arrived at Hakodate in a small coaster, after transhipping in Yokohama, *Tzu Hang*'s crew was complete, except for Henry Combe, an old friend of Clio's and a keen sailor, who was temporarily at a loose end. Clio told us that he was very keen to come with us.

'But how do you know that we are going to like him?' I asked her.

'Everyone likes Henry,' she said, 'and anyway he's bought a new movie camera and a dry suit for diving in cold water; but you'll have to write and ask him. I told him I'd tell you.'

I wrote off to Henry and asked him to join us at the beginning of April if not earlier, wondering what he would think of the tawdriness of our surroundings and the discomforts of our bath, but, like Clio, when he arrived he took it all in his stride.

Meanwhile the weather got colder and colder. Christmas came and from every store in every town, 'Jingle Bells' alternated with 'Holy Night' on their tape recorders and loudspeakers. As the ferry boats left and arrived at all the hundreds of ports throughout Japan, their loudspeakers tinkled xylophone recordings of 'Coming through the Rye' and 'Auld Lang Syne'. All Japan was tinkling. The first 'Jingle Bells' was heard on November 1st, and the last on January 1st, and all this time the selling spree went on. The Japanese have adopted not only Christmas, but also Valentine's Day, Father's Day, Mother's Day, and they already had a Boy's Day and a Girl's Day. Soon there will be as many days to inveigle the customer into buying as there are fiestas in Spain.

On New Year's Eve Clio, Beryl, I, and Kochi walked into Mori at midnight, because we felt that we had to be up and doing something, and also that we had to pay our respects to *Tzu Hang*. We went to the Buddhist temple, where we heard that people came to pray. A clear night and a bright moon. There wasn't a sound to be heard, nor a light to be seen as we walked through the *Minato*, but only the sound of our own boots on the frozen road and Kochi's soft padding. Even the piles of refuse that had accumulated outside each house since the first snow fell, and the mounds of frozen urine at the corners of the houses, almost on the pavement, failed to offend on a night like this.

We went up the temple steps, but there was nothing going on, only a boy and a girl hand in hand on the steps. Mori was sleeping like the *Minato*. We made our way back to *Tzu Hang*, made her a little Japanese bow and wished her well, apologizing that she was cold and deserted for the time being. Somewhere behind us a temple bell pealed once in acknowledgment. Then we went back to the floor and the *futons* and the icy cold of our shack.

Up to the New Year, the changing season, the slipping of *Tzu Hang*, the novelty of our situation, and the successive expectations of Clio's arrival, Kochi's arrival, and Christmas, had made the time pass merrily; but for the next three frozen months it was almost a struggle for survival.

Every day we went for long walks into the country, and it was the country behind the village that made life not so bad after all. At one farm there were some thoroughbreds and a stallion recently imported from Ireland, but the real racing studs were still farther to the north. There was always work to be done on poor frozen *Tzu Hang*, and Beryl was employing two women, so wrapped and padded that they could barely turn round in the cabin, to scrape the paint. She also had a pet *Daiku* or carpenter, who was repairing a broken rail caused by a swipe from a floating crane, while *Tzu Hang* was still at anchor in the harbour. The *Daiku* San and Oshii San between them made us a new rudder to replace the oak rudder that we had had made in Chile, as the worm had got into it. The *Daiku* San always carried dried fish in his pocket which he ate himself, but with which he also won Kochi's heart.

On our walks to exercise the dog we used sometimes to plough through the snow straight across country, but more usually took a regular circuit keeping to icy paths and cart tracks. Whichever way we went our path led sooner or later to the river, where the patient, hardworking peasant women were standing in the water in high rubber boots, loading stones with cold, red hands into horse-drawn carts for the stone-crushing plant. Kochi was allowed off her lead as soon as we were across the railway line, and it was lovely to see her as she ranged about on each side, her wolf tail carried high, except when she was galloping. When we put her back on the lead she would cast herself down on the snow in protest.

It was usually dark by the time that we got home, but the little shops were always open and busy, a warm light shining out into the iron-bound night. We stopped to buy chocolate, or *saki*, or plastic bags of oysters in brine, but without their shells. Perhaps a fisherman or a farmer would be sitting at the counter having a glass of *saki*. After a drink or two they'd muster up courage to call on the foreigners. We sat for hours talking to tiddly Japanese, bowing and smiling, and absolutely determined not to offer them any more to drink, lest they should stay for ever.

One afternoon Clio and I were besieged by a drunken fisherman. We rushed here and there like the defenders of Rorke's Drift, trying to prevent his ingress and stay concealed ourselves. When he outwitted us I had to take him by the seat of his pants and throw him out. He tottered down the road, the toes of his woollen socks extending six inches beyond his feet and flapping as he reeled. He had left his boots at the door.

'You can't let him go like that,' Clio called to me. 'He'll get frostbite.'

The temperature at the time was well below zero, so I ran after him and put his boots on, like a child, while he hung on to my neck. Then I handed him over to his friend who came down the road to meet us. The friend boxed his ears so that he fell to the ground, then he picked him up and they went off together, arm in arm.

Osanai, when he came on a visit, stayed for ever. One day, having run out of conversation, I gave him a copy of *Playboy*, which Jack Lewis, of Lewis, Addison, and Steele, had sent up from Yokohama amongst some other old magazines and paperbacks. As Osanai turned the pages he kept shaking his head as if he never would have believed it of me, saying as he did so, 'Oh, ho, Smeeton San.' Next evening he asked us all to supper. We were all sitting; Osanai, Mrs Osanai, several children and ourselves, packed on the floor round a small table, and drinking a glass of *saki* before supper, when Osanai excused himself and disappeared into another room. He returned with a packet of photographs half shielded against his thigh, which he passed to me in the surreptitious manner of a Port Said salesman. I should have recognized it, but thinking that they were family photographs and not having my glasses with me, I asked him to show them to Beryl. Osanai looked surprised, but nevertheless he handed the packet over to her.

Beryl is very good about family photographs. She put the packet on her lap, and with a look of pleasurable anticipation reached for her bag and found her own glasses, which she carefully adjusted on her nose, and then stooped to study the photographs which she expected to be of Osanai and all the children. One look and she gave a wail of dismay, pushing

The harbour of Mori in Hokkaido, North Japan

10. *Tzu Hang* is hauled ashore for the winter

11. Food and livelihood from the sea

them over to me. 'Filthy pictures,' she gasped. I handed them
back to Osanai, who looked rather disappointed. He brought
them round next day, and I had to explain again that I really
did not want to see them. He shook his head in doubt and I'm
sure remained convinced that I was a secret lover of porno-
graphic art.

Henry was due to arrive at the end of March. *Tzu Hang*
looked dreadfully unready for the sea, and I began to expect
that Henry would turn round and go home again when he saw
her. The wind blew as cold as ever, but now and then there
were warm days which began to take the snow away, although
it continued to freeze hard every night. *Tzu Hang*'s deck was
covered in ice. We chipped it off and sent it clattering to the
ground and, as soon as the fleeting sun had dried the decks, we
started to pay and caulk them, while the painters worked on
her topsides: scraping, sanding, and generally scarring them
with marks that she will carry to the end of her days. They were
house and fishing-boat painters, and looked at us in puzzled
wonder as we complained about the scratches.

Clio went to meet Henry and they arrived one night at the
station. Kochi stood on her hind legs against the chain, sniffing
each carriage door as it went past, as she always does when she
thinks that she is meeting someone.

They were loaded with luggage, cameras, diving suits, a
tripod, duffle bag, a suitcase that contained at least five suits
which Henry found of an irresistible cheapness in Hong Kong;
and the lot was topped by a birdcage with a small, singing bird,
a present for Takahashi San. Henry, forewarned by Clio,
showed no surprise at our house; he did not falter at the womb-
like concrete bath, nor at the ravaging draughts in the outside
privy, nor at sleeping on the floor. In the morning, when we
walked between the piles of rubbish that the melting snow
exposed and saw *Tzu Hang*, unpainted and desolate, so high
and dry above the sea, he was as cheerful as ever. He was tall
and gay and twenty-five.

He arrived at the right time, because now there was a regular
flurry of activity. The painters worked on the topsides while we
hurried to finish the caulking of the deck, so that their paint
would not be covered in dust. Two stainless steel tanks—fuel
and water—were fitted. The new rudder was shipped and the

Daiku San finished his work on the rail. He had made a firm friend of Kochi by giving her dried cod, which he always carried in his pocket. Ten days after Henry had arrived *Tzu Hang* was in the water again. The same process was reversed, the crane pulling from its berth beside her round a block anchored in the harbour; but it took most of two days before we got her out to her anchors.

During the winter we had scraped and painted the masts under cover of the smokehouse. Now we arranged for a freighter, which was coming into the harbour, to put our masts in again. With the help of most of the staff of the *Kaisha*, we passed them out of the window and loaded them on to bicycle trailers again. Down on the wharf we laid them carefully and unscarred beside the wharf shed, reassembled the cross trees and refastened and lashed the shrouds and stays. Next morning the freighter appeared and moored to the wharf about a hundred yards farther away than we had expected. We put *Tzu Hang* alongside the wharf in front of her and then carried the mizzenmast alongside. The derrick swung out, its cable was attached to the sling, and the mast was soon picked up and lowered into position.

'Well, that's one. That was pretty good,' I said to Beryl as we tightened the rigging screws.

'Like clockwork,' said Henry as he and Clio came up from fixing the step. At that moment there was a rattle of machinery and a shout from Henry. I looked up to see that the Japanese had had a better idea. A better idea than that of carrying the mainmast to the side of the ship. They had led out the derrick cable, attached it to the head of the mainmast, and were now winching it in along the ground. I let out such a roar of dismay that all work stopped, and we were able to rescue the mast before any major damage was done.

By now we had a hundred helpers, or at least advisers, and as usual no one in command. The Japanese seem to do things without an obvious leader, by communal instinct, in a buzz of activity which to a foreigner seems quite undirected. We attached the derrick cable to the sling again, and the mainmast began to lift; but this time the masthead caught in the mizzen shrouds. The derrick continued to hoist in spite of our shouts, but fortunately the sling was near the point of balance and, although the butt of the mast went up and the head stayed caught in the shrouds, there was no undue strain until the derrick operator started jiggling his machine about in an endeavour to set the masthead free. Suddenly it came away, leaving the mizzenmast shuddering, while the butt began a slow and death-dealing descent. No one, not even the mast, was hurt; but we were not through yet.

It normally takes only two people below to step the mast, that is to guide the butt into the step. Today there were at least eight and only one knew what he was doing. Henry arrived with a Canadian dollar that we had left in the house, just in time to put it under the butt of the mast. He had to fight his way through sixteen legs to do so. 'Lower away,' I called, and at this moment my helpers caught sight of the silver dollar in the mast step. There was a shout of dismay as they all dived to retrieve it, but the mast came down like a safe door, and somehow both fingers and dollar escaped capture.

There was still a lot to do, but by the end of the month we were ready to go. 'Before you go,' said Takahashi San, 'please come to the wharf side so that we may say good-bye.'

Everyone was there: the Takahashis, Yasuko, Osanai and all his family, and all the little Yoshikos and Toshikos who had so often paid us visits. 'Fat San' was there and Oshii San and many others. They threw paper ribbons from the pier into *Tzu Hang*'s decks. Mrs Takahashi's eyes, and Yasuko's, spouted tears and—how strange is life—we almost shed a tear too.

They had been very good to us. Perhaps kinder than we might have been to them if the situation had been reversed.

I hope not. Yet, of all the crew, only Kochi was unhappy to be at sea.

6 To Attu—
Across the Bering Sea

We left Mori, in its ring of snow-covered mountains, on a day of no wind. The white fishing boats spotted the sea, and the murmur of their engines sounded above the slow wash of the waves against the breakwater. We motored out past the red lighthouse, past a fisherman casting resolutely from the sea wall, and through the channel of black net buoys. Once outside we got up sail, but only drifted slowly towards Tomakomai, fifty miles away. We arrived there next morning and found a modern industrial port occupied with the pulp and paper industry, and, like all Japanese ports, in the throes of new development.

We tied up to a dredger and looked around. When I proposed to leave its steel sides for a better place across the channel I started the engine without turning on the fuel cock. This results in a tedious process of bleeding the fuel lines, and since I can blame no one but myself, I think of it as a peculiarly cruel and underhand blow of fate, especially as I can never remember the correct procedure. Now we had Henry with us, who had done some motor racing, and on the strength of this experience had been appointed engineer. I could regard my negligence with equanimity. Henry was soon on his stomach over the engine, his long legs projecting into the cabin, screwing or unscrewing nuts which need snake wrists, X-ray eyes, and six-inch fingers to get hold of. I read the instruction book, Beryl started her litany of 'it's no good trying any short cuts', which she repeats on these occasions, and Clio, Kochi, and the cat got themselves out of the way. When we got the engine going again we moved over to a quiet berth on the other side of the channel.

Here, next morning, we were visited by a Japanese artist,

who was also a 'Speedo' skating champion, a black belt at Judo, and had once been a sprinter of some repute. He was tall, had a keen, aquiline and aristocratic face, and he took a huge bag of our washing away in his car to 'get it done for us'. In the evening he came again to take us all to the public bath, and when this was over we returned to his house to find that the yard and garden were full of familiar and rather disreputable clothes, drying on the line. His round little wife had washed everything herself.

We saw them several times and on the day that we left they came to lunch before we sailed. When his wife said good-bye her black eyes went hazy with a facile emotion. Inspired with wine, and grateful for the enormous wash, so neatly folded, I gave her a kiss, a mere peck on the cheek. If I had lit a bomb under her the result could not have been more surprising. She gave a gasp, and then with flushed cheeks shot like a rocket to the deck. As I followed her up the ladder she caught me by the arm and dragged me vigorously to the mast, where we stood, leaning close and arm in arm, while she called for a photo. The 'Speedo's' dark brows contracted and I remembered that he was a black belt in Judo, but fortunately she seemed satisfied with the photo, and they set off in their car to the harbour control tower, in order to see us leave the harbour.

As we left the deck the breeze came suddenly over the hill behind us, cool on our cheeks. We got up the main and the genoa and were soon sailing quickly down the harbour. The control tower sent up the flag signal 'WAY', 'Wish you a pleasant voyage,' while all the ships in the harbour hooted and whistled. From the balcony of the control tower we could see the 'Speedo' and his wife waving their handkerchiefs. I hoped that my indiscretion had been forgiven.

'Did you see her reaction when I gave her a kiss?' I asked Beryl.

'You don't kiss in Japan,' she replied coldly.

We sailed due south for four miles to avoid fish nets, and then turned east along the coast, finding next morning a fine rocky shore to port, with snow mountains behind. We went into Samani Ko, a small fishing harbour with a good breakwater, its entrance guarded by a rocky promontory, like a haystack, which felt as tipply when we climbed to the top. It was one of the quietest anchorages that we found in Japan, but the one where we suffered most from the student menace ashore.

The curiosity of the Japanese students, the black-uniformed, peak-capped bane of visiting yachtsmen, was the worst cross that we had to bear in Japan. The plague waxes and wanes in virulence with the school holidays and reaches its peak in summer, when a visiting yacht should never tie up to a wharf. Even at anchor during summer holidays, if we went below for tea or a drink, we rarely had long to wait before there was a crash as some inexpert orsman in a borrowed boat rammed *Tzu Hang*'s hull, prior to discharging its cargo of booted teenagers uninvited on to the deck. At the wharf side they drop on to it as lightly as a sack of coal.

Ashore, in Samani Ko, they followed us until one of them, who was imitating us for the amusement of his friends, came too close to Beryl and with one of her violent gestures she caught him a blow in the face so that his cap fell off and he nearly sat down. He became the laughing-stock of his friends who turned like a pack of wild dogs to rend a wounded mate. I could see from the delight on Beryl's face that it was no mistake, and that she had done something she had been longing to do for months.

The giggling students who followed us in Samani Ko were annoying, but the officials could not have been kinder. The mayor sent his car on two successive days to take us for drives into the country. From the centre of Hokkaido a range of mountains runs south-east to Cape Erimo, the south-eastern point of Hokkaido. Between this and the coast, the coastal plain and the valleys running up into the mountains provide the horse-breeding lands of Japan. We went to Hitaka to see the government horse farm, where they were crossing country-bred mares with a Breton or Percheron stallion to breed farm horses. The work is heavy and the fields are generally very small, so that they need a small and sturdy horse, who can get into the corners and who does not till a whole field as he turns.

We saw an English thoroughbred and her foal, recently imported, at another farm, and some thoroughbred yearlings at the Yamade stud farm. It was like meeting old friends from home. I wanted to ask the mare how she liked it here, how she was treated, and what she thought of Japanese grooms. There was no need to ask. They all looked well and happy and were quiet and easy to handle. There were large fields, white-railed paddocks, lovely Dutch barns, and good houses; a feeling of wealth and spaciousness that goes with thoroughbreds.

Tzu Hang sailed from Samani Ko and rounded Cape Erimo on May 3rd, and on May 4th we were overtaken by a deep depression, bitter cold, and strong winds gusting up to Force 8. The old mainsail split and in taking it off, the main halyard, which had been carelessly fastened to a shroud, came undone, and the halyard went up to the masthead, so that we were forced to jog along under jib and mizzen. All the Smeetons and the dog felt seasick, but Henry and the cat remained disgustingly well. Next morning it was quiet enough to send him aloft to recover the halyard. With two youthful and strong people on board, Beryl and I began to think that this trip was going to be a sinecure.

Up to now we had been making short day or night trips, so that Kochi had been able to have regular runs ashore. Although she had to put up with the boat, we couldn't persuade ourselves that she liked it, or that she was not nervous on the deck. When she wanted to go on deck—only to relieve herself—she stood with her front paws on the ladder until someone came to hoist her up from behind. She then waited in the shelter of the cockpit, wrinkling her aristocratically curved nose to windward, her great golden tail down, until one of us took her forward on a lead. There she'd spend an interminable time, moving from one side of the deck to the other as the ship rolled, squatting down and getting up again, until it looked as if the object of the journey would never be achieved. When it was, there were shouts of 'Good Kochi, clever Kochi', and with her tail high she'd make a rush back for the cabin hatch, scrambling over the dinghy amidships in order to keep as far away from the sea as possible.

The cat, Pwe, is a tried and trusty mariner, veteran of many sea miles, several desperate immersions, and innumerable escapades in foreign ports. The boat is her home and she is happy at sea. She has no troubles with her toilet as a large sawdust-filled bowl is provided. Kochi liked her, having been brought up with a kitten, and was always anxious to play with her. Pwe, when sitting on a knee, was liable to take a swipe at Kochi, who is more than knee-high, as she passed, but if no knee was available, in the interest of warmth she'd cuddle up with Kochi on the same seat. Kochi would allow the cat to take food off her plate and they'd sometimes lick the same dish together. When we entered Kushiro on the following morning they were both sitting together in the lee of the doghouse, taking an interest in the sight of land.

Kushiro is a large fishing port, said to send a thousand boats out in May into the Bering Sea. Once inside the harbour we were soon picked up by the *Kaijōhowancho* who took us to a berth in a corner, not too well sheltered, backed by a high wharf where fishing boats unloaded. It was too rough to lie alongside, so we anchored off with long stern lines to the wharf, opposite a fish factory which discharged oily pink refuse into the sea. We got ashore by dinghy, bouncing in the backlash from the wall, and climbing up a smelly iron ladder provided for us by the fish factory, to the top of the wharf.

No sooner were we secured than a yachtsman appeared. He was perhaps the most northerly yachtsman in Japan. He was wearing his yachting cap and waved to us from the shore, until I brought him out in the dinghy. He was a business man who had recently returned from America where he had been getting orders for tins from the American and Canadian salmon trade. He brought out a whole wad of hotel bills and postcards to show us where he had been, and asked us to come ashore to see his factory.

It was a large modern factory some way out of town, and from the gallery outside his offices he could look out across the factory floor and see the tins start as tin sheets, and pursue a rapid course over rollers and on electro-magnetic belts, being cut, soldered, labelled, and packed, until they trundled out of his sight to the dispatch room and on down to the railway station, with only a hand here and there to help them on their way.

'Please, no photos,' he said to Henry who was handling his camera, and I thought of Shuji Watanabe, the yacht designer, who had said to me in Aburatsubo:

'The Japanese, you know, are very good at copying, and sometimes improving a little.'

As we were being conducted round, our guide saw the sill of a big shutter which had been caught by a lift truck and bent up.

'Get that fixed,' he said, like an inspecting general, and by the time that we had returned it was welded and done.

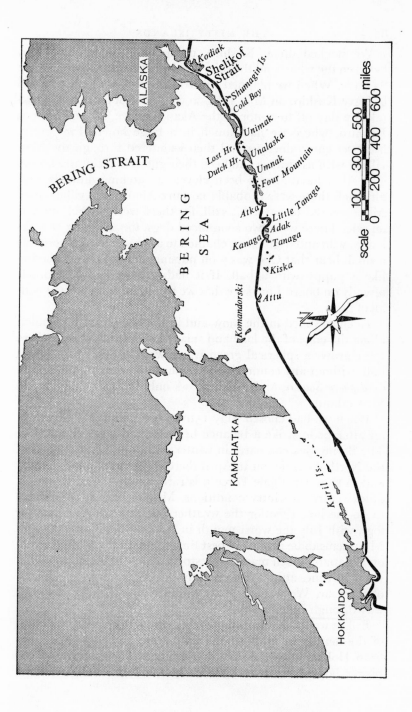

We stocked up at Kushiro, doing many overloaded trips between the wharf and the ship, and by May 17th we were ready to leave. When we planned this trip in Mori we had intended to leave Kushiro on May 15th, so we were not far out. We had taken a day off to motor to the Akan Reserve, fifty miles from Kushiro, where we had lunch in a large hotel. Two pretty hostesses entertained us and then wandered through the Ainu village with us as if we had been their guests in a country house. The Ainu have always been clever at catching animals, and although there were probably no pure Ainu in the village they still appeared to have this skill, for there were several animals on sale. There were two coon-faced dogs, the wild dog of Hokkaido, wild and frightened, chained to a wooden box. There was a small bear that Clio was soon nursing, and a fox cub playing like a puppy with a ball. If it hadn't been for the animals already on board I am sure that we would have had to sail with all of them.

Kochi revelled in the snow and in the opportunity to gallop along the edge of the lake and splash into the icy water, where there grows a spherical green water weed, like a green tennis ball, without any connection to the bottom, known as Marimo, *Cladophora Sauteri*, and which grows only in one other lake, in Switzerland.

When we had chosen May 15th as our sailing date it was in an attempt to strike a balance between bad weather and fog. The Bering Sea compares in winter with the stormiest parts of the North Atlantic but in April there is a general improvement and in summer a gale Force 9 is rare. After August there is a quick return to wintry conditions. May to August then seems to be the best time for the weather but it is also the time for fogs, with July the worst month in the year. Half-way through May seems to be about the best time to start. The typhoon season in Japan, which may send a storm along the Aleutian chain, starts in June, although there may be a typhoon in any month of the year. We wanted to be within reach of shelter by half-way through June.

Before we left Kushiro the harbourmaster showed me a chart of the density of fishing boats in the sea areas stretching out from Hokkaido to the Aleutian Islands. The majority of the bigger boats were now between 300 and 500 miles offshore, with a few eager boats farther away still. They were all in the warm current, the Kuro Shio, which runs up the coast of Japan and across the Pacific south of the Aleutian Islands, the same current that we used to bathe in in Canada and think so cold, and that brought the Japanese weed that sometimes fouled our propeller. The Alaskan current is a cold current that runs in the opposite direction, a branch of the Kuro Shio that turns northward on the Canadian coast, circles the Gulf of Alaska, pushes through between the Aleutian Islands, circles the Bering Sea, and sends one branch, colder still, down the Kuril Chain and down the coast of Hokkaido.

'Keep in the cold current,' the harbourmaster had said, 'and you won't meet any fish boats. They are all fishing in water over five degrees Centigrade. You should stay in three degrees Centigrade. You want to keep clear of them because they never use their radar until they are on the way home. They are too busy when they are fishing and too tired when they are not. Just sleeping you know.' We bought a sea thermometer to take the water temperature and set forth.

The harbourmaster sailed with us as far as the breakwater entrance. He would have liked to come with us all the way. He was an old Navy man for whom I felt a natural affinity. He shook hands with one of those deep meaningful looks that the Japanese give so readily and stepped quickly off *Tzu Hang*, as his launch came faultlessly alongside. We freed the headsail, as *Tzu Hang* leaned to a light south-easterly breeze, and waved good-bye. It was goodbye also to Japan. We were very glad to be going, but there is never a parting without some regret, and we were leaving much kindness behind.

That night Beryl and I began to wonder whether in fact we were going to leave Japan at all. We were becalmed in fog, which wrapped its deathly dripping tentacles about us, and surrounded by fishing boats. The cold current did not seem to have penetrated as far down the coast as here. We did not dare to run the engine because its noise prevented us from hearing the boats about us, and yet without it we were powerless to get out of their way. It was the worst night of the whole journey and not for one moment were we out of the sound of a hurrying boat. They attacked us from all angles, a sudden haze of light coming out of the blackness and as suddenly disappearing again. I do not know how many times they narrowly avoided collision, but their captain's nerves must have been of hardier stuff than ours, for by the time a light wind came and we were able to get under way again, Beryl and I felt like giving up sailing for good. Clio and Henry seemed to take our near misses with the same unconcern as we supposed the Japanese did, for whom it was only routine, a part of their regular life. They were small boats, very well lit, although we could only see their lights from a hundred yards away, and were probably only fishing for short periods offshore.

The following day we had a fair wind from the south-west and were able to set the twins, sailing up the coast of Hokkaido and well offshore, but passing many net buoys. The next day was again fine and clear. *Tzu Hang* crossed the meridian that she had crossed before in the Bass Strait, so that we might now say that we had sailed round the world, or at least that we had crossed every meridian under sail. It was cold—only forty degrees in the cabin. We began to see more interesting sea birds: a puffin and various skuas, long-tailed, pomarene, and one great skua. Kochi wanted to play with Clio on deck, though she took care to remain well amidships.

We got a distant glimpse of the Kurils, now in Russian hands. On May 21st, with 275 miles on the log, we heard that Hokkaido was expecting fresh winds with fifty knot gusts. The glass was dropping steadily and as the wind rose we stripped down to storm jib, trysail and reefed mizzen. At night there were snow flurries and we found it too cold to make it worth-while sitting on deck. We hove-to and turned in.

This became the pattern of an unhurried journey, which was more protracted than it should have been owing to our readi-ness to heave-to rather than face the cold night watches on deck. We had plenty of strong winds and on May 27th Typhoon Amy, the first of the season, was reported to be south-east of Tokyo and coming our way. The next day to my relief Amy was reported to be breaking up, and had been downgraded to a mere storm.

It was a fine cold day with every watch enlivened by the birds. There were shearwaters, fulmars, grey fork-tailed petrels which were always playing about the log line, many skuas, and some kittiwake that accompanied us. We often heard the shrill

scolding of a skua trying to make a kittiwake disgorge its breakfast. More often than not the kittiwake had had no breakfast,
and the skua would eventually leave it for another. We had a
small passenger, a water pipit, that came on board. I suppose
that he had been blown off course on his way up the Kuriles.
We called him 'Fred'. At first he was very assured and strutted
about the deck picking up imaginary insects. In his early days
he sometimes took off on brief flights but was always attacked by
the skuas, who luckily seemed to be unable to estimate his
uneven land-bird flight. He'd almost disappear, a valiant little
dot, and then come struggling back to us forlornly, low over the
grey hungry sea, so that we had to heave-to, to get him safely
on board again. He'd crash-land on deck and then seek shelter
under the dinghy. Clio tried to give him water and something to
eat. Daily we saw that his morale was falling and that he was
weakening. One morning a vicious sea washed down the deck
and as I looked aft I saw Fred rolled, tumbling head over heels,
right to the very point of the stern.

'No more of that,' he decided and fluttered through the hatch
and down into the cabin. Clio made a cage for him out of
basket and hung it on the deckhead. Pwe sat underneath it
malevolently and planning how she might get at him. At about
tea-time she lost interest and we found that Fred was dead.

Grey seas, grey skies, and a cold wind that flicked the icy
spray at our cheeks. A desolate sea and a desolate sky. Nothing
to be seen except the birds. The brown shearwaters up from
Australia; passing close to us, still and tranquil in spite of their
fast movement, like a child on a swing, their eyes still, watching,
their heads not moving. And the fulmars; grey and white or
slaty grey, with shorter wingspread, drawing the same curves
over the sea, yet always seeming busier and more vigorous, a
little more streamlined than the shearwaters.

With four of us on board we divided the night watches into
two-hour watches. It was too cold to stay out longer. I took the
first from eight to ten, Beryl the second from ten to twelve,
Henry twelve to two, and Clio two to four. If it was necessary to
stay on deck Clio sang mournful songs about 'little boxes' or the
sad story of an engine driver who ended up with his head in the
firebox, her current favourites. If I was not already awake and up
I awoke to a violent shaking at five minutes to four, and to her

voice calling 'Your watch' as she turned again for the cockpit. Sometimes, if I was up during her watch I'd brew her a cup of cocoa, otherwise she'd brew me a cup before turning in. These were moments of good companionship while the others slept.

On May 29th we had 970 miles on the log and were moving along comfortably under deep reefed main, storm jib and reefed mizzen, when we saw a ship behind us. She turned out to be an American survey ship and she altered course to pass close alongside us. Clio and Beryl raised some whistles from the crew who turned out to line the rail as she rolled past. We were so muffled up that it was surprising to see them coming out of their warm quarters wearing comparatively few clothes. I hoisted the 'Wish you a pleasant voyage' signal, but heard that when they arrived at Kiska they reported meeting a yacht who had hoisted the signal 'May we be of any assistance to you', which is a better story.

The next day, 300 miles from Cape Wrangel, the north-western end of Attu, and about the same distance from the coast of Kamchatka, a very tired sandpiper tried to come on board and twice fell into the sea. This sort of thing always distresses Beryl, who before now has dived into the sea to rescue some forlorn little traveller. Thank goodness that each time he succeeded in getting off again before his feathers became too wet, but I do not think that he could have kept going much longer. Perhaps he was also bound for Attu, or perhaps he had been blown off course from the Kamchatka and the Kuril chain.

Anything unusual, any relief from the empty, grey, heaving wastes, is of interest at sea. On May 31st with 1,200 miles on the log and only a day's sail from Attu we had a new interest. First we sighted a small cargo boat and a fishing boat, bound for the Komandorski Islands it seemed, and in the afternoon we sighted a white mound in the sea. On sailing up to it we discovered that it was a dead grampus, with what looked like harpoon wounds on it.

We hoped to see Attu next morning if our navigation was correct, and I had been lucky to get a good fix on May 30th, the first for several days. On the following two days we had no chance of a fix, sailing under such low overcast that the masts seemed to scrape the clouds. We were running by dead reckoning. At nine in the morning, scanning the near horizon with its dull, leaden background, I saw some white patches that did not change their shape. They looked like badly rubbed out chalk marks on a blackboard, or slopes of a hill, so grey that it merged in the background, with all its upper slopes buried in cloud.

'Land ho!' I called, and everyone came on deck.

'I'll believe it when I see it,' said Beryl, looking in the wrong direction like a cat when it is offered food.

'I see it, I see it too,' called Clio, hanging on to the shrouds, with Henry scoffing at her, and telling her that it was only a cloud. But she and I have the best eyes and we were right.

We were soon able to make out Cape Wrangel, and beat up towards it all afternoon. *Tzu Hang* was sailing hard and the wind was rising all the time. We could not get into Chikagof harbour before dark, and once round the island we would be sailing along a leeshore. Better to stay in the lee of the island and to sail round the point early next morning. We hove-to on the tack that would carry us clear of the point, so that we could round it in the morning. Next morning to everyone's disappointment, Cape Wrangel was nowhere to be seen, but we soon raised it again and were able to lay the course to clear it comfortably.

We did not know much about Attu Island, except that *Tai Mo Shan*, built in Hong Kong like *Tzu Hang*, before the war, had sailed there with a strong crew of submarine officers and a doctor. She had put in to Chikagof harbour and had found a thriving Aleut village, a Russian church, and an American trader. We did not know whether the settlement was still there or whether it had grown. We knew that there was Loran Station manned by the American Coastguard, at Massacre Bay, at the south-eastern end of the island, but this was an open anchorage, with little shelter available to a ship of *Tzu Hang*'s size.

All morning we sailed down the northern shore. Sea lions came rushing out to meet us, bellowing at the tops of their voices, and in one place a whole pack of them, their heads high out of the water, eyes wide and whiskers writhing, all bellowing indignant protest, hurried towards us, like a crowd of Victorians in stiff high collars bursting out of some indecent show. Above the steep cliffs there was yellow tussocky grass and grey-green tundra recently released from the snow. Stony screes emerged from the snow-filled gullies and reached down to the edge of the cliffs or into the sea. Where the soil clung to the cliff tops the puffins had made their burrows. They dived out of them, dropping for the first twenty feet before they had flying speed, then shooting out over the sea. On the surface they flopped out of the way of the boat so overloaded and under-engined that they could not get out of the water. They were all tufted puffins, with a yellow crest hanging each side of their faces, like straggly golden hair escaping from a hat.

We sighted Gibson Island, the flat-topped high islet which marks the entrance to Chikagof harbour. Both Henry and I spruced ourselves up although we had seen no sign of human life. I do not know what Henry expected to find, for he pulled out an old white-topped yachting cap, and sat at the tiller drinking tea and looking incongruously dressed in these surroundings. I thought he looked more like the captain than I did, but when we arrived there was no one there to see. The channel led round Gibson Island, past a low green island called Kennan Island, and then between some rocky outcrops, where seals were basking, and the eastern shore. We followed it, curving left-handed until the entrance was closed by the rocks and islets, over long strands of slowly waving kelp, until we anchored two hundred yards off a broken wooden pier.

There was no living thing to be seen nor any house nor habitation, but only the debris of war. The beach was lined with rusty barbed wire and there were wrecked lighters and boats lying almost on the grass above the beach, where high tides and winter gales had put them. There were one or two mooring buoys in the harbour, and two that had broken adrift were on the beach. There were foxholes and trenches and gun pits, but of the church and the Aleut houses and the store, there remained only the level green platforms on which they had once stood. Above them the still, sad mountains disappeared into the cloud, the snow lay deep in the gullies, and the slow swell reached up the beach and murmured against the stones. There was a cathedral stillness and the sound of the ripples was the murmur of a congregation; until the silence was broken by a skittering in the water as an eider drake landed near us, and his loud laughter echoed from the rocky shore.

As soon as we were safely anchored, out came the Avon dinghy and both it and the old pram were put in the water.

. Ainu carvings in the Akan reserve

13. Chikagof Harbour in Attu, Aleutians

Henry was taken ashore first, to film the arrival of the dog and the cat after two weeks at sea. The cat came first in the Avon. Her ears were flattened as she peered over the inflated rubber bow, her tail lashing slowly, the cautious leader of the assault. As the boat grounded she sprang out on to the pebbles and took a few paces forward. There she stood scanning the ground ahead like any good scout, until a wave followed up the landing and pricked her to a further advance. A few steps, another halt, until satisfied that there was no danger in the immediate vicinity of the beach, she continued her crouching advance to the shelter of some driftwood and long grass.

Next came the dog. Kochi was also in the bow, tail down, ears cocked, never very assured when on the water. Suddenly she realized that after all these days she was going ashore and as she neared the beach, with one tremendous bound she landed in the ripples. Without a moment's pause she took off as fast as she could go, across the beach, up the bank, through the grass, round and round, up and down, revelling in the glory of being able to stretch those lovely limbs at last; proud in her speed, sending the cat flying, in pure delight at the opportunity for unrestricted movement.

In spite of the dreary debris, which included the concrete bases of old Nissen huts, workshops, and water tanks, Chikagof harbour was still, because of its wildness, an exciting place to find. Henry, Clio, and Kochi, all long-legged and lithe, had soon disappeared round the point above Kennan Island, while Beryl and I went exploring in another direction. Presently a whitish-yellow fox, the colour of a Siamese cat, with a brown mask, came picking his way along the beach as if the country round the point had become too crowded. When they returned Clio was swinging an old Japanese helmet in her hand.

'Look what I've got,' she called.

She is an inveterate collector of useless objects from the beach, from smelly shells to driftwood and coloured stones. The helmet had a bullet hole through it just above the ear.

'I don't expect he felt that one,' I said, pointing it out to Clio.

'I don't think I like it now,' she said after carrying it a little farther, and laid it gently on a stone.

I had not made any inquiries from the American authorities, before leaving Japan, about visiting Attu. There is not normally

G

any necessity to do so. And I supposed that there would be some facilities for entry on the most westerly outpost of the U.S.A. Probably the worst that can happen to a yacht that visits a place without applying for permission is that it will be told to move on, whereas a yacht that asks for permission before leaving its starting point might have this refused. Since we now had discovered that Chikagof was unoccupied, Beryl and I decided that we had better announce our arrival to the U.S. Coastguard in Massacre Bay.

Next morning Beryl, Clio, Henry, and Kochi left to walk the eight miles to the Loran Station. The cat and I set off to accompany them part of the way up the hill. The cat soon gave up and returned to the beach. When I came back I found her on a log near the dinghy and very pleased to see me again. It was a long wait without my happy companions, which I spent in cleaning up and collecting pinewood for the cabin stove. The glass was falling and the wind began to blow onshore. I wondered whether I would have to move the boat to a more sheltered place without them. It was getting near supper-time when I heard their clear voices and their laughter coming down the hill. I hurried ashore to greet them. They were loaded with fresh trout and spare ribs and this was their story.

The track had wound up and down hill between the steep tundra-covered slope, past a bronze plate put up to commemorate the last stand of the Japanese defenders, who had died there. Presently they reached the highest point of the track and could look down to the Loran Station and the curve of Massacre Bay. As they approached the station they saw a solitary, bearded man coming towards them His head down, his hands were in his pockets, and he kicked at stones as he walked. Even from the distance at which they saw him he looked a lonely and disconsolate figure. Suddenly he looked up. He must have been a man of keen eyesight and quick perception, for he turned round immediately and took to his heels. A few breathless minutes later—they were told—he burst into the dining-room where the crew of the Loran Station were assembled for a cup of coffee and a sandwich and shouted at the top of his voice:

'Hey you guys, there're two broads and a man in a red coat coming over the hill.'

Complete silence fell on the gathering, for these men were at the farthest outpost where broads did not exist, let alone walk over the hill. Then two bearded men of action—it was a fashion then to grow long beards at Massacre Bay—each with a half sandwich in their hands, ran out to a jeep and drove to meet the invaders.

The jeep pulled up beside them Two hairy-faced coastguards stared at them round-eyed.

'Jump in,' said one, and the crew of *Tzu Hang* climbed in to the back of the jeep. They drove back the short distance to the station; no other word was spoken. Each man still clutching a half-eaten sandwich in his hand, found himself speechless and dumbfounded by this visitation, as it were, from the skies.

On arrival at the station they were taken to the C.O.'s office, and soon there were repeated knocks on the door, letters to be signed, requests to be made, and reports to be presented. Never, said the C.O., in all the history of Massacre Bay had so much business been done in so short a time. Last came the cook, in cook's hat and white apron.

'Excuse me, sir, but the young lady's dawg is looking rather thin. Would it be in order to give it a meal?' Clio went out to supervise.

After they had been given lunch and the C.O. had sent a message to the Navy Base at Adak, asking permission for us to enter the harbour, Beryl decided that it was time to marshal her forces for the return march. Kochi was found with digestive troubles outside the kitchen door, and Clio, who had been summoned for yet another discussion on dog's rations, was found surrounded by the rest of the crew of the Loran Station inside.

'It's just as well that you didn't sail into Massacre Bay,' said the C.O., 'because one of the buoys has drifted out of place. Can't put it back because we haven't got a boat.'

'No boat?' asked Beryl, surprised that there should be coastguards without a boat.

'No,' said the lieutenant, 'they took it away from us. One of our chaps got the "Outer Island Stare", and before we realized how bad he was, he'd gone off in it. Next stop America. He didn't get very far and they got him all right, but it gets people down, being so far away, so they took our boat away, lest someone else should try it.'

The jeep took them to a break in the track, a couple of miles on their way. They were loaded with a present of a dozen spare ribs for Kochi, and six lake trout for ourselves. We had spare ribs for dinner and trout next day, two marvellous meals, while Kochi did very well on the remains.

Henry and Kochi walked over again next morning to find out the result of the message to Adak. They required more information as to why we wanted to go there, the yacht's registered number, and various other questions, some of which Henry was able to answer and some that he couldn't. There was, however, a firm request from the U.S.A.F. at Shemya, one of the Semichi Islands, twenty miles to the eastward, to visit them. News travels fast in the Aleutians. By the time Henry got back a certain coolness had developed between him and Kochi, who after two miles had turned back to the Loran Station, in the hopes of another bone.

During that day and night a storm passed south of us and was now well over by the Pribiloff Islands, giving us a favourable wind for Shemya. I decided to leave, thinking that I could get the answer there about our visit to Adak. We left in the morning over the slowly waving kelp fronds, and past the glistening rocks, where the swell sucked. Because we had been there and walked about it, and enjoyed it, the bay no longer seemed as derelict as when we came in, and in a way we were all sorry to leave it again so soon to the little cream-coloured foxes and the eider ducks.

We had a quick passage across to Alcan Harbour in Shemya, but found it very exposed to the north-east wind that was now blowing. We sailed in to have a look at the anchorage, but it was too rough for us and the broken-down pier gave little shelter. In these waters it is just as well to be always expecting the worst, and this was bad under the present conditions. We turned round and sailed out again, finding a strong current which set us towards some rocks, so that we used the engine in order to point a little higher and avoid them. I could see that Henry, rather a purist in these matters, didn't fully approve.

As soon as we were clear of the harbour we set the twins and rolled off towards Adak. We could see the aircraft taking off and landing on the Shemya airstrip; off on, and back from, their ceaseless watch and ward over the huge cold areas of sea and sky. Beneath them big screens and domes stood grouped, as still as sentries, or turning slowly, questing, in perpetual vigilance. *Tzu Hang* rolled off along a course that must often have been followed by Russian fur traders, also under sail and bound on rather similar tasks, both in search of sea otters.

We had heard that the sea otters were coming back again after the population had been so depleted by the traders that in spite of the strictest protection it had barely survived the normal depredations of animal life. We did not know where to find them, but to find them and get some photographs was one of the objects of the voyage. While the others were down at supper we were rolling along in great style. I was on watch, listening to their laughter and trying to guess at the cause of the joke. I sat relaxed in the cockpit, feet across on the opposite side, leaning forwards and backwards to the roll, and like Shakespeare's shepherd blowing my nail, for the north-east wind was bitterly cold. I glanced forward. Right ahead of me, the wave lapping up its side, was a great black rock.

To say that my heart jumped would be an understatement. I hauled on the tiller wondering by what strange mischance I had not seen it on the chart. I saw that we would never avoid it if it extended at all under water, and as I looked, horrified, struck dumb, for I called no warning, I saw the rock slide forward and alter shape. It was a whale, a humpback, the most horrible and frightening whale that I had ever seen, and we missed it by a few feet.

We sailed on through the night under twins, and slap through a vast fishing fleet of big trawlers steaming every which way. It was quite impossible to guess their movements. We passed one big boat, bringing in a trawl or a seine over its side. It was quite hove down, and under the bright arc lights we could see the dark glistening net coming in, and oilskin-clad figures hurrying about it.

We lost the Shemya beacon after sixty miles—the last beacon that I was to hear on that set, for it never worked again until I gave it away in Canada. It was of no great loss to us, as there are few radio beacons in the Aleutian Islands, none of them of great range, and of little use to a ship that wants to cruise in and out of the islands. Everything is covered by Loran, which all the fishing boats rely on, but which was no use to us.

On June 8th, with 280 miles on the log, early in the morning I saw auklets flying south. I felt sure that they were heading for land not far away, and by 6 a.m. I was able to make out a point of land that we had already passed and which was now on our quarter. The sights of the sun are so rare and the currents so variable that we were rarely sure of our position until it had been fixed by the sight of land. Presently we were able to identify the point as the western end of Tanaga. We decided to go into Hot Springs Bay, round Cape Sudak, the eastern end of Tanaga, because Beryl announced that she could do with a hot bath.

Tzu Hang gave Cape Sudak a wide berth as there is shoal water and kelp stretching some way out into the Kanaga Pass, the passage between Kanaga and Tanaga Islands. As we turned down the passage, before doubling back behind Cape Sudak peninusla, Bobroff Island was to port, a 3,000-foot volcano, sprouting directly out into the sea. We skirted the edge of a kelp bed and as we did so noticed some black heads sticking out of the kelp like fish-trap buoys. At a second look I thought that they were seals, but there was something quite different in the shape of their heads from the seals that I had seen so often; something about the white cheeks or the grey whiskers that bothered me. They were not seals at all but sea otters. Any number of them, and I felt that just this sight alone had made the trip worthwhile. Their heads kept popping up amongst the kelp and they seemed to be holding kelp stalks in their paws and chewing away at it. Although we saw much more of them at closer range, we were never able to decide whether it was the kelp itself that they were eating or small shellfish attached to it. Later on when we anchored near a kelp bed we could hear their champing and chewing through the hull of the ship.

The weather was fine although the hills were lost in clouds, as they were on practically every day of our voyage through the islands. A few miles up the southern side of the peninsula, two miles short of the head of the bay, we saw a small cove behind Bara Bara Island, opposite a place where there had once been an Aleut village. This looked more sheltered from the north-east wind which was still blowing, than Hot Springs Bay. If it was to change to south we knew that we had only to cross the bay, so we decided to anchor there and forgo the search for the Hot Springs.

It was the most lovely place. As wild as one could find any-where. We were surrounded by bare grey-green hills, which reminded me of the Shetlands, and sometimes the cloud lifted to show the snow on the higher hills. We had anchored on sand in seven fathoms, four hundred yards off a black sand beach, and two hundred yards off the kelp beds which fringed the rocks round Bara Bara Island. The island was connected with the shore by rocky tidal pools and jagged spurs.

On the north side of the peninsula that now protected us there were Rough Bay and Gusty Bay. On the south side of the sound there were Annoy Rocks, Explorer Passage, and Eureka Bight. All the names bring pictures of fur traders, risk, and fortune.

We went ashore. Beryl in search of Aleut remains went one way, Clio and Henry in search of sea otters went another way, Kochi put up a fox and pursued it in a friendly manner in another, and I, without going anywhere in particular, dis-covered two glaucous gulls, a black oyster-catcher, a snipe, some sandpipers, and two teal. None of them showed any fear and the teal behaved like tame ducks, swimming about and bobbing their heads as if they were on a private pond.

Between us Beryl and I collected a good supply of driftwood. This was always one of the pleasanter chores. Although there are no trees in the Aleutian Islands there is plenty of far-travelled driftwood, which takes such a pounding on the beaches that it is often found in stove-sized pieces. We had several saws on board and were able to saw up longer pieces to the correct size. All the time at anchor we had the cabin stove going with a large pot of water on the boil. From time to time the lid of the pot lifted slightly and allowed a little steam to escape. It was a comforting sound, like someone puffing quietly at a pipe.

At some time during the night I put my head out of the hatch. It was half light. The still, bare hills enclosed us and the cloud roof was low above us. The kelp swayed gently in the small swell and the ripples murmured on the beach. All else was silent except that from the direction of the kelp beds there came a sound of munching and an occasional splash. The sea otters were having an early-morning snack.

7 Sea Otters, Sailors, and Foxes

We should have stayed longer in the little bay behind Bara Bara Island, but with the whole chain of islands ahead of us, who was to know which was going to be best? Even now, I cannot decide which anchorage I liked the most; but the best for sea otters was certainly this one. They became scarcer as we sailed eastwards.

Henry and Clio went off to film sea otters, both cluttered with equipment, while Kochi was left with us. Henry was wearing his black skin suit, as he hoped to get some underwater pictures of sea-otters feeding, and had his oxygen tanks and underwater camera equipment with him. Clio was wearing a blue, quilted jacket, her long legs as usual in tight blue jeans. The whole expedition looked very dashing, and we didn't see them again until six in the evening.

Beryl and I worked on *Tzu Hang* until lunch-time. While on deck we heard the hum of a distant aircraft and then saw it emerge from the cloud and cross the Kanaga Strait a few miles away, a moment of flying before disappearing again. *Tzu Hang* was hidden like a smuggler's boat in the cove; but those who fly aircraft in the Aleutians are a special brand of pilot, always with wits alert, for the clouds are low, the mountains high, the winds strong, and the beacons few. Although we were some way off and well to one side of his course, the pilot saw us. A few minutes later the aircraft suddenly flew close round the spur above us and zoomed low over *Tzu Hang*. Its wing tip was just on the level of Clio and Henry, who were climbing the grassy cliff to look at an eagle's eyrie. 'Reeve's Aleutian Airways' was painted in large letters on the side.

Beryl and I went ashore in the afternoon, with Kochi. Kochi had sat the whole morning on the deck, looking in the direction in which Clio had disappeared, and now had to be restrained from following a cold trail. We examined the remains of the Aleut village, which consisted of two turf-roofed pits called *Barabaras*, almost indistinguishable from the surrounding grass. Then we climbed the steep tundra slope to the top of the hill above the bay. At the top, Kochi put up a brown and white ptarmigan which curved away round the hill. A little farther along the edge of the hill we could look over the point which formed one side of *Tzu Hang*'s anchorage, into Hot Springs Bay.

Four sea otters were lying on their backs in a row in the kelp below us, each with a cub resting on its stomach. They looked like four women waiting outside a baby clinic. Sea otters used to spend much more time on land, but were driven to a seafaring life in order to preserve their society. Now they very rarely come ashore; but they pay the usual penalty that a landsman pays when he takes to the sea, that of being unsuitably clad. The sea otter has a beautiful furry coat, splendid for Arctic winds, but he has to be continually at work on it in the water. He spends a great deal of his time in grooming, and he does it in the most delightful way, like someone who is determined to get clean in cold water. He rests on his back as if in a bath and busily brushes under his arms and over his shoulders. He picks up one leg and rubs it vigorously and then the other, rubs his chest and stomach, and then reaches round to scratch his back.

When Beryl and I got back to our bay Kochi was soon off on Clio's trail. After collecting Pwe from the ship we walked round behind Bara Bara Island and along the stony beach in search of them. Presently we met Kochi coming back again, picking her way awkwardly amongst the round, polished stones; but her golden tail was waving to show that she was still enjoying her day. Kochi likes to keep in touch with all her people. It is one of her instincts inherited from ancestors that wandered with scattered nomad bands, their sheep and camels, on stony hills and valleys and across dusty plains. She turned back immediately and round the next point we met Henry and Clio.

'Did you get any pictures?' I asked them.

'Yes; but not underwater,' said Henry. 'Couldn't move because I was all tangled up in kelp. I didn't like it at all. Bloody cold too.'

'Did you get any out of the water?'

'Yes. I think I got some smashing pictures of two otters swimming and playing together. A hundred feet anyway. I could have got some more, but ran out of film. Clio, the nit, had gone to sleep with all my film.'

'I wasn't asleep, Henry. There was an eagle, a Steller's Sea Eagle I think, sitting right above me. I was looking at that.'

'She was sitting in a fox's earth with all my film. I was fit to be tied. There was this old sea otter combing his whiskers about three feet away. I was behind those rocks. I couldn't shout and tried to signal her, but she was communing with eagles.'

'Why are you so wet?' Beryl asked her. Henry in his skin suit was dry, but Clio was soaking wet.

'I fell in.'

'Right on her backside off Bara Bara Island. You never saw anything so funny', said Henry.

'Well, you wouldn't try it,' she said. It was obvious that they had enjoyed their day ashore too. They walked on to collect their equipment, while Beryl and I followed at cat's pace. Pwe is now fourteen but can still do a couple of miles at her own pace, and provided the way is deserted.

Beryl looked out of the hatch when she got up to start breakfast.

'They're watching us,' she said.

We knew who, but we had to leave them. We had to drag ourselves away, for there were so many things still to be photographed and investigated. Clio's eagle was one of them, but we did not get close enough to identify it. It was now twenty-five days since we had left Japan. The bread was finished, and we had eaten two hundred eggs. The Japanese eggs had very hard shells and we did not find a bad one. They weren't finished yet, but other stores were getting low and Beryl, who had made some soda bread, issued an ultimatum. If we wanted to eat proper bread, we had to sail.

And what a day it was to sail on. It started grey, but a fresh north wind cleared the clouds away and soon the snow-covered mountains, glaciers, and volcanoes shone above us. The sea sparkled, the wind nipped cold, and all the world felt good and clean and fresh. I thought that I would just like this adventure to go on and on. One trip like this merely skimmed the surface. I thought of the soldiers and sailors posted to stations here. It was the sort of place that Beryl and I would have loved to come to when I was a young soldier, with uninhabited islands waiting to be explored, sailing, shooting, fishing, and ski-ing and these marvellous mountains to climb, right at the door.

We sailed between Bogroff Island and the north coast of Kanaga, under Kanaga Volcano, which is 4,400 feet, snow-clad, and extinct. We had intended to anchor behind Round Head Point, the north-eastern point of Kanaga Island, but the bay was unattractive when compared with the one we had left, and the bottom felt stony. We brought the anchor in again and set off for Sweeper Cove, the U.S. Navy Base on Adak.

It was a lovely fast sail down the mountainous north coast of Adak, with the mountains still clear above us. By the time that we had got down to Zeto Point, the northern entrance point of Kuluk Bay, and sailed into a sheltered anchorage behind the point, it was too late to attempt Sweeper Cove. We were obviously back in civilization as there was a constant stream of car headlights running backwards and forwards round the edge of the bay.

'I wonder if they'll let us in?' I said to Beryl.

'Of course they will,' she replied. 'They can't very well send us on without food and water.'

'What about that man and his wife sailing from Japan, who sailed into a U.S. Navy base, and they just revictualled him and filled up his tanks at sea, and sent him off again?' I asked.

'Listen to your father, Clio, he's being ridiculous as usual.'

'All I wish is that I had the permission I asked for,' I protested.

'Well, you do your face up, Clio,' said Beryl, who remembers how easy it was to enter forbidden places when she was Clio's age.

'I think we had all better spruce ourselves up a bit,' I said. 'Henry's looking like an adolescent Sikh, and I feel pretty dirty.'

Next morning, all of us shining with health and cleanliness, we got up our anchor and sailed for Sweeper Cove. We beat up the harbour and into a narrow entrance between a lighthouse and a breakwater. Inside there were a row of piers and one or two small Navy ships. We continued to tack up the harbour

under short sail, wondering where we might go. We had not
long to wait, as a small tender put out to meet us, with several
men on board in ski caps and windproofs. We backed the headsail and waited anxiously for someone to break the silence.
Presently a young man in a blue peaked cap put up a megaphone and hailed us:

'May I have the name of your ship, please?'

'*Tzu Hang*,' I shouted back, 'from Japan and Attu.'

'Are you able to follow us?'

'Yes, I have a motor.'

'Will you have the kindness then to follow us, please? We
will show you to a berth.'

I do not know whether it was because I was unsure of our
reception, or because of the politeness, the efficiency, and the
paucity of words used, but it made a lasting impression. We had
an almost exactly similar reception from the British Navy,
sailing one day into Gibraltar.

As soon as they had shown us our berth we went alongside.
There were men to take our lines. First on board from the tender
was the station doctor.

'I needn't ask if any of you are sick,' he said, 'but you'd
better just tell me if you've been in contact with any infectious
diseases.'

'Well, except for two stops in the Islands at Attu and Tanaga,
we've been at sea for twenty-six days,' I told him.

'O.K., Captain,' he called up to the wharf. A tall, broad-
shouldered man, also in mufti ski cap and windproof, scrambled
down the ladder. 'Captain Bartol,' he said, introducing himself. 'I'm the C.O. here. We got your message from Attu and
have been expecting you, but didn't know where you'd got to.
Now, is there anything we can do for you? First of all, I'd
better tell you what we *can* do for you. We can let you have a
bachelor officer's quarter, so that you can get showers and your
clothes washed. You can't really stay there,' he said laughing,
'but you can use it during the day. Then I understand that you
want some supplies. Well, today's a holiday. That's why we're
all dressed like this, but we can get the Commissary open for
any supplies you want now, and then you haven't got to rush
away, have you? We can fix up the rest later. We can let you
have some fuel. How much would you need?'

'Ten gallons,' I said.

'Well, don't foul up our accounting. We leak that amount every day.'

It was a kind reception and made us U.S. Navyphiles for life. They would not stay for a drink, but promised to get in touch later. We were driven in a car to the Commissary, where Beryl got fresh bread and fresh eggs, although some of the Japanese eggs outlasted them. Then we were taken up to the washing machine and to boiling hot showers.

On Sunday evening, after a flurry of washing and drying, we were taken out to dinner at the Club. So magnificent a club that it was difficult to believe that we were in the Andreanoff Islands or indeed in an Officers' Club at all. I thought of the dusty Army Clubs that I had occasionally frequented, the Saturday-night hops in Loralai or Poona, the stringy chicken and the caramel custard. No wonder that we preferred to spend Saturday night out in camp, with the prospect of chasing or shooting something on the following morning. But here it was different. Here there were great red curtains, red carpeting, white napery, and red wine. There were coloured waiters in white jackets and a butler to carve the turkey, or the chicken, or the duck, whichever you preferred. There was white wine if you wished, and oysters fresh from the Chesapeake, or fresh salmon from the coast, or lake trout from Oregon. There were the biggest and juiciest steaks that I have ever seen.

Our host was an airman, the C.O. of the squadron there that kept a continuous tally on all sea movements, flying no matter what the weather, quartering the seas like albatrosses in the Southern Ocean. The acquisition of fresh Chesapeake oysters was no problem to them. He was a perfect host: grey-eyed, tall, and saturnine, with long, bony fingers and supple wrists that kept his hands in perpetual and eloquent gesture. He and another of his guests, a member of the Nursing Service, were keen on long, country hikes or 'tundra stomping' as it was called. They were considered to be slightly mad by the others, he explained. She had a cool, efficient manner, grey hair, slim figure, and young face.

Next day Captain Bartol's daughter arrived on the back of a Vespa on the wharf to ask us up to dinner. Her father picked us up in his car. He was an enthusiast, proud of his Command, proud of his family, and even proud of his violent winds. After dinner he took us for a drive to show us round the station. He drove us to Adak Forest, where about twenty trees have grown a few feet in ten years, and he took us to see the bald-headed eagles, one to every telegraph pole and the rubbish dump, waiting for the rats to come out. He said he wished the American emblem could find a more worthy occupation.

We sailed next day, leaving the harbour as we had come in, under sail. We were bound for Little Tanaga, for Chisak Bay, on its south coast, but only a day's sail away. The day before we left we had had a visit from a U.S. Coastguard officer. He explained that he was at Adak representing Customs and Immigration in case, as sometimes happened, a Russian or Japanese trawler asked permission to enter, usually because they had some badly injured man on board.

'It's extraordinary,' he told us, 'how often they get themselves caught up in some wire rope or machinery.' He asked us where we were going. I told him, and he said he wouldn't bother us as long as we were on our way to Canada and not staying in U.S. territory.

'Well, thanks very much,' I said. 'Sorry I didn't know you were here, or I'd have come and reported to you. Is there anything else you want to know?'

'No,' he said, 'that's all. I just wanted to check that you were going through to Canada.'

This was just the sort of reasonable attitude that we expected, and we thought no more about it, only remarking how nice it was to be back amongst officials whom we could understand, and who understood us, and did not bother us with endless petty regulations.

The north coast of Adak is steep and, as usual, disappeared into the clouds. We passed the narrow entrance of Kagalaska Strait which separates Adak and Kagalaska Island, a regular passageway between the topless hills, and then turned south down the next channel, Little Tanaga Strait, between Little Tanaga and Kagalaska. Here the tide was running like a river past the black rocks along the shore, and we slid through the pass with a following wind, watching the coast go by as quickly and smoothly as the landscape from a railway carriage window. The western shore was hazy and the mountains lost in cloud.

So were the hills of the eastern shore, but we were close enough to appreciate the different textures; the soft grey-green of the tundra, the brighter shore grasses and wild wheat, the soft browns and reds of eroded earth and land slips, the grey screes and, here and there, the bleached bones of piled driftwood, all the way from Canada or Alaska.

We passed between Silak Island and the eastern shore, where the navigable channel is reduced to less than half a mile. As we slid swiftly and silently towards it we heard a steady, growing roar. 'What's that noise?' asked Beryl.

'A jet taking off from Adak', I answered.

'But it seems to be coming from over there,' she said, pointing in the opposite direction.

I looked in the direction she had pointed and saw that it came from sea lions on the rocks opposite Silak Island. They were packed like brown cough lozenges in a box, side by side in rows. As we came down the narrow passage between them and the island they raised their heads and roared either at us or at new arrivals from the sea. They looked like bathers who had taken every yard of beach and were now objecting to a new arrival, which is exactly what they were doing. They were drying their sleek, stout bodies, which varied in shade like any group of bathers, from coffee to cream, and hoping perhaps for a little shaft of sunlight to complete their comfort. I almost felt surprised that there were no striped umbrellas.

At the bottom of the Strait, on the Kagalaska side, we could see a great flying buttress of rock standing in the sea and supporting the cliff; and across the entrance to Chisak Bay, off Agony Point, there was a tall, isolated pinnacle. Round Cape Chisak the cliffs came down like elephants' feet, with deep caves between them. As Chisak Bay opened we could see that its entrance was almost closed with rocks and islets, but the channel was easy to discover. The wind was blowing straight out of the bay, so we brought down the sails and came in on the motor. Little Tanaga consists almost of two islands, connected towards the northern end by a narrow isthmus. The southern halves enclose Chisak Bay and the northern portion Scripps Bay, which is the smaller and said to be subject to williwaws.

Chisak Bay is full of islands and skerries and surrounded by low, green, rounded hills. There were birds everywhere: puffins, both tufted and horned, black guillemot and pigeon guillemot, eider duck, Pallas' murres, and harlequin duck. We anchored towards the head of the bay. There was a fresh wind blowing.

Clio, Henry, and Kochi went ashore to explore, and walked over to Scripps Bay. They found a steep slope down which they could glissade, and came back some hours later, like children, with green backsides. I did not like this particular anchorage. The winter before a young Norwegian skipper had been drowned while going ashore in his dinghy, and there was a spooky feeling about the place. There were other anchorages in this lovely bay quite free from any sense of tragedy.

Next morning Henry and I rowed off to one of the islets to try to film eider duck and puffins. Beryl stayed on board to fix a leak over the chart table, and Clio took her lunch and disappeared over the hills with Kochi.

Henry and I were not very successful with the puffins. While he was looking in one of their burrows one popped out immediately above his head. Henry waited for hours, looking as inconspicuous as a straw stack in a stubble field, but no birds returned while he was there, although many came to look at him from a distance. We were unlucky also with the eider duck, as the females all left their nests as we approached; but a black oyster-catcher re-established Henry's morale. This bird was very keen on being photographed and piped and complained if he was not actually pointing the lens at her. She was prepared to pose at close range, and even whistled up her two children to be included in the picture.

While Henry was sitting it out with the puffins I rowed over to Little Chisak Island and found that there was a sheltered place to anchor. I also saw a sea otter on land. He had a very dark coat and his whiskers looked extremely white in contrast. He had the same caterpillar gait of a land otter, but it was the gait of a fat, hairy caterpillar, rather than a thin, smooth one. He or she took to the sea when I arrived and swam past me several times in order to get a good look at me.

Clio didn't come back until after six, and I was glad to see her come striding easily over the hill, with the dog beside her. She had managed to get a photo of Kochi following up a fox's scent, and the fox sitting outside its earth, watching the dog just below it.

Next day we moved *Tzu Hang* to a little bay nearer Cape Chisak, and better protected by the islands at the entrance. It was a very good anchorage and one of the most beautiful. On one of these little islands there was a wooden cross, showing that someone had been drowned there; but it must have been some time ago, as it did not feel a tragic place.

The little bay in which we had anchored formed one side of a grassy spur that joined Cape Chisak to the island. Just over the spur was another bay looking out on to Little Tanaga Strait. Both bays were piled high with driftwood and on the strand of the far one was the backbone of a whale.

Clio and Henry went off to photograph her fox, but when Beryl and I came ashore a few minutes later we found a fox sitting in the grass above the driftwood, watching the photographers disappear round the edge of the hill. The foxes, like all the birds, were very tame. They used to be trapped by the Aleuts, but the Aleuts have gone from almost all the islands, and I suspect that the little blue foxes, having multiplied exceedingly, have become degraded. This one had a blue coat except for his brush, which was a sandy cream in colour. He was not as big as the English fox, nor did he look so alert. He had a shorter muzzle and a puppyish face.

Beryl and I took the cat for a walk on the hillside. We felt that spring had really come to the Andreanoffs. The tundra was studded with lupins and aconites and if one looked closer, with many kinds of small mountain flowers. The birds were all nesting, the longspurs fell like drifting leaves towards their mates, singing as if their little hearts would break for joy, and even the foxes yapped away huskily, though whether they were barking for love or at us it would be hard to say.

We had been told that Great Sitkin Island, fifteen miles to the northward, was the place for foxes, and we went there next day. We had a fast sail, through narrow passes and tide rips, into Yoke Bay. The bay that we had left was narrow and full of islands, but this was a vast amphitheatre, with a long, curving, sandy beach. Great Sitkin is an active volcano of 5,700 feet. The cloud curtain sometimes lifted high enough to show us the lower snow slopes, but we never saw the top. There was not the same sense of security that we found in Chisak Bay, but the weather was fine and we were sheltered as long as the wind stayed in westerly quarters. *Tzu Hang* was dwarfed by the scale of her surroundings. We came slowly in, until it seemed that we were almost on the beach, but after anchoring found that we still had a long way to row.

We had come to photograph foxes and no sooner had we anchored than a small blue fox came titupping along the beach inspecting the tide line for any food that might have been washed up. He paid no attention to us, but trotted along the edge of the ripples, pausing sometimes to smell and examine something in the sand.

The beach curved away for ever behind him, smooth and brown, but half a mile in front of him it narrowed and merged with the steep cliffs and the boulders at their feet. No other thing except the ripples moved in all the great arena. He seemed the loneliest little fox in all the world, and soon he had shrunk to a mere mouse, and then he was gone.

'The fox that walked by himself,' said Clio.

'Well, I'm going ashore to get some pictures,' said Henry. 'That one looked as if he was specially ordered, didn't he?'

'We'll put you ashore this end of the beach; then we three, Kochi and Pwe will take the two dinghies and row right round to the other end. Then we can meet in the middle,' planned Beryl.

We put Henry ashore and then cut across the head of the bay to the other end of the beach, keeping well out so as not to frighten any foxes. Henry soon looked like a dwarf on the sand.

At the far side of the bay we found a stream running over a shingle bank and then drawing wide, wet patterns over the sand to the sea. Easterly gales had tried to dam its exit with sand and stones, but the stream had busily removed the sand, leaving only the stones to contain it, and even these had been swept aside in places.

Behind the shingle bank there was a wide pool, and beyond that the stream followed so tortuous a course that a pin ball might have drawn it. In places it was so narrow that we could jump across it, the banks about four feet high. It came from a long valley that disappeared some miles away in clouds. We pulled the dinghies up the shingle and explored the stream for a short distance. When we returned to the beach we took it in turns to hold Kochi while the others walked on so that she might really stretch her legs in catching them up.

Henry was very pleased with his photography. He had found a fox sitting on a rocky spur that divided the beach.

'It let me get right up to it,' he told us, 'within about six feet, before it went down its earth. The place is full of holes and you can hear them barking at you from inside.'

Kochi was already investigating the place by the time we got there, and even Pwe showed some interest; but she would not venture into the earths, although the rough little barks would hardly have frightened a beetle. We decided to put some food out for these hungry little creatures who seemed to get their living from shellfish and other beach snacks. Unfortunately, it was discovered and eaten by Kochi, who then took herself off, since she was no longer hungry, in pursuit of our intended guests. We left her, and Clio rowed in again after supper. Just before dark she returned with Kochi sitting in the bow. Because Kochi was back, she was welcomed and all things forgiven. She had so won our hearts, although she gave little in return, that none of us would have slept very well if she had remained on shore.

We spent another day in this wide bay. I went to the rocky spur and sat for some time, in the hope of seeing more of the foxes. Presently the vixen appeared, sat on a ledge outside a crack in the rocks that formed the entrance to her earth, wrinkled her nose and screwed up her eyes as if she was short-sighted. She then examined me, sitting on a rock a few yards away, her eyes suddenly grown round and suspicious. I was soon dismissed as a new fixture, or at least harmless, because she turned round and brought out on to the ledge first one skinny little rat of a cub and then another, carrying them in her mouth while they cried and whimpered so loudly that the fox came round from the other side of the spur to see what the matter was. Now the whole family were assembled there, but they had none of the pride and self-sufficiency of the English fox. They were poor little beachcombers in a society which did not have to excel in fitness and intelligence to survive. A little regular hunting would have done them no end of good.

Meanwhile, Henry had gone fishing, with a big game rod and two hundred yards of stout nylon line, a mackerel hook and some mussels. He succeeded in catching three grilse from the little stream that we had discovered the day before. The grilse were splendid eating, but what really pleased Henry was the tackle that he caught them with. When we joined him neither Clio nor I nor lunchtime could get the rod out of his hands, and he was as serious and preoccupied as if he had paid a hundred guineas for a few days on the Spey.

In the morning we sailed for Kasatochi, an extinct volcano sticking directly out of the sea, about twenty miles to the east-ward. A good day for the Aleutians, a day of light wind, with the genoa set, the sunlight filtering through light overcast, and a day so warm that Pwe spent the whole time on deck. We could see the blue lower slopes of islands to the southward, but for some time we could see not the slightest sign of Kasatochi which was standing somewhere high in front of us. When its outline appeared ahead of us in the light haze, like a faint shadow on cloud, we altered course to pass south of it. Soon it began to take shape, although it would not bare its head to us, and we could see the red and grey boulders at its foot, and the steep green slopes running up to a suggestion of the crater's edge. On the eastern side, sheltered from the light wind, the kelp beds were close to the shore. We found our way in between some outlying patches and anchored on stones. The glass was so high and the sea so calm that we felt it safe to leave *Tzu Hang* under Pwe's charge. We found a channel through the inshore kelp and then pulled the two dinghies high up on to the rocks. The beach was piled with large boulders and driftwood, with steep, grassy cliffs above. As we scrambled over the boulders Beryl suddenly called excitedly and dashed off, with Clio gaining on her in hot pursuit.

'What on earth's happened; have they been stung?' I asked Henry, but he was as puzzled as I. Beryl kept her lead and suddenly, diving behind a boulder, pulled up a huge, rope-covered, glass ball. We have collected glass balls from various seas and beaches, but this was the biggest yet. 'I'm sure this is a Russian,' she said, although it had no mark to say so.

We scrambled up a steep cliff of loose earth and stones, and over the broken edge on to the tundra. The sunlight filtered through, making the lupins and aconites glow in the grey-green moss. Song sparrows, Alaskan grey-headed rosy finches, and longspurs filled the air with song. We climbed up a spur, from where we could see the precipitous northern face of the island, with five-hundred-foot cliffs dropping sheer to the sea. Two sea lions—one chocolate and one light brown in colour— were fighting on the rocks below, and we could hear their angry roaring above the wash of the waves. In a bight in the coast a black rock thrust its corrugated back out of the swell and then submerged, leaving a frothy white ring spreading on the surface.

When we reached the lip of the crater, Clio and Kochi first, and the others rather out of breath behind, we could see nothing. The light cloud rolling in over the southern and lower edge, which we had just been able to discern, disappeared down the steep inner side. The slope looked very steep indeed, and I began to fear first that Kochi, who had disappeared inside, might lose her footing or became crag fast; secondly that Clio would follow her and that I should have to follow, too.

'Kochi, Kochi,' she called, and the echo piped back from the far wall.

On the way down we found the slope above the earth cliff steep enough for a glissade. My glissade ended as so many glissades have done, in an upside-down toboggan run on my back. I began to wonder just how I was going to stop it when Kochi, flying down the hill and quite disregarding all the forces of gravity, caught me by the windproof and brought me to a halt. A very exciting game she thought it; and I was glad of her assistance, although it wasn't only the windproof that she got hold of in her eagerness.

It stayed light for most of the night now, but the birds at last became silent, and the only sound to disturb us as we slept was the rumble of the chain on the stony bottom and the lapping of water against the ship's side.

Another fifteen miles to the eastward was the island of Kon-iuji, also volcanic in its origins, the home of seals and innumer- able seabirds. It had no safe anchorage nor even was an open anchorage like that at Kasatochi mentioned in the Pilot, nor had I any detailed chart. The cliffs at its western end were dotted with glaucous gulls, covering the whole face of the cliff, standing on their rocky ledges as white and upright as mile- stones. We sailed or rather motored along the southern shore and could see that the top of the cliff was riddled with the burrows of auklets; we could see them sitting along the cliff edge, a row of little figures, the Koniuji Home Guard.

A little farther along the coast we came to a beach brown with sea lions. A shallow stony shelf stretched out from the beach and we were able to anchor on its edge. It was not a comfortable place as the swell was much larger than it was at the Kasatochi anchorage, since it was not under the lee of the island.

Several large male sea lions had selected their areas, and were defending them loudly and lustily, while their females surrounded them, stretched indolently on the rocks about them, any way up, with here and there a flipper waving as if to emphasize a point in their conversation, all of which seemed to be carried out at the top of their voices, like women enjoying a sauna bath. We watched one old sea lion, a dark chocolate, whose whole front was red with blood. A lighter-coloured male wallowed slowly over the beach towards him, and the noise of the onlookers rose like the cheers and the jeers of an excited football crowd. He closed to within three feet of his selected adversary and no doubt the hearts of the sleek brides beat quickly in anticipation of the coming battle.

It was not a rough-and-tumble free-for-all, but seemed to be a carefully ordered affair. They both stood as high as they could, heads up and mouths open, roaring as they confronted each other.

'Gentlemen of the French Guard, fire first,' said the newcomer, but the old, darker sea lion refused. Suddenly the younger dived at his opponent's bloody breast, and worried at him with all his terrific force and strength. The old bull raised his muzzle to the clouds and bellowed, 'Look at the chicken,' he seemed to roar, 'he couldn't hurt a cod'; but it was probably much more insulting than that.

When the younger bull failed to tear him apart, he let go and bared his breast to his adversary. Then the old man dived in and heaved and tugged while the younger bull raised his muzzle and bellowed insults in his turn.

This went on for several exchanges, until the younger rolled away, but not into the sea. Honours were apparently even. He left his opponent bloody but unbowed. Perhaps the younger was an established male who only wanted to win extra wives. There were one or two male sea lions on the edge of the beach or in the sea itself, who had either been pushed off or were perhaps selecting the meekest adversary, or even giving the girls a look-over before they became engaged in combat for their sakes.

We sailed that afternoon for Deep Cove, on the northern coast of Atka, and on the way saw a strange animal. In all the thousands of miles that *Tzu Hang* has sailed we have seen nothing that could be described as mysterious or unaccountable, except this one beast that we all forgot about in the interest of arriving at Deep Cove.

Clio, Henry, and I were on deck when it occurred.

'Look, look,' cried Clio, suddenly pointing close off the weather bow. 'What is it, what is it?'

Close off the port bow an animal was lying in the water; it looked to be about the size of a sheep and had long, pepper-and-salt hair like a cairn terrier, of a reddish-yellow colour. As the bow approached, it made a slow, undulating dive and disappeared beneath the ship. What most impressed me was the length of its hair, about four to five inches long; and when I first saw it on the surface the hair was floating round the body like weed growing on a half-submerged rock. I never saw its head, but Clio, who also saw it come up on the other side of the ship and look at us, said that the head was more like the head of a dog than of a seal, with the eyes close together, not set on the side of the head like a seal's. Henry confirmed this impression, saying that it had a face like a Tibetan terrier, with drooping Chinese whiskers.

In Steller's account of his exploration with Bering and the ships *St Peter* and *St Paul*, from Kamchatka to the North American coast in 1741, he writes of an animal which he called the 'sea monkey', reddish-yellow and about four feet long, which has never since been identified, so that naturalists have thought it never existed. Steller, however, was a very acute and literal observer, unlikely to imagine anything that he did not see. They were observed several times on this voyage, which is described in the book recently published, called *Where the Sea Breaks its Back*, by Corey Ford. It was only after reading this account in South Africa that Clio remembered our own strange animal and wrote to remind me. Clio, Henry, and I had all forgotten the sighting, but now we all believe that the animal we saw was the same creature; neither sea lion, seal, nor sea otter, that Steller describes in some detail.

Atka has so many sounds and entrances that it is difficult for a stranger to choose first the most suitable, and then to recognize it. A rocky islet guarded the entrance to Deep Cove; but, instead of following the channel up the sound, after we had passed it we turned to starboard into a shallow cove, and anchored near its head in three fathoms. It was the anchorage that I liked the most, and we called it Caribou Cove.

The cove was walled by cliffs and the entrance was protected by the other side of the sound. A long valley swept away from its head. No sea could reach in there, but only wind. It could come, in winter anyway, screaming down the valley and rip away the surface of the cove. Even now it was blowing quite gustily, and I was glad that we had not tried to stay at Koniuji. The holding ground was good. I thought that if we had a strong enough mooring we could have kept *Tzu Hang* there all the year round.

We rowed to a shingle beach and pulled the dinghy up. A stream, as at Yoke Bay, had cut a channel through it. Behind, except that we were walking on tundra and not on heather, we might have been in the highlands of Scotland, and everywhere there were tracks of caribou, imported to this and to some of the other Aleutian Islands, where they have thrived.

We found a good set of antlers sticking out of a small bog. Henry, in an attempt to get them, was soon up to his waist himself. We pulled him out and later found another fine head sticking out of an even smaller bog hole. We got hold of these, but they were still attached to the unhappy caribou that had met his end there.

I should have loved to spend days there, a week at least, with all that great valley to explore and somewhere the caribou herd waiting over the skyline. Ours was the fate of the restless wanderer; the skyline is never an end but only a bound, and something—so much—lies beyond. We had to be moving and we decided to sail next day.

8 The Misty Islands

That night a wild wind came whooping at us, rushing down the valley and swirling round the stony hill that made the southern shore of our bay. *Tzu Hang* swirled this way and that at the end of her anchor chain, while the glass plunged and the rain rattled on the deck. Since our anchor seemed so securely fastened in the sand, and the weather was so unpleasant we decided not to sail that day. We had a long lie-in and spent the morning on board. Ashore for another walk in the afternoon with the distant skyline and the soft going on the tundra tempting us to go farther, the rain gone, and the soft green of the hills dappled here and there with sunshine. Henry searched the stream for fish but found nothing, nor did we see any sign of life other than the caribou tracks.

Having wasted a day of strong winds we had little enough to sail with next morning. Beryl wanted to see the Aleut settlement in Nazan Bay, on the east coast of Atka, the only purely Aleut settlement remaining in the islands, for the Aleut are disappearing from their islands in a voluntary but encouraged migration to the Alaskan towns, towards education, medicine, shops, and centralized authority. Some remain, or at least for part of the year, because they are able to draw a hard living allowance when in their village, and these hardy ones are concentrated in Nazan Bay, where they are well looked after by the U.S. Government.

We had intended to cross the mouth of Korovin Bay and to go round North Cape, but it was soon obvious that we would not be able to get there before dark. When I read the instructions in the Pilot I became confused by the number of islands and reefs that it referred to, and in the inner bay the holding ground was said to be poor and it was open to the north-east.

I had no detailed chart. I did not like the idea of going in, perhaps largely because Martin Harbour on the north coast, and now directly south of us as we crossed Korevin Bay, was described as offering good shelter to small craft in all weather.

'Couldn't you walk over to Nazan Bay, if we went into Martin Harbour instead?' I asked Beryl.

'Oh yes,' she replied, as delighted at the thought of a long expedition on foot, as at the idea of entering the paragon of harbours, which had the additional blessing of a 'sticky bottom of mud and sand'. We turned south and went in immediately through a narrow entrance guarded by rocky spurs.

Martin Harbour is the grandiose name for the anchorage at the head of a sound about a mile and a half deep. The head of the bay shelves gradually to a mud beach enclosed by a low bank covered with reedy grass, which separates it from a marshy valley. A stream winds through the valley from a kloof in the hills above, about a mile and a half away. On each side the hills climb steeply. Like Caribou Cove it was reminiscent of the Highlands but not on such a magnificent scale, yet it is as wild as can be, without a sign that it ever knew hut or house or landing stage.

We had just got ashore when we heard a motor-boat coming up the sound and a party of Aleuts arrived in an open plywood boat with an Evinrude outboard motor. They were the Proko-peuf family—nearly all the Aleuts have Russian names—and they were shooting seals. They were much better dressed than any of us, in good U.S. Service parkas, U.S. rubber thigh boots, jeans, and peaked caps. Their clothes suited their features, which had an Eskimo-Indian look, with a liberal addition of white blood. Mrs Prokopeuf seemed to be the leader of the party and they all came on board to tea. They thought that we were a wreck when they saw us, they explained, and if they were disappointed to find that we were not they did not show it.

Beryl asked them the way to Nazan Bay. There were two ways, they said—straight over the hill if you could find it, or round the shore to the camp that they had just come from, their summer fishing camp at the head of Korovin Bay, and then across the spit to Nazan Bay a few miles farther. If Beryl came this way they asked her to call in and see them. They went off to try to shoot a seal, while Clio took Kochi for a walk round

the bay, Henry went to investigate the fishing, and Beryl and I
set off on a reconnaissance of the direct route. We climbed the
hill to the watershed, but the ground undulated away for a few
miles and then fell steeply. Fog was rolling in from the sea and
climbing the eastern slopes. We could see nothing beyond it
and I was very glad that we were safe in Martin Harbour.

Next morning Beryl, Henry, and Clio walked to Nazan Bay,
but as Kochi was on heat and there would be dogs in the village,
she was left with me. There was no question of their going over
the hills as there was a heavy fog and we could not see the shore
of the bay around us. They pulled the dinghy up on to the top
of the reedy bank and set off round the shore. For a long time I
could hear their voices, with Clio and Henry trying to persuade
Beryl to take a short cut and Beryl wisely insisting that she was
going to keep one foot in the sea.

They came back in the Prokopeufs, motor-boat in the evening. They had had quite a journey, for the coast as far as the
Prokopeufs' camp was very irregular with numerous spurs and
gulleys, which had to be surmounted and crossed. The Prokopeufs had a small wooden shack and were netting salmon in a
stream beside it. Their sturdy, gentle-eyed daughter, Theresa,
had shown them the way to the village, which was easy walking.
It was a scattered collection of white wooden houses and gaily
coloured roofs dominated by the green onion domes of the
Russian church. The houses, the bright parkas of the children,
the many-coloured dogs, and the washing on the clothes-lines
all brought colour and movement to the drab grey background
of tundra, sea, and sky. Beryl, Clio, and Henry told me all
about it later. It was just as well that they hadn't tried to come
the direct way, Mrs Prokopeuf said, because even Aleuts got
lost. A year or two ago her son, aged thirteen, had wandered off
in the fog and had been lost for five days. The Americans had
been looking for him with aircraft but men from the village found
him in the end, 'They knew he'd come to the sea,' she said.

'But poor little fellow, he must have been starving,' said
Beryl.

'No. He wasn't so bad. He had slept under the lip of the
tundra where it curls over on a stream bank, you know. I
guess he found some berries or something to eat. He is an
Aleut,' she finished proudly.

Mrs Prokopeuf had known hardship herself since she was on Attu when the Japanese invaded. Some of her people had been killed and she had been taken away to Hokkaido. I thought that if she and her man left the Islands and went to Alaska as so many had done, they would often think, like the Men of the Hebrides in the Canadian boat song:

> From the lone shieling of the misty island
> Mountains divide us and a waste of seas
> Yet still the blood is strong, the heart is Highland
> And we in dreams behold the Hebrides.

The sound of the motor died away as the boat turned seaward at the entrance to the sound. Presently there came the crack of a rifle, a noise that the hills caught and mumbled about. 'If I was an Aleut, I should never leave,' Beryl said, turning to the galley and to the fresh salmon that they had brought from their net.

I took Kochi ashore in the dinghy to collect the clothing that Clio and Beryl had washed in the river the day before, and that I spread out in the vain hope that it might dry. By the time that I had collected it I could just make out Kochi on the hillside a mile away. Indignant about her desertion by the walkers in the morning, she had gone off the moment that she put her foot ashore. She was a good six miles over the hills from the nearest dog, so I wasn't worried. When I got back to the ship I could see through the glasses that she was gnawing some caribou bones. She didn't come back for her supper, so we left the rubber dinghy ashore so that she might sleep in it. That would teach her a lesson we thought.

A couple of hours later, when the light was beginning to fail, I searched for her with the glasses. I saw her making her way homeward. She found the dinghy on the bank and examined it, but she had no intention of spending the night there. She jumped down on to the beach and trotted round until she was exactly opposite the ship. Then she sat down to consider the situation. She does not regard us as her masters but as her companions. She does not try to please us nor does she ask for help. Presently, a decision made, she got up and trotted round the beach, her tail high. On the way there were various distractions. She frightened some harlequin duck out of the

stream and put a fox up in the rocks, which she hunted for a
short time. When she came level with *Tzu Hang* and found that
she was no nearer to us her tail drooped.

She made another pause to consider a new plan. Then,
decision made, up went her tail and she trotted round to the
other side of the bay opposite *Tzu Hang*. Again there were
distractions and this time she almost caught a squawking water-
bird that she came on in the reeds. Finding that she was still
no nearer the ship, her tail drooped and only waved when she
had made her decision. She trotted slowly back to the head of
the bay which was perhaps the closest distance to *Tzu Hang*.
It was almost dark now. She waded straight in and swam out
to us. Of course we were waiting to pull her into the dinghy
and to tell her that she was a good dog. Our good resolutions
had gone by the board. She was rubbed dry and cosseted and
given some food, all of which she considered her due.

From Martin Harbour we sailed for Seguam, having light
airs at first until the wind came easterly, so that by nightfall
we were still off the north coast of Atka. The wind was fresh
easterly the following morning with heavy fog. We beat up
against it for Seguam and presently caught sight of irregu-
larities in the fog texture, whites and darker patches, which
turned out to be snow and rocks on a mountainside not very
far away. We held on until we could see the shoreline and then
tacked off into the fog again. By darkness we were close inshore
but decided not to go into anchorage in Finch Cove at the eastern end of the island, since the wind was easterly, the fog thick,
and it was already late. We hove-to on an offshore tack and had
a quiet night.

In the morning I could just make out Moundhill Point, the
eastern end of Seguam, before the fog closed around us, so we
knew approximately from where we were starting. I laid a
course to pass just north of Chagulak Island about fourteen
miles to the westward.

After sailing our distance I thought that I could see the
island momentarily on the port bow. I altered course on the
assumption that I had seen something so that we would leave
the island to starboard. We continued for another ten miles and
then took down the sail. I guessed that we were now north of
the pass between Amukta and Yunaska Islands. We could see

and hear nothing, no sign of land. A large yellow sea lion came and inspected us. Kochi barked nervously but Pwe was very bold, knowing from long experience that she is safe on *Tzu Hang*. The shearwaters kept swinging past us and disappearing into the fog. They were the only guides that we had, for I knew that they would not be flying into cliff faces. We could hear the sound of tide rips and believed that they were caused by the currents in the pass between the two islands. At ten in the evening I motored north for two miles until I thought that we were out of danger. There was no wind and we turned in.

At about two in the morning I heard the tide rips again and on looking out found *Tzu Hang* revolving slowly while they chattered all round. I went back to my bunk and lay listening. I heard Beryl stir.

I called her softly, 'We're in those bloody rips again.'

'I don't see that there is anything to worry about,' she said, 'I should think they'd take us around the rocks, not on to them.'

'No. But I don't like not knowing where I'm going.'

'Well, I don't see how you can tell anyway. I think you're better in the rips than trying to motor in the dark.'

The rips seemed to quieten and I dropped off to sleep again. I awoke at four and found *Tzu Hang* rocking violently and the roar of strong tide rips all round us. It was beginning to get light. *Tzu Hang* was spinning so violently that it was impossible to follow the compass. This was too much for me. I roused all hands and we started the motor. *Tze Hang* came under control immediately. I assumed that we had been carried down into the pass between Yunaska and Chagulak and set off to the north. As the light came our friends the shearwaters started to fly past us heading north or south. I could use them as pilots. With the daylight came breakfast and while we were all down below except for Clio at the helm, I heard her singing. 'I see a mountain, I see a mountain,' she sang.

I hurried on deck. 'Why didn't you tell me?' I asked. 'I did. This is me telling you. I see two.'

There were two single snow peaks sticking out of the fog to starboard and I was able to get a bearing on each before they disappeared. I cut a template from a piece of paper, and then slid it up and down until it fitted two mountains in the vicinity. They were Carlisle and Herbert Islands in the Four Mountain group, and we were in the pass between them and Yunaska, about twelve miles farther on than the log had given us and about twelve miles to the south. We had in fact been carried during the night from the Bering Sea into the Pacific. I knew exactly where I was now, and we continued to the north.

By midday the fog had cleared sufficiently for us to see Uliaga Island to the north. We could make out the lower slopes of Kagamil, and Kagamil Pass was clear. The fog rolled through Carlisle Pass like the cannon smoke at Balaclava. We turned eastward, aiming to sail through the pass, and to anchor in a bight on the east side of Kagamil. Ships are strongly recommended not to anchor in the Four Mountain group because of the tide rips, but there seemed to be no reason why we should not anchor there, since apart from the fog the weather was fine.

Soon Kagamil and Kagamil Pass were blotted out completely, while south of us we could see a narrow black band below the fog. It was the northern coast of Chuginadak. This soon disappeared also. Unsure now of the set of the current, but allowing for its probable flow through the various channels, I set a course that I hoped would bring us to the south-east corner of Kagamil. As we approached it the various signs so necessary for navigation in these waters appeared.

There were swirls and rips to show conflicting currents, and then the wind began to fluke first one way and then the other, as it blew round the mountain. Then came a change in the movement of the swell, and a tide line of scum from breakers and broken pieces of kelp. Finally there were hundreds of murre on the water, a sure sign that high cliffs were near.

We kept on through the dank murk until we saw some white patches showing through, which turned out to be bird droppings on steep cliffs. Then there appeared a quick-drawn pencil outline of a rocky point, as quickly rubbed out again. Round the point the fog cleared slightly and we were able to follow the coast more easily. As we felt our way into the bight where we intended to anchor, the peak of the volcano showed for a moment high above us, lined with streaks of black lava and snow gullies. The sun was directly behind it and as it showed above the fog it blazed with golden light. We anchored on sand and cinders off a driftwood beach.

The driftwood was piled on the beach and had been washed up between the narrow banks of a small stream. We rowed ashore and as we scrambled over the logs a fox that had been watching us from the top of the pile disappeared within their protection and barked at us from inside as we passed. Above the bank of the stream, on a grassy meadow, stood a small wooden hut.

It had been a trapper's hut, for it was full of fox traps, but it had been deserted for some years. There was a grave outside the hut with a wooden double cross above it, roughly nailed together. The trapper's possessions littered the shack. There was an old gramophone and records from the 'thirties. There were some newspapers from 1938. There were his tools, his axe and spade, his spring traps, a box bunk, a half-empty tin of coffee, with other tins on a shelf. There were also a pair of home-made wooden skis, too small, we thought, for anyone but an Aleut. Death had come to the house and we wondered how it had happened.

'I think he died in his bunk and some Aleuts came in a boat and found him. Then they buried him and left everything as it was,' I suggested.

'I think he died and his wife buried him and then rowed over to Nikolski. It's only about twenty miles away,' said Beryl.

'I think his wife died and he buried her and rowed off to look for another one,' Clio guessed,

'Well, I think he was evacuated after Pearl Harbour, they just whipped him away. He probably bought the papers when he first came. They'd be about three years old anyway. I don't know about the grave, perhaps it was his wife's,' was Henry's suggestion. We never discovered the answers.

Next day there was still fog to seaward and all that we could see of Umnak was the snow-white cone of Mount Usefidof, showing above it. We climbed a part of the way up the hill behind the house and slid much of the way down. It was very like Kasatochi, but on a grander scale. There was a little sunshine and the longspurs and rosy finches on the slopes and the Seguam winter wrens in the driftwood were all busy.

We set off next day for Nikolski with the snow mountain still shining like a beacon above the fog. As we crossed the strait the fog thinned and finally disappeared. About half-way across, when Clio was at the helm and the rest of us below, there

Yoke Bay in Great Sitken Island, Aleutians

15. Clio and Beryl with Pwe and Kochi land in Yoke Bay

16. Theresa Prokopeuf, an Aleut girl
from Atka

was a sudden thump below the keel as if we had run into a heavy log, followed by a quick series of bumps that made the hull ring. We started for the deck and at same time saw Clio's anxious face looking down the hatch.

'What are you doing?' she called.

We were on deck in time to hear a loud roar from Kagamil, a receding roar, which I recognized at once as an earthquake. It was reported on the news that evening, its epicentre in the sea about sixty miles away. We had had an earthquake at sea when in the Aegean. That one gave a single loud shock like a depth charge. This one gave a quick series of jolts over a period of about three seconds. There is a record of a steamer reducing speed until it could have its propeller examined under the belief that it had damaged it against some underwater obstruction, after experiencing an earthquake in these waters.

Apart from the U.S. Navy and Air Bases and the Aleut settlement at Nazan Bay, Nikolski is the first outpost of Western civilization. It boasted a store, a post office, several scattered houses, and an airstrip. We walked to the airstrip to look at the fuselage of a cracked-up aircraft of Reeve's Aleutian Airways which had come to grief in a windstorm. They were dismantling it piece by piece and flying it back to their base. We met some of the crew from the big radar station on the hill above Nikolski, who drove us up to their station in search of a few gallons of fuel with which to top up *Tzu Hang*. The domes and screens, their shoulders hunched as if to face the rain, had an architectural beauty, perched so high on the hill, as well as an air of alert watchfulness.

'Did you feel the earthquake?' I asked one of the crew.

'I'll say,' he replied, 'I thought that the Aleuts had blown their raisin still!'

'We're all allowed a free telephone call home,' said the other. 'You know how it is. The folks see that a severe earthquake has been recorded with its centre near Umnak and they begin to think that we're all under the ruins. Actually it did no damage at all.'

Beryl and Clio went to the ranchhouse of a sheep station which has its headquarters at Nikolski. They returned in the dinghy with Art Harris, a big man, the owner of the ranch, and with half a sheep.

I

'You did well to send your womenfolk,' he said, 'otherwise you'd have to pay for this.'

He was very keen on Aleut remains and ancient artifacts, and perhaps talking about this brought him to the subject of eggs. He told us that the old-timers were so used to the eggs that were shipped to Alaska, packed eggs, that they used to prefer their flavour to fresh ones. He had heard eggs described in the old days as being 'real fresh. You can eat 'em without ketchup.'

From Nikolski we motored across to Ananuliak Island which is separated from the northern point, Nikolski Bay, by a pass known as Seaweed Pass, where the Pilot told us we might anchor in good holding ground off its south-eastern side, sheltered from northerly and westerly winds. There was no wind at all and we anchored as close as we could to the kelp bed. The island was interesting because of its sea-birds. Puffin, pigeon guillemot, glaucous-winged gulls, and eider duck were all there in great numbers. It was known locally as Rabbit Island and there were some large yellow rabbits which kept Kochi entertained but which always had a burrow at hand.

The pigeon guillemot, so like the black guillemot except that the white patch on their wings is cut by a small black triangle, were breeding in holes and small caves in the rocks at the foot of the cliff. When coming in from the sea they sat in groups on the rocks at the sea's edge to dry, before hopping up and into their nests again. If a glaucous-winged gull came gliding along the cliff face they all hurried back into the sea in obvious agitation. For them, the whole process of nesting seemed to be an anxious one.

The tufted puffins were much more extrovert. 'With a nose as strange could be, of vast proportions and painted red,' they dived out of their burrows at the top of the cliff, plummeted downwards till they had flying speed and then zoomed off across Seaweed Pass. They seemed to find all the food they wanted, for large numbers were always sitting on the water amongst the seaweed.

Henry crouched for hours just above their burrows but, though they'd fly up and have a good look at him, they never came right home.

The glaucous-winged gulls were hatching, and Clio found a

spotted baby which had fallen out of its nest, which is the most carelessly scraped together affair on the top of a rock. The gulls are egg robbers themselves, but no one seems to bother them. The spotted baby, which looked like a piece of plum duff, proved irresistible to Clio and she picked it up with the usual result, all of which Henry was able to film, although he had unfortunately run out of colour.

The eider duck, as always, had hidden their nests with care, a regular little house inside a clump of tussocky grass or reed, beautifully lined with down.

We left next day after lunch and in a flat calm motored eighteen miles up the coast to Inanudak Bay, helped by a strong tide. Inanudak Bay is a deep and wide entrance from which several fingers run inland. By the time we got to the head of Hot Spring Cove a fresh wind was blowing. We rowed into the beach and although we could see some steam rising farther up the valley did not feel inclined to wander. The wind blew violently during the night and we were heartily glad to be away from our last anchorage which was open to the south. In the morning it was still blowing southerly and we decided to make use of it. *Tzu Hang* sailed out at great speed in the calm water, making a good seven knots, but in the lee of the land as we left the sound the wind was fluky.

The fog was pouring over the hills, and streaming over our heads for some miles to leeward. The smoke of a volcano came rolling off the hill also, lying below the fog.

Soon we found ourselves trying to sail in the most extra-ordinary conditions, at one moment becalmed, at another wishing that we had the main off. At one moment the wind blew violently from the port side and at another switched suddenly to starboard. All round us willywaws caught at the sea and tore from the surface a myriad drops, whisking them away like smoke from a bonfire. Wherever we looked we could see one of these fires burning. We put double preventer guys on the boom to protect it, and made for Ashishik anchorage at the end of Umnak, but the wind backed easterly and we had to give up the idea. We had intended to go to Bogosloff Island, a volcanic island which is always changing its shape, but only suitable for a fine-weather visit. Now, with the glass falling and the dreaded south-easter blowing, we gave up that idea too.

As soon as we were into Umnak Pass and no longer protected by the mountains, we were in fog again, with a heavy sea
running. By 0400 hours we could see the light on the radar
tower at Koriga Point, Unalaska. We spent the whole day
flogging up the coast and hove-to for the night off Cape Wislow.
Next morning we made sail and by noon were beating into
Dutch Harbour. It had taken us two and a half days to get
there, a distance of about fifty miles.

We had pictured Dutch Harbour as a Navy base far bigger
than Adak, and we had written to the Secretary of the Navy for
permission to enter. His reply could have only caught us with
difficulty, but after three days' head wind, with the fog rolling
through the passes ahead of us, we felt that we were entitled to
claim some respite. As we beat into the harbour the wind eased
so that we could make in one tack the last stretch along the
outside of the sandbank that makes the eastern shore of the
harbour. *Tzu Hang* was sailing well and came quickly down the
bay. We could see a mass of barracks, water towers, and fuel
tanks behind a substantial T-shaped pier. Yet there was no
ship to be seen, nor any movement visible. It began to look as
if the whole vast camp was entirely deserted. We handed our
sail and motored towards the pier, when to our relief we saw a
truck come down the road and drive along to its head. By the
time we arrived alongside, George Wright and two Aleuts were
there to take our lines. He moved us round behind the head of
the pier where we made fast.

'I knew all about you,' he shouted down to us, as soon as he
saw the ship's name.' I have just finished reading Annie Van
de Wiele's book, *The West in my Eyes*. You want a bath, don't
you?'

His wife, Helen, was soon on the pier too, full of excitement
at the thought of visitors.

It was the eeriest place. Silence and desolation hung heavily
on the air. George Wright and his wife and one other American
looked after the Shell Oil plant and John Lawrence, also with
his wife, looked after U.S. Navy interests for four months of the
year. Behind their three houses there were now empty barracks,
empty offices, and empty barrackrooms, deserted roads and
barrack squares, silent workshops and storerooms, empty
dining-halls and an empty school. Children's weather-faded

toys lay broken and unloved beside the road above the silent playground. No hum from the generator in the power house standing silent with is still-crated reserve on the floor beside it. A window in one of the married quarters was swinging loosely on its hinges with no one to fasten it. Amongst all this and quite unaware of any sense of desolation the five survivors of the once teeming multitude of sailors and marines led their lives. They were like five bees clinging to an empty hive.

Both of the men were ideally suited to their jobs, which took up very little of their time. George Wright could never find enough time for his interests. He read, he dug for artifacts, he was an ardent rock-hound and stone-polisher, and a maker of strange home-made wines and home-made beer. John Lawrence was a compulsive hunter and fisherman; a vigorous man who loved to get the best out of life. He told us that when he was in the marines in New Guinea anything with four legs went into his stock pot while the others lived on K rations. 'They were always round for my stew,' he said, 'until I told them what was in it. Lizards and all sorts.'

We met him first when he drove up to the Wrights to enlist our help in getting a halibut, that he had caught on a long line, into a truck.

'How the hell did you boat that?' asked George.

'Well, I don't really know,' replied John, 'and when I did there wasn't much room for both of us until I tapped him on the nose. And do you know what, there was another one on the line at the same time and I lost the bastard.'

The fish filled the boat. It was six feet long and must have weighed 300 pounds. We got it into the truck with great difficulty and then took it to the empty playground and hoisted it by the tail over a child's swing. Its nose just swung clear of the ground.

'What are you going to do with it now?' I asked.

'I'm going to cut it up tomorrow and freeze it,' he said. 'I get 200 lb a month free airlift back to the States. We ship all kinds of clams and fish back. Keep the whole family stocked up for the winter.'

It was July 12th. The Bering Strait was ice-free and the first ships were on their way to the north and round Point Barrow to the Mackenzie. Mackenzie Bay is clear of ice from the middle of July until the beginning of September, but from the time the ships passed Icy Cape to Point Barrow and along the north coast the ice would never be far away and the gap between the shore ice and the drift ice liable to close when onshore winds blew. They were likely to meet floes anywhere on this stage of their passage.

The firstcomer was a red-and-white-painted ship, the Canadian Coastguard vessel, *Camsel*. As she headed up into the harbour the Captain and the Chief Engineer on the bridge saw *Tzu Hang*, also painted red and white, tied up to the wharf, and as yet unable to recognize her as a yacht, the Chief said to the Captain, 'By God, look at that. Someone stole our paint last year.' They were very smart and efficient, the new Canadian ensign matching their colour. When they found out that we were a Canadian yacht they couldn't have been more helpful. We had baths and lunch on board, our battery charged, and a carton of fresh vegetables, bread, and butter was sent over to us. The *Camsel* had a small helicopter like a goldfish bowl in which we were all taken in turns for a ride.

That evening a big tug, the *Neptune*, came in; she had a long scow in tow. It was loaded with all kinds of equipment for the Dew Line—airstrip track, snocats, D4 cranes, trucks, tanker lorries, and lumber. The tug was commanded by a well-known character on the coast nicknamed 'Whispering Smith'. He looked as if he had been hewn out of oak and sounded as if he had the vocal equipment of a foghorn.

After much delay owing to all the good-byes that had to be said, we left about midday, and when we got out of the bay we saw the fog rolling through the Akutan and Akun passes. *Tzu Hang* groped her way across them and then followed the coastline into Lost Harbour on the western side of Akun. The fog was beginning to lift as we got out of the Straits and into the shelter of the sound so that, although it was eleven at night, there was still plenty of light for navigation.

The wind blew furiously all next day and we were glad to be at anchor. We went ashore. Beryl and I collected driftwood and then took it back to the ship to saw up for firewood, Henry, Clio, and Kochi went for a long walk round the bay in search of glass floats. They were gone a long time and when they returned seemed to be loaded each with a great burden. They had found sixty-two glass balls, most of them attached to the head line of a net that had broken away. It had been washed up and covered with sand. They saw one ball and when they picked it up found all the others buried but still attached. We stowed them away in the canoe stern, together with a three-legged Kaffir cooking-pot and other useless treasures.

With the wind down and moving round to the west we sailed next morning, but north about, by Akun Head, rather than through the Akun Strait where the tide runs up to twelve knots. I should have liked to have gone that way but found the language of the Pilot too intimidating. As we rounded the Head a herd of seals came bellowing to see us just as they had done at Attu, but this time I felt it was to say good-bye rather than to welcome us. There was still fog about, but is was lifting and lying in streaks across the slopes on each side of the Strait.

Unimak Island is the last of the Aleutian Islands and is separated from the mainland peninsula by the Isanotski Strait. This is a narrow passage only used by small fishing vessels and has a six-foot-deep bar across its northern end, so that it can hardly be called a strait at all. The Unimak Strait is a deep-water passage between Unimak and Uminak and is the high road to the North, leading to the Bering Straits, Icy Cape, Cape Barrow, and the Arctic Sea. It is an immensely romantic passage. With the wind swinging all the time to the north-west, and the day turning clear and cool, we could see all of it, the far side dark and rocky, with snowfields above, and in the midde the low black headland known as Scotch Cap.

We headed for the channel between Seal Cape, the south-west end of Unimak, and Ugamak Island, and all the way was black with shearwaters, sitting on the water or swinging in writhing skeins over the sea. There were various kinds, the pink-footed, the broad-billed, and the dusky shearwaters. It seemed to be a meeting-place for all that had come by different ways from the southern seas, some up the Japanese coast and along the Aleutians, some up the Californian coast and across the Gulf of Alaska. As we sailed close to Ugamak Island with sea lions covering the beaches, the veil of low-flying shearwaters was sometimes so thick that it hid them completely. When we rounded Seal Cape, Scotch Cap showed black and clear against the sunset, which lit up the snows on the volcanoes and showed us Shishaldin, nearly ten thousand feet high, puffing away from its snow-covered peak.

At about 0730 hours on July 15th we picked up Cape Lazarof at four or five miles, but fog was all round and no other land in sight. We laid a course for Cape Pankoff, 1,200 feet high and twenty-one miles away, on the end of the Ikatan Peninsula. The fog gradually closed in on us until visibility was reduced to one mile, and the wind began to freshen from the south. There are two coves, one on each side of the low isthmus, known as East Anchor Cove and West Anchor Cove; the latter, which connects Cape Pankoff to the Ikatan Peninsular, is exposed to south-westerly winds, the former to those between north and south-east. We picked up the coast entrance to the West Anchor Cove and sailed all the way along the cape for about three and a half miles, keeping the breakers just in sight, under the fog, and sometimes the grassy slopes behind.

The lighthouse on Cape Pankoff loomed large and we must have been quite close in. As we turned the corner for West Anchor Cove we met a run of killer whale, about seven of them, and three came rolling and blowing lazily over to inspect us at close quarters. Nothing is more beautiful in the animal world than the dorsal fin of a killer bull showing like a sword above the surface until, like Excalibur, it disappears.

East Anchor Cove is a lovely place and we tucked ourselves in behind a curving red beach. South of us and clear from the fog because we were on the lee side, green grassy slopes ran up to the ridge which stretched with one deep gully between the points of the cape. To the west was the low isthmus connecting the cape with the Ikatan Peninsula. Henry and I rowed ashore to investigate. Over the grassy bank behind the beach a wide meadow and marshland stretched across to West Anchor Cove. We walked down to the beach and came upon the tracks of an enormous bear. I had never seen anything like them. They followed the tide line and were so fresh that the bear must have been on the beach when we came in. There were also tracks of a wolf in the sand.

We went back with fabulous tales which neither Clio nor Beryl believed. The wind piped up violently during the night as another depression with gale force winds passed over us, so that we decided to stay another day. Ashore we walked across to West Anchor Cove to find the fog and sea rolling in hideously. There were many bear tracks but we found no bears. I took a shorter cut back to the beach and sat down on the wreck of an old boat until I heard the others arriving. I looked over the bank. I had come through long wet grass and made a wide track. They were following my trail and I heard Clio say, 'This is the way it came. Look, this is the way it came. It's going to the beach again.' This was the last of the Aleutian anchorages. We left them with regrets but the sight of the bear tracks held a promise of other interests.

9 The Photogenic Bear

We had waited in Dutch Harbour for more film to arrive, and eventually left without it. George Wright said that he'd send it on to Cold Bay where there is an airport. There is also a Customs officer that I didn't know about. Cold Bay is a wide bay twenty miles deep with low rolling tundra where the wind always seems to blow and where the huts and buildings cling, unhappy and without beauty, to the cold, bare ground.

It is only a step across from East Anchor Cove to the entrance. We had a little wind as we sailed over, but once inside it freshened considerably and we were soon beating up towards the port at the north-western end of the bay. We found a small coaster there, the *Alaskan Trader*, which had left Dutch Harbour on the same day as *Tzu Hang*. When we approached them to tie alongside the captain called down to us that there was a storm warning out and that we would do better to tie up to a buoy.

'Come alongside tomorrow,' he called down, 'if it's all clear. Come to breakfast.'

We hooked on to a mooring buoy not far away, which was covered with droppings from cormorants and seagulls and smelt like a fish-meal factory. The storm didn't materialize and next morning we slipped the buoy and went alongside the *Alaskan Trader* for breakfast.

'Where were you during those two gales?' asked Captain Mackay, a tall, spare man of about forty-five. 'I dragged my anchors all over the place, even out of Lenard Harbour. I have been steaming ever since I left Dutch. I'm going to put my second anchor ashore and get a heavier one shipped out. There is something wrong with it, it won't hold at all.'

Lenard Harbour is a deep re-entrance on the other side of

the bay, supposed to be well sheltered, with good holding ground, but subject to violent squalls. During the gales we had been at anchor in Lost Harbour and East Anchor Cove.

After a tremendous breakfast we went in search of the post office. Captain Mackay was already ashore when we left, but his crew of about six men were at work on the bow, cutting through his main anchor cable. A sling was rigged to a derrick and fastened to the second and lighter anchor, outside the hawse hole on the starboard bow, ready to lift it up and swing it on to the quay as soon as the chain was cut. They had almost finished cutting through a link of the main anchor cable. The crew then stood well back, while one of them started to drive a steel wedge into the cut to break the link.

'But why have they got the strop round the other anchor?' asked Beryl.

'I can't imagine. You don't think they're cutting the wrong chain, do you?'

'I'm sure they are. Hadn't you better tell them?'

'They must know what they are doing,' I said, and anyway it was too late. With a final thwack the link broke and the 750-lb main anchor, with a few feet of chain, plunged with a splash into the sea. A cloud of rusty dust hung round the hawse hole. There was a stunned silence and then a rush to look over the bow.

'Where's our anchor?' they asked, looking at each other doubtfully.

'We cut the wrong ruddy cable,' said someone at last.

It was Sunday and there appeared to be no one about anywhere, so we came back to *Tzu Hang*. Presently Captain Mackay came below for a cup of coffee. He shook his head mournfully.

'Seamen,' he said. 'There aren't such things these days.'

'You'd better have something in your coffee,' said Beryl. Captain Mackay agreed.

A little later he was called for by one of his crew. After a few words he came down again.

'More trouble,' he said, 'she wants to see you.'

'Who?'

'The Customs officer.'

I went up to the wharf and found a very austere person

waiting for me. She was not wearing uniform but nondescript clothing under a loose-fitting open waterproof coat.

'Why did you not report to me?' she asked aggressively.

As I had no means of telling what or who she was I asked why I should have done so.

'Well,' I explained, 'I couldn't report yesterday because I came in late and we tied up to the buoy on account of the gale warning. I've been ashore this morning, but I saw no one at the airport and there is no Customs Office down here. I simply didn't know that there was a Customs officer here, and anyway we reported to the coastguard at Attu and at Adak.'

'You have no right to put in anywhere except at Anchorage, which is a Port of Entry.'

'But we had to put in somewhere for water and stores.'

She ignored this but told me that she would advise Anchorage, and that I was not to sail until I had an answer. Half an hour later she was back. She told me that we were to go direct to Anchorage without putting in anywhere.

'But this is a sailing ship,' I said, 'we can't just go four hundred miles out of our way and up a long narrow sound without putting in anywhere. We may want water.'

'Well, it's nothing to do with me. These are the orders I've been told to give you.'

'I'd better talk to the man.'

We went to the office and eventually got him on the radio telephone. He didn't sound too bad.

'We can't have you sailing all over the Bering Sea without letting anyone know,' he said.

'But I didn't know that the Bering Sea was yours,' I said. He laughed at this but continued to insist that I must report to Anchorage. I saw that it was no good going on with the conversation, as to him two hundred miles up a sound was two days' steaming at the worst, so I said I'd do what I could, but remained determined not to go.

At 0330 next morning we heard a shout from Mackay, who told us that the wind was bouncing him on to the pier and he would have to leave. We got the engine going in a rush, cast off, and hooked on to our buoy again. *Atlantic Trader* disappeared down the bay heading for Lenard Harbour, and as we did not see her again we never heard how she managed on one anchor that didn't hold. Perhaps more chain was the answer. We moved back from our buoy and tied up to a halibut boat that had come in. They, and an engineer called Vymer, who lived happily with his pretty Aleut wife in a house on the hill, were very helpful. Vymer fixed our voltage control for us and the halibut boat gave us some excellent halibut. Both of them told us of the Customs officer and her husband. She was also the magistrate as well as the assistant postmistress and he was the postmaster and the assistant Customs officer. They seemed to have got all the power in Cold Bay into their hands and it didn't do to argue with them.

'But why don't you go to Sand Point, in the Humboldt Strait between Popof and Unga Islands, in the Shumagin Islands?' the captain of the halibut boat asked. 'They have a Port of Entry there for Canadian halibut fishermen.'

We decided to sail immediately and to open a flank attack from there.

We didn't get there very quickly because the wind was dead on the nose as we left Cold Bay. I have never been so pleased to leave any place as Cold Bay. Vymer loved it because of the sport, the goose, duck, and big game shooting, but we met no one who did not complain of the unhappy concentration of authority, and I personally felt as if I had arrived in Koluchin-skaya Guba, on the other side of Bering Strait. We anchored east of Fox Island but did not go ashore and went on next day through a maze of islands, proceeding mostly under power. These were frequented waters and we met several crabbers; one of them in his ship called Le Roy gave us three hoots as he passed. Everywhere we saw the pink plastic buoys that mark crab pots. Pavlof Volcano, its snowy cone covered with ashes, was smoking away, giving a hearty puff from time to time, which billowed out over the crater's edge. We sailed into an anchorage called Coal Bay, behind Seal Cape, and had a quiet night.

Sand Point, which we reached next day, is a small port with a factory where king crab are processed and packed during the summer months. Everyone there, except the Customs officer, a young preacher, a nurse, the radio operator, and three American Scandinavians who ran the store, was occupied in either the catching or the processing of king crab. Inge, Helfe, and Rita ran the store, and Hazel was the radio operator, but I do not remember their surnames, only that they were great fun. The Customs officer was a small man and very eager to be helpful. He arranged to call up the Chief Customs Officer at Juneau the following morning.

Next morning I sat beside him and he had my story written out on a piece of paper.

'I know all about him,' bellowed the Chief Customs Officer over the radio. 'He should know the regulations. He can't come in like he did to Attu without reporting.'

'But I did report,' I whispered. 'Let me talk to him.'

'He would like to talk to you himself, sir,' said the Customs officer.

'No, I won't talk to him,' shouted his superior. 'He's broken every law in the book, and he must stay with you until he gets my orders.'

There was nothing to do but to wait until the instructions arrived. Meanwhile everyone knew that we were in trouble, and everyone knew who had been the cause of it, so that we had a lot of sympathy. Every radio-telephone conversation is listened to by the fishermen, and now they came with salmon and halibut as gifts, and to say that they hoped that we didn't think all Americans were like the one in Cold Bay.

We had arranged to take Rita, Inge, Helfe, and Hazel for a sail on Saturday morning. At about half-past eight a strong wind blew in from the south, making our anchorage untenable. Fishing boats started up their engines and cleared out of the harbour. We hoisted the main, rolled in a deep reef and tied it down again.

'I don't expect that they'll come out in this,' I said to Beryl, 'but we'll have to go anyway.'

At nine o'clock, the time that we had arranged, we could stay no longer. Just as we were about to get up the anchor, the cold rain slatting down, a motor-boat arrived and all the Scandinavians and Hazel piled on board. Water ran off their oilskins and off their noses but their faces were alight with pleasure. We soon had the main up and the anchor in and were off down the Strait, towing the motor-boat. We beat round the sandspit which gives the harbour its name, and across to a bay well protected from the south wind, on the Unga Island shore.

There they left us and took the motor-boat back, all soaked to the skin and completely happy.

Next morning while we were all ashore the wind came from the north again so that we had to move *Tzu Hang* a mile farther up the coast, where she could get some shelter from a rocky point and was no longer close to a lee shore. Kochi had found something to hunt and was temporarily lost in a maze of thick wind-packed bushes. Clio elected to stay at the old anchorage since she thought Kochi would return there. But Kochi, from somewhere on the hill, saw us move and came down to the shore near the new anchorage, where I saw her picking her elegant and unruffled way along the rocky beach towards us. When the Scandinavians and Hazel arrived for lunch in the motor-boat we collected her and then Clio from the other anchorage. That afternoon we had a good sail back to Sand Point, and Henry succeeded in filming *Tzu Hang* from the motor-boat.

On the wharf outside the crab factory there were tanks full of king crab groping hopelessly at the edges but unable to climb out. If a king crab is held by the legs and stretched out it measures about four feet across. They are caught in big wire pots about six feet by six by four, which are hoisted and lowered by power blocks on the crabber's derrick. The pots are buoyed with pink or orange-coloured plastic buoys, and a crabber, which usually has several pots stacked in the stern, is bright with these buoys and with gaily coloured polyester fibre rope. They are usually good powerful sea boats and very well kept up, since there is plenty of money to be made in king-crab fishing.

The crabs were taken from the tanks on the wharf in a type of lift truck, which raised a load of sadly waving crabs over a chute and then let them go. They slid down to a killer, who smashed the shell over a steel blade and twisted the two halves of the legs off the carcase. Then off went the legs on conveyor belts and the carcase into the sea below.

All the meat is in the legs and claws, and these now went through a steaming, crushing, and separating process, until they emerged on a conveyor belt as crab meat and were carried between a row of packers who picked and packed in various grades as the meat went by. There is something pathetic and

hopeless about the big crabs in the tanks, who keep gesticu-
lating hungrily towards their mouths, or search feebly for some
escape from their inevitable and ghastly end, but when it is all
over they make marvellous eating.

Judgment day arrived. I was given a cruising permit and
ordered to go in my own time to Ketchikan, where I might be
liable to a fine of 3,000 dollars for failing to report my arrival
at Attu. I was told that I might put in a plea for mitigation,
which I did immediately. Although I had reported at Attu and
again to a representative of the Customs Service in Adak, it
left Beryl and me with an unpleasant feeling that rather over-
shadowed the rest of the cruise as far as Ketchikan. It made us
inclined to hurry on to learn the worst, rather than stay and
enjoy some of the anchorages that we discovered.

The first of these was in Mitrofania Island which we reached
after a day and a night of light wind on our way to the Shelikoff Strait between Kodiak Island and the mainland. It is
uninhabited and is shaped like the cone of a crater with one
lip broken away and sunk beneath the sea. We found shelter
in the most easterly bight, with steep cliffs and caves on both
sides of us. A very quiet night. Clio and Henry would have
liked to have stayed and explored the island, but we went on
and spent three days beating into strong head winds, when we
might well have been quietly at anchor and gained as much
ground.

On August 3rd we were well into the Shelikoff, with Kodiak
Island showing clearly to starboard and snow mountains to
port. We had a following wind and sailed quietly across until
close to the Kodiak shore, but we had tide and current against
us. In the evening *Tzu Hang* sailed into Uganik Bay, round the
Uganik Peninsula, round Miner's Point and Broken Point,
avoiding several salmon nets tended by an Indian and his wife
from a camp on shore. We came to anchor in three fathoms
off the mouth of the river. It was a lovely evening and very
still. A bald-headed eagle was circling above trees near the
shore, and we could see a heron standing on a shingle bank in
the river mouth. The Indian and his wife left in their boat with
an outboard motor and we had the place absolutely to ourselves.

We took both dinghies ashore early next morning. The head

Back in the fir trees on reaching Queen Charlotte Island, B.C.

18. Anthony Island totem in British Columbia

19. Beryl and Pwe enjoy the sun

of the bay was surrounded by a steep grassy slope, and behind was marshland and grass, cut by a small stream in a many-looped pattern to the river. It was much the same sort of land as we had found at East Anchor Cove, but the grass was quickly lost in foothills covered by scrub oak and other trees.

Beryl and I took Kochi and walked round the head of the bay to the far side, while Clio and Henry went off up the river to photograph bear. I can only think that we expected to get a picture of bear because this was Kodiak Island, but the moment Beryl and I left the beach and went to the bank of the little stream, we saw tracks of bear all over the place. Perhaps they scooped salmon out of the water, because a path was trodden along both sides but we saw no fish, and it didn't look like the sort of stream that a salmon would use. Kochi seemed quite ready to stay with us as if she was a little nervous of the smell of bear.

We explored farther round the bay following a bear's path which climbed along the southern side about a hundred feet above the water, on a steep slope through low scrub. At one point there was a bear's seat, where the grass and bushes had been flattened, and where the users of this path obviously sat to look out over the bay. I could picture one sitting there, watching the salmon-fishers and humming Pooh's song about his toes, tiddely pom. We turned from there, tiddely pom, walked back to where, tiddely pom, we'd left the boat, tiddely pom, for rowing.

It was a long time before Clio and Henry appeared in the Avon dinghy, coming down the river. When they got out to *Tzu Hang* I could see that they were bursting with news.

'Any luck?' I asked.

'We got some pictures of harlequin duck,' said Henry.

'That all?'

'No, the river was full of salmon. I got some pictures of salmon going up.'

'Nothing else?'

'Yes,' said Clio, 'we climbed a tree and got some pictures of an eagle's nest with a brancher sitting in it.'

'Oh, come on,' I said, 'what about the bears?'

'You tell him, Henry.'

K

'No, you tell him,' said Henry.

'Let's go below and you can tell us both.'

Clio and Henry told us their story during an early lunch. It had been the most exciting day in Clio's life and perhaps in Henry's.

They had started up the river and presently left the dinghy on the bank. After photographing the harlequin duck and the salmon they found bear tracks in the grass. These eventually led them into thick oak scrub and after ploughing around for some time they decided that they were making too much noise to find a bear and that they'd sit down for a rest. Henry took off his glasses and his camera equipment and put them on the ground. Clio had sat down beside a bush a few yards away, and Henry, leaving his equipment on the ground, walked over and sat down beside her. They were talking and laughing, but not making too much noise, as they felt that they were in bear country.

'I don't think it's any good going any farther,' said Henry, 'it's too thick. Let's go back to the river again.'

'Shall we have a look at that ruined cabin we saw in the trees, where the eagle's nest is?'

'Yes,' said Henry. 'Come on. Let's get going.'

'Well, you pick up your stuff then.'

Henry stood up and as he did so a large bear stood up on the other side of the bush.

'He looked at least seven feet high,' said Henry. 'Well I remembered that you said no matter what happened I had to take pictures, so I walked slowly backwards to my camera, then, watching the bear the whole time, I stooped down for my glasses. Of course I couldn't find the bloody things, and all this time Clio was sitting right under the bear.'

'I couldn't see it,' said Clio, 'because I was so close to the bush. I could only see Henry stalking backwards with his eyes absolutely popping out.'

'Eventually I got my glasses,' he went on, 'and the camera, and started filming. Then the bear turned round and shambled off a short way. Then he turned again and tried to come in below us. I think that he was trying to get our scent because he kept stopping and wrinkling his nose, and then trying to get below us.'

'What did you do?'

'Well, we kept moving parallel to him and trying to keep below him, but we were very close all the time in that scrub, you know.'

'And one time we crossed the stream and scrambled up the bank,' Clio took up the tale, 'and there he was standing right in front of us as we came up.'

'I was scared sick,' said Henry, 'and if Clio hadn't been there I'd really have taken to my heels. I began to feel as if he was hunting us, but perhaps he was just puzzled. Then Clio, the nit, stopped to take her boots off.'

'Why did you do that?'

'Well, I think he was really a nice bear. He didn't look at all angry, but I just thought that if he did come after us I'd throw my boots down to keep him interested.'

'Well done, and did you get a lot of film?'

'Oh yes, Henry was jolly good. He was filming away like mad. And I finished my roll. Hope they all come out.'

We should have stayed there another day, but we left after lunch with a favourable tide.

We sailed for Strawberry Inlet where the Wakefields had started the king-crab industry, at Port Wakefield. As we turned into the sound we found ourselves in different country. The coast was bare and precipitous but inside the sound there were fir trees on the lower slopes, and grass, with the hills on each side, bare on their upper slopes, reaching up to about 3,000 feet. It looked like good sheep country, but I believed that there were only bear and elk there. The most notable thing about Kodiak Island for us were the trees. Here they started. Poor little sticks by Canadian standards, but we hadn't seen any since we left Hokkaido.

In the big earthquake that hit Anchorage while we were in Kagoshima, parts of Kodiak Island had sunk four feet. A tidal wave had swept into Kodiak Harbour and we had already heard the tale of a fisherman on his radio telephone who had said: 'Well, there's something bloody funny going on because I've just gone past the school.' We had been told not to worry about alterations in depth because everywhere the depths were greater than shown on the chart.

As we sailed down the sound we passed the rusty remains of

the deserted Iron Creek cannery. A little farther on, off another cannery, we tried the anchor. It didn't hold so we brought it up again and went on past Port Wakefield, where the factory ship *Akutan* was tied to the wharf. We went on still farther to a shallow bay. The anchor didn't seem too eager to hold there either, so we gave it only a slight pull and let out plenty of chain.

How lovely it is to come to anchor late on a summer evening, with high bare hills all around, and dark fir trees brooding on the lower slopes with the light failing and a star showing. For a moment the boat lay still and dark as if waiting to be accepted by the watchful hills. Then suddenly there was light below, and sound. Someone passed up the anchor light. A mile away we could see the lights of Port Wakefield. We heard the sound of an outboard coming towards us and a motor-boat with two young men in it circled the ship. They came alongside. One of them was a Wakefield.

'Father says that if you'd like to make fast to the *Akutan*, the ship there, he can give you a mooring buoy in the morning.'

'We've got our anchor down now, may we come in the morning? Would you like to come on board?'

'No thanks. We'd better get back. 'Bye for now.'

'Good-night, and many thanks.' The boat roared off, splitting the quiet evening.

'Now then,' said Beryl, 'what about an omelette—and what about a drink?'

The earthquake had put the crab factory at Port Wakefield out of commission but operations were continuing with the factory ship, *Akutan*. Port Wakefield, like Sand Point, was really a company village, but it had the air of being a well-run and well-organized affair. There was a store and a laundry and well-built cedar boxes for married and bachelors' quarters. There was an air of well-being and happiness and it was all based on the king crab. The inhabitants might well be happy, for they lived in lovely surroundings, there was plenty of sport, and lots of good pay.

Wakefield himself, the founder of all this property, was a big, quiet man, and a charming host. In the evening he brought down one of the company directors who had flown up from New York. He was called Slocum, a relation of Joshua, and we were

delighted to get his name in the visitors' book. In the evening
we went to a beaver lake, but saw only one lodge and there
was only one couple working there. They had been busy
round the edge of the lake felling small fir trees and bolstering
up the dam in places. We waited hopefully but the mosquitoes
were attacking us in hundreds and we were all soon prepared
to forgo the pleasure of seeing beavers if only we could escape
from our attackers. Apparently there was a much better dam
with several lodges farther up the stream.

When we left by the Kupreanof Strait we had a following
wind. The strait is wide to begin with but the final exit is very
narrow between wooded shores and with a two-to-three-knot
tide behind us we shot between them like a canoe down rapids.
We then sailed across Narrow Strait and anchored in a tree-
girt cove called Neva Bay. A bush pilot, seeing us in the small
bay, circled the cove and then sideslipping round some trees
landed his Piper Super Cub beside us as easily as if he was
bicycling round a street corner and then stopping with a foot
on the kerb. After a word or two he took off again for Kodiak,
banking slightly on the water and taking off on one float on a
turn.

We left next morning, motoring through a narrow pass
between islands and through a still narrower channel to
Kodiak Harbour, where a good municipal fishing-boat harbour had been made, full of all kinds of fishing craft and one
yacht, owned by Dr Bob Johnson, who was soon on board
Tzu Hang. Bob had built himself a house overlooking the sound,
with a huge living-room, its ceiling supported by slightly
curved laminated beams, so that it gave the impression of
being in the interior of an old sailing ship, a living-room big
enough to accommodate a riotous young family without their
getting in the way or making the place untidy.

Bob's mother was gay and vigorous and lived in a house
nearby. She drove us to her house and Bob picked us up later.

'Your mother is wonderfully spry,' I said to Bob.

Beryl burst out laughing.

'Spry,' she said, 'I bet she's no older than you are.' On
second thoughts I had to admit that Beryl might well be
right.

It is about 650 miles from Kodiak to Cape Muzon at the

north side of Dixon entrance, the great entrance between Charlotte Islands and Prince of Wales Island, between Canada and Alaska. In fact we didn't intend to enter by Cape Muzon but farther to the north between Cape Decision and Coronation Island, and it was for Cape Decision that we sailed when we left Kodiak Harbour on August 11th. We had a light wind and a clear day and used the engine a great deal, but by dark Kodiak Island was still to be seen behind us.

After making no progress during the night we motored on again until a breeze sprang up at about four in the afternoon. It was the greatest spell of engine work that we had had during the entire trip, the horizon clear all round. We saw a flight of golden plover. I cannot think why they were flying such an offshore route, but they were only an hour or two from land. We saw also a black-headed gull, all kinds of shearwaters, Alaskan terns, and our first mollyhawk. On the next day the wind moved slowly round to the west and we made $6\frac{1}{4}$ knots for most of the day. In the evening there were all kinds of storm warnings behind us in the waters we had left, the Shumagins and Shellikoff Strait, but our wind stayed steady in the south-west. For the next two days we made excellent progress, although we were unable to get a sight. On the twelve-to-two watch one night, after striking the genoa and setting the jib, *Tzu Hang* made sixteen miles. Great going for her and an easy motion down below with the wind abeam or on the quarter.

There was rain all next day and most of the night, and early in the morning of August 16th by dead reckoning we were fourteen miles off Cape Ommaney and heading for our passage.

For three days we had had no sight and we had been sailing across the current which sets northward up the Gulf of Alaska. I made a good allowance, calculating it at about half a knot across our course. On this last day with nothing but fog in front of us and fog all round so that we could only guess at the horizon, I got a noon sight that put us a long way south of our estimated position. A sight with a false horizon due to haze or fog will give the sun greater altitude than it has and consequently put the ship's position, in the northern hemisphere, farther south than it is in fact. I therefore did not accept this

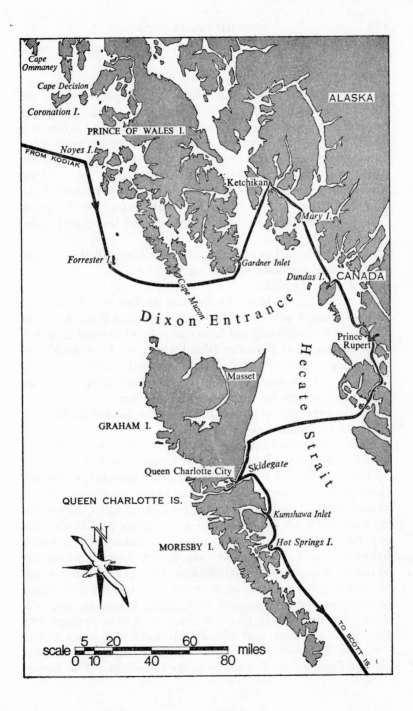

as my latitude, but at least considered that we might be much farther south than we had expected.

We sailed on, past our distance for Cape Ommaney, past our distance for Coronation Island and Cape Decision. We listened for some noise from the blank wall ahead. There was none. Then we saw the outline of a ridge coming down to a point, a point on the end of a peninsula, running south-west. It was only a hazy glimpse which soon disappeared but the direction of the ridge was what counted. We were a long way south after all, and this looked like Noyes Island off the middle of Prince of Wales Island. We laid a course for Forrester Island, in order that we might keep well off shore during the night.

The fog wrapped us all night, and *Tzu Hang* sailed on. When Clio woke me she had seen nothing.

'Only fog,' she said.

We were approaching our distance for Forrester Island and as light came I saw flock after flock of puffins flying low over the water but radiating out from one point. I guessed that they were coming from Forrester Island which the Pilot mentioned as being popular with the birds, and sailed round it, judging its position from their flight. About an hour later, when we were on a course for Cape Muzon, the fog cleared and we could see Forrester Island for the first time, behind us. We had cleared it by about a mile.

The sun came out and the end of our passage was a brilliant day. The Canadian border was just below us and as we turned up Clarence Strait for Ketchikan, we saw whales in the channel, their spouts showing like shell bursts in the sea. We put into a narrow inlet—Gardner Inlet, with an island filling its mouth. Both channels on either side were navigable and in the bay beyond there were two fishing boats, salmon seiners, which left by the other passage as we came in. The bay turned slightly so that it was completely landlocked. All round the shores and all up the hills so close around us stood the tall firs and cedars of our own country, moss-draped, silent, brooding, and still. There was little life in them. A few deer, a bear perhaps, but they were too dark and still for birds. In the water it was different. There were little grebe round the edges, and marbled murrelet and a loon swimming in the centre, and if we looked long enough surely a bald-headed eagle somewhere high on some bare pinnacle of fir. As if to welcome us four Canada geese came winging in a half-echelon over our masts, following the line of the coast. All this and the smell of the firs was the very essence of home.

10 Back to B.C.

In the morning both the cat and the dog were eager to get ashore. We launched the dinghy and first Pwe and then Kochi jumped in and then waited for their crew to row them to the beach. They regard themselves as first-class passengers.

Beryl had made a canvas sling for Kochi, with a handbag handle over her back, so that we could heave her in and out of the dinghy. As soon as Kochi was laced into this sling she regarded herself no longer as a first-class passenger, but as first-class luggage instead. She could then be hauled up a quay wall on the end of a rope without any sign of nervousness. When she came alongside in the dinghy she waited, quite relaxed, until she was swung up to the deck by her handle and hauled on board. Only then did she remember that she had legs, and walked off to the cockpit, where she waited to be undone.

We sailed out of Gardner Inlet by the other entrance and found a fresh, cold breeze blowing down Clarence Strait. We beat across and into Nichols Passage and eventually, with the wind failing and the tide about to change, took down our sails and motored up the eastern entrance to Ketchikan, past wooden houses balanced over the water, past wharves, fishing boats and fuel docks, past a little airways office with a blue Piper Cub float plane hauled into a garage beside it. We spoke to the coastguard vessel and they directed us to the fishermen's harbour, farther down the channel. We turned in, out of the swift-flowing tide, and made fast to a float reserved for visitors.

Next morning to the Customs Office, and here at last I was dealing with regular Customs officers in a busy port. I told my story to one of them. He handed me another piece of paper from the head office in Juneau to say that I was liable for a fine of 3,000 dollars for transgressing the laws of the Public Health Department.

'I don't think that I should let that worry you too much,' he said. 'We'll do some telephoning. I know that the Coastguard have a man at Adak who represents the Customs Service and you saw the Health Officer there. You should have put in for a cruising permit from Adak, but I don't see that you're too much to blame for not knowing that. But you'll pay for the telephone call?' he asked.

I could hear the head man grumbling away at the other end of the line like a bear being smoked out of its winter cave. 'Well, he's cost the Department a fortune in telephone calls, he'd better pay fifty dollars to cover them,' the receiver growled. I nodded and it was all fixed up.

'But what about the other fine?' I asked.

'Oh, I should forget all about that now. You won't hear any more about it. I think your case was a little misrepresented,' said my man. He was the nicest of Americans and I thought him the best of Customs officers.

I do not know whether it was because of the relief at the casting away of our burden, but Ketchikan seemed a gay place, full of helpful and enthusiastic people. On the day that we had rounded Cape Muzon it had been so warm that Henry had taken off his shirt in the cockpit. It was almost the first time that we had been outside without a windproof for nine months. In Ketchikan everyone was complaining about the heat, which we revelled in, but on the following day we would have preferred to have had wind.

It was a baking, still day as we sailed under power down a long steep-sided sound, with the tide against us. We anchored at Mary Island, a low wooded island, on our way to Prince Rupert, the Canadian Port of Entry. It was our last anchorage in Alaska. A fisherman brought his salmon troller alongside and then allowed it to drift away as he stepped out of his house to speak to us. To him a yacht was the mark of an amateur and he didn't consider us to be sailors at all.

'Hello, Buddy Boy,' he hailed me. 'Reckon you're not well acquainted round here. You're in the wrong anchorage. Never seen anyone anchor there before. Been fishing round here all my life.'

It seemed all right to me, and the whole bay was marked as an anchorage. I told him that it looked as if the weather would stay fine, and I wouldn't move now. Indeed I saw no better place.

'Well,' he said doubtfully, 'if you're satisfied I won't say any more, but I'll go and anchor in the right place.' He moved off a few hundred yards and let his anchor go, but he didn't stay there long. He was soon off fishing again.

It was a still afternoon. There was no sound except the drumming of a woodpecker, and occasionally a distant fishing boat's motor. We went ashore and in a peaty pool at the edge of the trees found several small sandpiper. They were wading at the edge of the water or running in eager little dashes along its bank. Clio and I sat in some tall grass and they came so close that I might have caught one in my hand. Henry came up and filmed them and they were quite unafraid. We motored off again next morning, still in calm weather, bound for Brundige Inlet in Dundas Island, also uninhabited and our first anchorage in Canada.

In the Aleutians every anchorage was surrounded by bare hills; now every anchorage was surrounded by trees. Brundige Inlet went in for several miles, like a river between low rocky banks with trees growing just above the tide line, their branches overhanging the water. At low water, when we went ashore, we could make good progress along the beach, but at high water we had to pick our way through the trees.

The others walked up to the head of the inlet. I took the Avon and rowed up to meet them and as I came round a point met Kochi, the leading scout, returning along the beach. She barked her deep 'woof, woof' when she saw me, and then withdrew to tell the others that the Brundige Monster was on the surface and coming their way. Sometimes I fear that she is not a very brave dog, though I do not think she would allow anyone to attack us without trying to protect us.

There are two approaches to Prince Rupert—one from the south-west up the wide main channel, and one from the north through a narrow passage. We took the latter, as it was shorter and more interesting. I had no detailed chart but I hailed a motor-boat with three Indians aboard, who had just come through.

'Sure it's all right,' said one. 'Just keep to the markers.'

'Are they red to starboard and black to port as we go through?'

'That's right. Bigger boats than you go through.'

'But we draw seven feet.'

'See here,' said the older man, who was wearing a red hunting cap and a red-and-black checked shirt, 'you just follow me and we'll show you the way.'

'But you don't want to go back now you've just come here?'

'Sure we will. Just visiting the wife's parents. No hurry. She don't mind.' He jerked his head at a broad-faced sturdy woman in a yellow jersey, who nodded agreement.

We saw a lot of Indians later in the streets of Prince Rupert and they seemed to be better integrated here than in our own part of the world near Victoria. Here they were making good money in logging and fishing, and farther inland as cow hands, in competition with other Canadians. The farther they are away from cities and civilization, the greater the equality with the Canadians of European origin, and consequently the greater their pride and the better the man.

The quickest way to destroy a race is to destroy its pride. This is what happened to the British Columbian Indian. The best way to rehabilitate them is to restore it. This is not done by benevolent protection, by putting them in reservations, by preserving old customs. It can only be done by urging and helping them to compete successfully with the dominant race in sport and work.

We were glad to have them showing us the way, and when we were through they waved and sped back again. We could look across the sound to a long and hazy array of wharves, funnels, chimneys, sawmills, and ships at anchor. The misty green hills, half hidden by the summer smoke haze from burning slash or forest fire, rose up behind. It was Sunday and nothing could be achieved by going over to the port now. We anchored behind a wooden spit while a man and a woman brought a motor-boat in to the beach. Four sturdy fair-headed little boys, in red lifejackets, disembarked and were soon searching for treasure amongst the rocks and driftwood.

Tzu Hang went across the sound next morning and tied up to the yacht club float. A Customs officer came aboard. 'Had a good holiday?' he asked when we told him that our last port was Ketchikan. It had been a very good holiday. He gave us a clearance form to see us to Victoria.

Next morning we sailed down Ogden Channel, the tide helping, and anchored in a small pocket in its side. At the bottom of the channel there was a seiner bringing in its net over a power block. When the purse came to the surface it had about twenty salmon in it, some of them good fish. The time that a seine may be left with one end attached to the shore before being hauled, is limited by law to twenty minutes only. This gives the incoming salmon a chance to find their way up the shores of the sound without running into a net. We saw them set their seine later on. Two fishermen in a powerful inboard motor-boat hauled one end to the shore. One of them jumped out and stamped up the steep bank, dragging the ropes attached to the net to a tree, where he made them fast. They did it all with such vigour and dash that they looked as if they were competing against some other boat.

Early next morning the water was glassy, and streaks of mist lay about the shores. All was grey and damp and still. A heron flew squawking from a dead tree lying in the water, its roots on the bank. In the entrance to the sound the rocky islets looked as it they had been cut out of grey paper and stuck on glass. Later, a light wind came and we motor-sailed across the Hecate Strait until we picked up the low shore of the Charlottes, and rounding the northern end of a shallow spit, made our way south for about twelve miles between the shallows and the shore to Skidegate Mission Cove, where we anchored at dark between the Indian village and Torrens Island. We had done 78 miles since the morning, but most of it was under power.

The Charlotte Islands are to British Columbia what the Hebrides are to Britain. They consist of two main islands, Graham and Moresby, divided by the very narrow Skidegate Channel, and numerous smaller islands. Skidegate Channel is shallow and only passable to a ship of *Tzu Hang*'s size at high water. The population of the Charlottes is small, being centred only round Queen Charlotte City, at the entrance to Skidegate Sound, and Masset, in Masset Sound in the north, both based on the fishing and lumber industries. During our time there the only houses that we saw were at Skidegate Mission Cove at a sawmill across the sound, and at Queen Charlotte City, a little village with a wharf, a fuel dock, and a few houses.

We intended to go through Skidegate Channel, and after filling up at the fuel dock, where there were a flock of turn-stones on an old float on the beach, we went a few miles up the sound to the beginning of the narrow channel. Although the coast that we had sailed down was low, the centre and the west coast of the Charlottes is mountainous, and the pass runs between low tree-covered banks, backed by steep forests. When we anchored and looked back we saw the tall scimitar of a bull killer whale's fin cleaving the water behind us. It sank below the surface and we didn't see him again. He was well up the sound and I wondered if he knew the passage and sometimes went through, but surely only at high water because at low water there is less than six feet in the channel. He was probably following salmon up the sound but only so far and no farther.

Behind us was a low islet and the sound stretching away beyond; in front was the narrow valley of the passage, walled in by huge firs, with the hills crowding in on each side. There was no sign of any living person except for the navigation marks in the channel, not even the distant whine of a power saw and the rumble of a falling tree, a noise that can be heard for miles on a still summer's day, and is so characteristic of British Columbia that it goes as unnoticed as the chirping of sparrows.

We walked along the bank to check on the navigation marks in the passage. There were deer tracks everywhere along the shore, as if they had a daily procession there, and we thought our anchorage one of the most beautiful that we had seen any-where in the world, only five hundred miles from our home.

Next morning I was ashore early to check the marks at low tide. The passage had shrunk to the size of a stream bed through which the tide was just beginning to flood. I was able to see exactly how the channel ran, but when I got back to the ship I found that Beryl and Clio had discovered that the re-mains of Haidar villages were all on the east coast, south of Skidegate. This was where they now wanted to go. It was just as well that they had changed their minds. We started off under the engine and had not gone far before Henry called that there was no oil pressure. There was a light wind just beginning, so we were able to sail back to Queen Charlotte City. If we had gone the other way we might have got into serious trouble in the narrow passage and the fast-running tide. We spent the next two days trying to locate and repair the defect, which we eventually discovered to be a leak in the cylinder liner, so that water was finding its way into the sump.

We sailed in the afternoon and arrived in Kumshawa Inlet, a few miles down the coast, by dark, anchoring round the northern entrance point, in a small bay. Next morning we all went in search of totem poles. We found the poles but there was little left to show that there had once been a big Haidar settlement. In this climate, where huge trees that have fallen are soon rotten, covered with moss and on their way to dissolution, the remains of Haidar villages have almost disappeared. A patch of meadow covered with tall green grass that the forest is encroaching upon, a few totem poles leaning this way and that, or, their bottoms rotten, fallen to the ground —this is all that remains.

Where there are traces they are barely distinguishable from the usual debris of fallen branches and thick undergrowth characteristic of these forests, but here and there are old cedar planks, two feet wide, split by hand from some great trunk, or perhaps a single archway, the entrance to a council house or chief's house. They seem to have preferred to build on or near a point giving two beaches facing north and south, which they could use according to the weather.

Most of the good totem poles have been removed to museums or parks, but there are still some remaining, perhaps twenty feet in circumference and sixty feet high, which give the impression that the Haidars must have been a fine people. They were great seamen and fishermen, hunted whale in their canoes, and were the scourge of lesser tribes down the coast. Perhaps their development had been arrested, or they were incapable of existence under another race, or the coming of iron destroyed them, as an old squaw said, but anyway they are scattered to the winds now, and the deer that they hunted and that clothed them, know their places best. Of the three sites that we saw at Tani, Skedans, and Kumshewa, that at Skedans was the most worthwhile seeing.

We spent one night at Thurston Harbour, a deep and narrow

inlet, slightly bent so that its inner end is landlocked. Like so many so-called harbours in these islands and along the British Columbia coast, there was nothing there, the only watchman a heron on a log, or an eagle high on some bare branch of fir, the only visitors the timid high-stepping deer, and brown-coated mink the only residents. It was still and warm, the silence almost uncanny, so that the rattle of a woodpecker's beak sounded loud and the scraping of his claws on the bark as he shifted position could be heard from the ship.

To our surprise we found a solitary and deserted mooring buoy to which we tied for a night as still as any night has ever been. In the moonlight the tall trees seemed to lean towards us, silent and waiting, holding their breath as if for fear that we would tell someone about them and the whining saw would come to cut them down. When we left in the misty morning they were still and silent, but perhaps later on when a breeze came they stirred and waved to each other and talked amongst themselves.

We needed a breeze because the engine had packed up completely, and to Beryl's relief Henry and I had now given up trying to make it work. We sailed to Hot Springs Island farther down the coast, a small round island with a well-sheltered bay on its eastern side. *Tzu Hang* ghosted in between reefs well marked by kelp and anchored in sand. From the beach an indistinct track led between salal bushes and over the mossy trunks of fallen trees to the southern side of the island, where a hut had been built on the rocks above the sea. A hot sulphur spring came out of the rocks above the shack in which someone had installed an old enamel bath, and either hot water or cold water—for there was a cold spring too—could be deflected into the bath by adjusting a piece of slate in the channels.

While Clio and Beryl were bathing and washing clothes, Kochi became bored with waiting and had gone off exploring. I had just come ashore when I saw a deer come down to the beach below me and start swimming towards the island which formed the other side of our anchorage, nearly half a mile away. His antlers showed like a branch of driftwood in the water. I heard Kochi's deep bark in the woods and knew she was on its trail. A moment later she appeared on the beach and stood on the edge of the water looking after the swimming

L

deer. At the same time Beryl and Clio arrived, smelling strongly of sulphur.

'Look at Kochi,' I said, never thinking that she'd start swimming after the deer.

'Kochi,' called Beryl, and immediately the obedient dog, as if taking this for encouragement, waded into the water and set off in the opposite direction in pursuit. As the deer scrambled out on the other side Clio and I started off in the dinghy, to try to intercept Kochi should the deer intend to swim farther. We were only half-way across and Kochi had just reached the other shore, when the deer came out of the trees on the south side, scrambled down the bank into the water again, and set off for another and larger island, still farther away. We were able to head Kochi off before she got into the water again. Swimming from island to island was nothing new to the deer and he was not hard pressed by Kochi.

We left by the northern entrance next morning, the tide just helping us through. We made a slow passage down the coast, passing a halibut boat that we had been told about, a boat of old fishermen unable to bring themselves to give up fishing, who worked the more sheltered waters east of the Charlottes, with plenty of escape holes available if the wind blew up.

There was something rather satisfactory about the engine being definitely out of action and knowing that we had only our sail to rely on. We decided to put into Winter Harbour on the west coast of Vancouver Island, if there was enough wind to get us up the narrow channel leading in from the sea. In the afternoon it began to freshen and we carried the genoa all night. All next day we made good progress, running with the twins and mizzen in front of a north-westerly wind.

In the evening *Tzu Hang* came racing down inside the Scott Islands, and through between Beresford and Lany Island. The Pilot gives warning of dangerous overfalls in this passage, but we had the wind with the tide and did not anticipate any trouble for a ship of *Tzu Hang*'s size. The sea was building up and breaking in the shallower water and *Tzu Hang* was really stretching her legs, feeling fresh and strong as she went through the tide rips. The little white horses welcomed her to their pasture, for they had seen her before, one summer, when she came that way.

It was a wonderful night with the hills showing in the moonlight, a ship coming up ahead, and the loom of a lighthouse over the horizon, and best of all the feeling of coming home. The wind had dropped by daylight. It fell so light that we could hardly keep our sails filled in the swell, so light that as we rounded the point to turn up into Winter Harbour we felt too close to the black rocks below the lighthouse, but once in their shelter, with the wind blowing down the channel, the sails filled evenly again and we were able to tack up between the trees. Soon we found ourselves in a wide reach and sailed across to the wooden jetties of the little fishing port. We came quietly alongside and threw a line to a man standing on the quay.

'You folks must be in trouble,' he said. 'Never seen anyone do that before.'

Winter Harbour, with its wooden quays and boardwalk, clings to the side of the hill, as if it is in danger of slipping into the sound. There are only a few families who live there all the year round, and a migrant population of fishing boats. The fishing boats were all out, and apart from the man on the quay the whole place looked deserted.

'Is there a store here?' Beryl asked.

'There's one store,' he replied, 'but I guess there's not much in it, and the folks are still mostly asleep right now.'

It was ten o'clock so it seemed as if time wasn't very important in Winter Harbour, and when Beryl got to the store she found that they had no bread, which was about all we needed.

With the help of a mechanic who was in charge of the ice plant at the Fishermen's Co-op, we managed to get the engine going again, but only for long enough to see us out of the harbour next morning. We had wind for the first day, but little on the second, and now that we were so near the end of our voyage, no one felt impatient at the lack of it. We slipped slowly down the hazy coast, and on this last full day at sea had a strange visitor. A red-breasted nuthatch came on board and ran rapidly up and down our sheets and halyards as if he was inspecting them for damage. He found nothing and as we were only a mile or two offshore he left for a more fertile hunting ground.

In the morning the smoke from forest fires hung a red veil above the hills. We were only twenty miles from Port Renfrew and had so little wind that we ended by putting the dinghy over and towing *Tzu Hang* towards the entrance, hoping to beat the turn of the tide. As we closed it another yacht came out of the haze ahead. It was Vivie and Raith Sykes who had sailed with us for Hawaii in *Tzu Hang*, ten years ago to the day. Now they had *Escapee*, a ship of their own, and the same size as *Tzu Hang*. We had warned them of our arrival by radio telephone from the Fishermen's Co-op in Winter Harbour. By booming out the genoa on the end of a boathook we just managed to lead them into the harbour. It would never have done to let them beat us. When our anchor went down we felt that to all intents and purposes we were home.

They came on board, and as we talked the sun down, fishing boat after fishing boat, salmon trollers and gill-netters, came chugging into the bay. They anchored and started to unload their catch. Suddenly it seemed as if *Tzu Hang* had got an audience, and perhaps she raised her voice a little as she told *Escapee* of all the strange places that she had seen.

11 Down the West Coast

When *Tzu Hang* brought us home—to the whine of a power saw and crash of a falling tree sounding across still water, to the smoky summer days and deep still fjords of British Columbia—we were unsure as to her future and as to our own. Whether to come ashore and make a home, or whether to start on another journey—that was the question.

A year later, when the geese were heading south, it had been decided. *Tzu Hang*'s anchor came aboard once more, and her red hull slipped past the dark trees and rocky shores of her old accustomed haunts. The year had been almost too good to all of us, so now Beryl and I felt that we had to go to sea again to appreciate its goodness. Clio was married and living temporarily in South Africa, Henry was back in England, and with nothing to keep us ashore, we set off for San Francisco, the Panama Canal, and the east coast of Canada. The kelp waved and the loon, many generations down from *Tzu Hang*'s old friend in Musgrave's landing, popped his snake head out of the water to see her go.

If Jorrocks had gone sailing he would have said that a small boat warning is an awful thing. With a warning out for the Straits of Georgia and Juan de Fuca, we thought so too; feeling almost as wet, sick, and unhappy as ever we have at the beginning of a voyage. We thrashed backwards and forwards off Discovery Island, making only a few yards on each tack against tide and wind, and put in to Victoria Harbour as soon as the tide had turned. We wrote a postcard to friends who were also planning a voyage and heard from them later to say that they had laughed so much at our description of rounding Discovery Island, and that they now felt that they could go anywhere. They still think that we were joking.

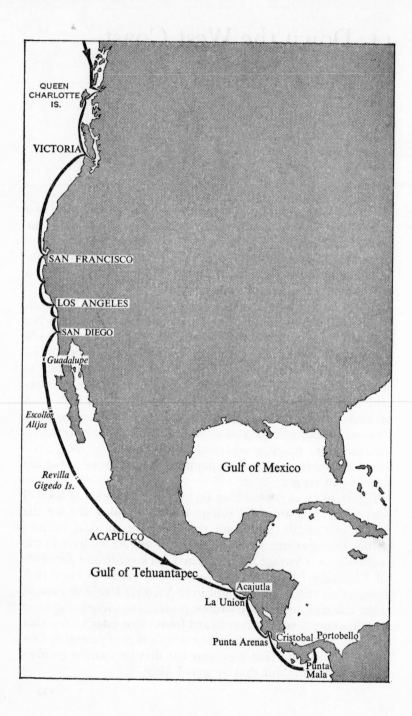

Next day, October 2nd, seasickness forgotten, we were off again down the misty straits and that night were well out to sea. This was the second time that *Tzu Hang* had sailed to San Francisco from Victoria. The first time was in November 1955, when we had met strong winds off the Oregon coast, broken a backstay, and made a slow passage for a ship of *Tzu Hang*'s size. 'You can expect the first gale on about September 12th, an old hand at Neah Bay had told us then, and he had been right to the day. Now we guessed that we might have the second gale or even the third, but anyway it is a stretch of coast to regard with respect after mid-September and until the end of April. We had plenty of strong winds and as the worn gear of the roller reefing broke, we were apt to have either too much or too little sail.

One day, after the glass had risen and the wind turned well to the north-west, while running under headsails, *Tzu Hang* sat up on the top of a wave and took off like a Flying Dutchman. Her stern was well down, and breaking water surged along the deck on each side of the cockpit coaming, so that I seemed to be sitting high and dry in the midst of a breaking sea. Her bow was up and on each side a bow wave arched up almost to the height of the light boards. She was behaving like a fast motor-boat except that there was no feeling on the tiller. If it had not been for this loss of control it would have been a most exhilarating feeling, but she ran on straight and true for twenty to thirty yards, and then slipped back into the wake of the wave with a lazy wallow, like a buffalo who makes an attempt to climb out of his mud pool, and then slides back in again to enjoy the easier life. She has ridden a breaking wave like this several times but we have always been below and I had never seen the arching bow wave before.

Now that the steering vane is so widely used, we are often asked why we do not fit one to *Tzu Hang*. She is a ketch with a canoe stern and a high freeboard. If we could fit a Hasler-type steering gear without destroying the lovely lines of her stern, the length of the steering oar would be so long that it might not stand up to the demands made on it during protracted cruising, and any other device would involve too much of an operation. She will have to continue to sail herself by a combination of sails and direction, which do not always give her her best speed nor an exact course. But she does quite well as she is. With the wind aft she will steer herself. With the wind abeam she will steer herself without the mizzen and it may be necessary to roll a reef in the main. Close hauled she will steer herself and with the wind on the quarter she will steer herself under her main and the jib boomed out on the other side. She usually has to have some assistance with shock cord, and she never steers herself very satisfactorily when there are three of us, as watches are not then so arduous and we take less trouble to make her do so. During our passage south we kept watches anyway, but they were not always very wakeful ones.

The last night of our journey to San Francisco found us racing down towards Cape Reyes, having sighted no ship until the last of the nine days of our passage. We started with some faint doubt of our ability still to handle *Tzu Hang* by ourselves. For our last long journey we had had Clio and Henry with us and had forgotten what it was like to be shorthanded. Now *Tzu Hang* was taking hold in earnest, flying through the dark water with a wild élan. We had the wind on the quarter and, because of the broken reefing gear, were carrying too much sail. Beryl, with a relieving tackle on the tiller, could barely hold her. *Tzu Hang* felt as if she was determined to round up before we had the light abeam, but I knew the wind would ease with the Cape behind us, so we hung on to our canvas, while the lights of a ship took a long time to overhaul us. Suddenly the lighthouse seemed almost too close, and under Beryl's promptings I began to wonder if I had not cut it rather fine. Then it was falling behind us so quickly that soon the lights of the Golden Gate were ahead of us. At daylight the wind dropped, but the tide, boiling under the bridge, carried us with it. Carried us to the company of other yachts from Canada, and stories to be told, but the only harrowing ones came from the trimarans, most of whom had run into trouble.

It is one thing to arrive in San Francisco, where there is such a warm welcome, but quite another thing to leave it, especially when there is no threat from approaching winter gales to drive you forth. We had fine weather, day sailing and night anchorages, all the way down to Los Angeles. We crept in towards the harbour in fog and smog and got a horrible fright from a huge black lighthouse that suddenly rose above us, marked by red and white rings at its top, and towering out of large white buildings.

'My God, that wasn't a lighthouse,' I said weakly, correcting the helm which was hard over to avoid the rocks on which we supposed it rested. 'It was a Japanese tanker.'

A few minutes later we discovered the breakwater and crept like a shrew along the wall of a room, until we found the entrance and the incomparable Peggy Slater, yachtswoman of every year, waiting for us at California yacht harbour.

It was just as hard to leave Los Angeles three weeks later, for a short last stop at San Diego to take on stores, and see something of the members of the Seven Seas Cruising Club, so many of whom had done remarkable voyages. San Diego, where the Navy ships came and went ceaselessly, where the Navy aircraft roared off the runway to sudden thuds as they cut in extra power, and where *Columbia*, sleek and polished, already preparing for the America Cup trials, slid through still water, with no apparent wind to move her. After loading up with stores we anchored off Point Loma to sort ourselves out and have a good night's rest before leaving. We sailed on December 19th with a very light wind and were becalmed in fog in the evening. We could hear a ship approaching and presently a bos'n's whistle and orders given over the loudspeaker, although we could not see it. A Navy ship home for Christmas.

We had decided not to visit any Mexican port, thinking that we might reserve Mexico for another visit by car, when we have swallowed the anchor, or perhaps because we do not like filling out too many forms too often. Still there were offshore islands, Guadalupe, the Escollos Alijos, and the Revilla Gigedo Islands, which someone had said were uninhabited. *Tzu Hang* loves uninhabited islands, and the sea elephants were there at this time in search of their brides. We decided to join them.

Guadalupe is a high island, its northern peaks being 4,000 feet high, lying about 200 miles south-west from San Diego and 70 miles off the Mexican coast. Any landfall thrills a sailor, even after a short passage. He develops an eye for landfalls, able to pick them out when a landsman won't see them, and he savours them like wine, comparing them with others that he has known. All are different. Guadalupe did not climb slowly over the horizon. It was suddenly there ahead of us, materializing grey and bulky out of a grey haze. It took us all day, in the light wind that we were still experiencing, to come within hailing distance of its shore, and it was dark as we rounded Punta del Norte and crept in to the cliffs in search of an anchorage. In and in we went without finding bottom until it appeared that we were almost on the rocks. The anchor was let go with a run in eight fathoms. We stretched the chain out towards the shore wondering whether we would have room if the wind came onshore during the night. We stopped the engine and the swell sucked and swirled on the rocks close to the counter. There were no lights to be seen anywhere. Suddenly almost aboard, came a hoarse rattling roar, the once-heard-never-to-be-forgotten bellow of a lovesick sea elephant. All night they rattled around us, like emetic-stricken giants.

As a result of this noise it was impossible not to be up early and I rowed Beryl to the shore to land her with a camera on the rocks. As we rowed, a bald head with great liquid eyes and a huge wrinkled nose emerged from the oily swell, so that it resembled that of a portly and resentful clubman, peering over his morning paper. He raised his wrinkled nose with a haughty and disgusted look and turned away from us to eye some sleek and mountainous females, reclining on the rocks. They were lighter coloured and their little noses seemed almost retroussé in contrast to the gnarled and hoary trunks of their suitors. Beryl jumped on to the slippery rocks and as she made her way to the shore to photograph the huge members of the harem, the male sea elephants and I, for there were several about me, had much in common. We all had large noses and we watched our women ashore with admiration and some anxiety.

On the southern end of Guadalupe there is a bay, well protected from the north and partially protected from the south by two islands. We decided to move from this restless place to the better-sheltered bay, where we hoped to be able to get more photographs. In the valley which ran down to a small stony beach a quarter of a mile from where we were anchored, there were some empty barracks and a few empty houses, and although we could see sheep on the hill we felt satisfied that the island was unoccupied. It was a strange landscape. Above us there was a large wall of grey mud running across the hill face, and there were chocolate and grey swirls on the cliffs. Farther down the coast there were tall cones of red mud, and layers of grey rock. The whole thing looked like a disastrous chocolate cake, half mixed, overcooked, and overflowing.

We sailed down the east coast, keeping close inshore, but seeing only steep hills and burnt rocks and an occasional hawk perched on a rock or wheeling against the sky. As we rounded the south-east corner, Morro Sur, and headed for Melpomene Cove, lovely name for an unlovely anchorage, the wind blasted first one way and then the other, threatening to catch us aback at any moment. It looked as if any anchorage in the cove, sheltered from the sea, would still be exposed to gusty winds from the hills and valleys. We took down our sails and motored in towards the beach, and only then did we become aware of a shoddy, military-looking settlement and a radio mast on a spit of land in the south-west corner, marked as a good landing spot on the chart. This changed our plans, for we had no permit to visit the islands, and no visa for Mexico. Such an isolated detachment would almost certainly be out of wine and cigarettes, and would probably try and hold us during lengthy radio conversations with the mainland. 'I bet that they're a penal battalion too,' said Beryl.

We turned *Tzu Hang*'s bow towards the sea and hoisted our sails. Two miles away we could see the white horses running before a fresh north wind, but here there was only a puff from the east, a blast from the west, and now calm. I picked up the glasses to study the settlement and saw men running to the shore. They began to launch a yellow boat that was lying on the beach.

'I do believe that they're coming out after us,' I said to Beryl.

'Well, let's get going,' she replied.

A sudden cloud of smoke, like a shell burst, told us that the motor had started, and soon I could see the little overcrowded boat reeling towards us with urgent faces and stooped shoulders showing in the bow. A bone in its teeth and the black exhaust fumes told us that this was urgent work. It was gaining fast and there was still a mile for us to go to those white horses and the fresh north wind.

'Have they got rifles?' Beryl asked.

'Yes, and they'll soon be in shot,' I answered, feeling rather like Midshipman Glover, a hero from one of the books of my childhood, when the British Navy ruled the world.

'Let's get up more sail,' she said.

We hoisted the genoa and all began to draw. *Tzu Hang* steadied and her speed increased, but better still we began to feel the lift of the swell. The boat was nearer now. Without glasses we could see the eager crouching crew, eight of them, yearning for fame or fortune, but preferably the latter. Then the true wind came fresh from the north. We eased the sheets and turned to a southerly course. Up went the jib, boomed out to starboard, and *Tzu Hang* stepped out lightly in the following seas.

'They'll never catch us now,' Beryl called, her face alight with excitement, but they still pressed on, and this feeling of pursuit and escape was really thrilling. Now we could see that the seas were getting rather too much for them. The boat was yawing violently and suddenly we heard the noise of the motor die to a more moderate note, as whoever was in charge ordered them home. They settled down to a slow wet plug to the shelter of their cliffs and their dreary isolation so far from their sun-baked homes. All at once we felt sorry for them, but it didn't prevent us from breaking out a bottle of Paul Masson's Beaujolais to celebrate our escape, although the unhappy results of capture may have only been a product of our imagination.

Two days later, after only light winds, we saw a big trimaran crossing our bow about a mile away. Presently they took down sail so we made over towards them to see if they were in need of any assistance. It was Christmas Day, but for the time being we had forgotten it. 'Only a little rudder trouble,' they called to us. 'Can you give us our position?' By good fortune I had just checked it and was able to give it to a girl who had a pencil and pad all ready. We left and then felt guilty that we had not stood by to make sure that they really were all right, but looking back I saw them get up the sail and make off again towards the coast.

This story has a sequel. Some weeks later Raith and Vivie Sykes who had also come south in *Escapee*, met some of the crew in Acapulco. They had left the big trimaran somewhere on the American coast and were telling the story of their trip north. One of their biggest difficulties was that they had no navigator on board and they seldom knew where they were, and never when they were out of sight of land.

For some days before they had met us they had been beating against the winds that had helped us so comfortably on our way, and after one or two long tacks offshore they had no idea where they were. It was Christmas Day, they explained, and they were feeling rather lost and forlorn with rudder trouble when, they said, 'Suddenly over the horizon in a red boat came Father Christmas complete with white beard and everything. We asked him where we were and he told us without even going below to find out, and then sailed away again over the horizon.'

Two hundred and fifty miles south of Guadalupe are the Escollos Alijos, fingers of bare rock thrust suddenly out of the deeps of the sea. We did not intend to visit them as they have no protected anchorage, but at least I wanted to see them as they were on our course to the Revilla Gigedo Islands. Once seen, they are in your pocket, and there is then no need to worry as to whether they are lurking in wait for you in the scariest hours of the night. We saw them in the afternoon, dark and desolate, with a white frill of breakers at their base. Bare rock, the tallest 112 feet high.

Five hundred miles south of the Escollos Alijos are the Revilla Gigedo Islands. We sighted Socorro from forty miles away late in the afternoon, and could see it clearly, a high bold peak, as we approached in the moonlight. We took down sail so that we might approach by daylight and then sailed down the east coast. Unfortunately Socorro also had a military encampment on it, although I believe that the other islands are really unoccupied. There seemed to be no future in going ashore here either, so we set off for Acajutla in San Salvador.

We had so far had nothing but light winds and easy going. Nor had the sea been very occupied. As we passed Socorro some huge fat porpoises came to see us, looking as if they had more than enough to eat and little work to get it. Just south of the island there were hundreds of shearwater resting on the water. Now we saw more porpoises, and two whales at different times came close to the ship, one of them a monster far bigger than we were. On one day we saw a yellow float and on going up to see what it was, found that it had a rope attached to it and what appeared to be a piece of white flesh on the end. Beryl tried to snag it with the boat hook and a small shark moved off and a large shoal of small fish spread away from it.

They looked like reef fish, and we wondered whether they had followed this float and bait all the way from the shore. We left the float bobbing on the water and sailed on none the wiser. We were able to bathe on nearly every day. If there were porpoises around we dived in without fear of shark, as we have a theory that shark will not come near porpoises. Only once did we give up our bathe because there were shark following the boat.

On January 10th we could see the lights of Acapulco reflected in the sky, and the following night had a witches' reel with black squalls. They circled round us and every now and then one would leap into the ring with *Tzu Hang* in a deluge of rain, shrieking and cackling, and then hopping out and leaving us in the wildest confusion. They then continued their solemn progress round us, their shoulders lit by lightning, mumbling and grumbling, while they prepared for the next dance.

All yachtsmen who have to traverse the Gulf of Tehuantapec at this time do so with their fingers crossed, hoping that they may tiptoe over and not disturb the giant on the other side of the hill. The Tehuantapecers are caused by a readjustment of pressures between the Gulf of Mexico and the Pacific side, and the wind can be violent. They can best be avoided by keeping close inshore and anchoring if the wind swoops down. We were well offshore and experienced two, but neither was very alarming. In the first we had a rough sea and a strong wind from the east, so that we hove to for the night as we did not wish to go farther south, but on the second occasion we were well across the Gulf and it sped us on our way, blowing from the north-east.

When this Tehuantapecer was over we were becalmed, as we were also after the first, but two days later we sighted the peaks of Volcan Fuego and Volcan Agua in Guatemala, standing like haystacks on the horizon. Soon after dark there got up a light northerly breeze which freshened strongly at about three o'clock and blew for three hours. The mountains showed clearly and with the strengthening wind there came the most marvellous smell of land, compounded of dung and honey. I realized that this was the land breeze and that it had accounted for the strange short swell that we had met with on the two previous mornings although no puff of the wind itself had reached us.

A day later we sailed into the harbour of Acajutla, which used to be an open anchorage off a ramshackle pier. Now a great new breakwater has been built and modern harbour offices, all air-conditioned, and soon there will be another enclosing pier. The harbourmaster still used his old office at the base of the old pier and I had a long hot walk to find him and the Customs officer. Having left the new bungalows of the new port, I found myself in a village street, where the road ran between ramshackle huts and little thatched stalls where watermelons and lemonade were sold. Children and dogs were everywhere, and slim dark-skinned girls walked barefoot along the sandy road carrying babies on their hips. There was a smell of rotting fruit and fish and the sweet scent of flowers, the smell that the land breeze had brought to me. The harbourmaster and the Customs officer were both taking their siesta and I was asked to come back in the morning. It was all in great contrast to the new port.

We had an introduction to Archie Baldocci in San Salvador. Archie is an American who lives in San Salvador and whose mother and wife are both from El Salvador. He has all the culture of Spain and Italy and the drive of America and at the moment was particularly interested in a fleet of shrimpers who were shrimping in the Gulf of Mexico. He is also an ardent pilot and has a small aircraft for business and a Mustang fighter for pleasure. We motored up to El Salvador to see him. He took us for flights round all the volcanoes, although he wouldn't stay over the active ones for long because the volcanic dust damaged the engines. For lunch and in the evenings he took us to some of the great Salvadorean families, all owners of large coffee estates, living in marbled halls and behind wrought iron-gates and screens, in rooms that seemed fit for vast receptions, but almost too formal for comfortable living.

When we left we were loaded with gifts for our voyage, and Señora Baldocci took us down to the kitchen in order to show us what she had got for us; there she was surrounded by little maids, fluttering and excited, so that the kitchen resembled a dovecote. Although there is a vast difference between the rich and the poor in El Salvador, the relationship between them, at any rate in the great houses, is most democratic. Something that we have noticed also in other Catholic countries.

When Archie Baldocci took us down to the airport he introduced us to Bob Love, another American, an ex-fighter pilot, who was agent for one of the types of small American aircraft, and who was also developing a property in Honduras. He also had a Mustang and promised to come and see us again—'Although it may be only from the air,' he said.

We sailed from Acajutla after breakfast on January 30th, and tacked out against the beginnings of the sea breeze, past the low rocky point of Punta Remedios, until we were well clear and were able to turn up the coast. From now until *Tzu Hang* reached Panama she would have to rely on these fickle breezes to make her passage, or on the wings that the dark fleeting squalls would lend her. All the way she'd have a contrary current against her. The Equatorial counter current hits the coast about the latitude of Panama Bay, and turns north along it almost as far as Bahia California, before it sets off again across the Pacific.

There was only a light wind and we sailed slowly below the volcanoes within sight of the coast road from La Libertad. In the evening I heard the drone of an aircraft engine and presently saw it high against the mountains flying west. A little later there was a sudden roar beside us as a blue Mustang swept past, a few feet above the water. It was Bob Love, who had come to check our progress. Up he went, as if on some gigantic swing, and made another run beside us; he seemed to be below the masthead and just beyond the bow he did a breathtaking, perfect roll, so that his turning wing seemed to skitter along the top of the sea. Next evening he and Archie Baldocci came to visit us again, both in Mustangs, the roar of their engines only sounding to us as they passed and climbed away, one moment at sea level and the next high in the mountains and turning for home. We anchored that night close offshore, on a long line to our Danforth anchor, and had an undisturbed night.

The night breeze had only blown for a few hours, so the following day we decided to put into Fonseca Bay and spend another easy night. As the wind had turned easterly we had to beat along the coast, and made slow progress against the current. We rounded Abalane Point, low, rocky, and covered with scrub, and found a still bay behind it, ringed by shores of dark mud. As the anchor went down the wind failed. The power had already gone out of the sun and all was still. In one corner of the bay a few houses showed and a dugout canoe driven by an outboard motor appeared from behind an island deep in the bay and came towards us. Presently it was alongside and some swarthy and friendly fishermen stepped on board. Beryl and I sat on the doghouse and practised a little Spanish with them, unaware until they evacuated the deck that trouble was approaching from the other side. As the fishermen left we heard the noise of an outboard behind us and looked round to see another dugout with two uniformed men, wearing steel helmets and carrying rifles, crouching in the bow. They clambered on board without asking permission, a corporal and a private of police or coastguards, we never discovered which. The fishermen were gone.

'What are you doing here?' asked the corporal.

'We've just come in for the night as there is no wind outside,' I replied. 'We put into Acajutla where I saw the Customs, and I have my clearance.'

'It is forbidden to come here, and you must now go to La Union to report to the harbourmaster. We will take you there.'

I had no intention of going to La Union, fourteen miles inside the bay, nor did we have a detailed chart, but although the policemen were small, they both had rifles and seemed very excited. Now—ominous gesture—they removed the paper wads that they had stuck in the barrels to protect them from the sea water on their journey. Beryl's Spanish is much better than mine, and she took up the argument.

'We can't go to La Union,' she said. 'We have no chart.'

'I know the bay like the back of my hand,' said the little corporal, 'I will be the pilot.'

'I've heard that one before too,' I thought.

'Well, if we can't stay, we'll leave. That's quite simple,' said Beryl.

'No, no,' said the policeman, 'you cannot leave now. It is my duty to take you to La Union.'

We tried to play on all his emotions, on his generosity, his common sense, and on his fear, but without success. He was determined to take us to La Union and the harbourmaster was the highest authority that he recognized or knew. Eventually

M

we gave in. 'I'll anchor before dark,' I said to Beryl, 'and they can bloody well stay on deck and I hope they have a miserable night.'

We started off, the private crouching in the bow and the corporal in the cockpit, but they had both replaced the paper wads in their rifle muzzles. Now that we had conceded that we would go to La Union our relations became more friendly. 'I wonder if the Señora would be so gracious as to give me a glass of water,' asked the corporal, 'I need it to drink my tranquillizers. When I become excited I have bad palpitations and the doctor says that I must take tranquillizers every two hours.'

After his tranquillizers he settled down in the cockpit and explained that he was very sorry to do this to us, but that he had been 'Muy castigato' for allowing a yacht to go without reporting once before. Beryl began to feel sorry for him, and after we had anchored, and heard them coughing and complaining about the cold on deck, we passed them up something to eat and a blanket apiece. Although we had some slight satisfaction at their discomfort, they had the best of it. They kept us awake with an interminable conversation, by shuffling and sighing just above our heads, and by frequent trips to the rail to ease their bladders as the cold struck them.

In the morning we anchored off the pier at La Union. The port is low and tawdry and devastingly hot until the afternoon wind blows. The harbourmaster endeavoured to make me pay ten dollars for harbour dues, but this I flatly refused to do, complaining that I had no wish to visit it in the first place, nor ever to return, and that anyway he had no official stamp for his receipt. He waived his claim as if he was doing me a favour and we left early in the morning without further trouble and found the land breeze still blowing to take us down the bay.

Nicaragua was enjoying one of its endemic revolutions, so we attempted no call there, but kept the coast in sight in order to make the best use of the land and sea breezes. Our next port was Punta Arenas in Costa Rica. *Tai Mo Shan* had had some difficulty in weathering Cabo Blanco at the entrance to the Golfo de Nicoya, but we just managed to scrape round on the day that we first saw it, and then spent all that night and most of next day beating up the bay, until we anchored amongst the merchant ships, between them and the shore.

When the Port Captain and Customs officer came on board next morning they suggested that we should move up to the pier. At first this looked a gay place to be as it was just off a bathing beach, but although the beach was bright with umbrellas and bathing dresses, my inspection with the glasses revealed that there was nothing very attractive either under or inside them, and in the afternoon a strong onshore wind made the anchorage uncomfortable. We moved round a spit of land to a narrow stretch of water, shallow and frequented by fishing boats, flies, and smells, at Estero. It was in the centre of the town, but farther up the river there was a yacht club that we did not know about. There was also a slip and shipyard run by Sammy Manly and his family. He came out from Whitehaven in 1906 to work on the railway and was then asked by the United Fruit Company to run a small yard to look after the banana boats that used to bring the fruit to the port. The United Fruit Company have gone from there, but Sammy Manly took over the yard. He was now eighty-two and full of vigour, and mended a water pump for us that had been giving trouble. As soon as it was fixed we left, but not before the customary financial brush with the harbourmaster.

Costa Rica is not a place that I wish to return to, but perhaps I misjudge it as we met no one and did not get up into the mountains. Unless one gets up into the mountains the coast of the Central American Republics is best avoided. It is too hot, the harbours too tawdry, and the port officials are too exacting.

We were now within a few days' sail of Panama and by then we might say that half our journey was done. Those last few days can be difficult. The trade wind blows across the isthmus and down the gulf and the current sweeps out of the gulf and round Cabo Mala, so that there is little hope for a sailing ship to make its way up the western coast of the Gulf of Panama. We left Punta Arenas on February 13th and in the early morning of the 15th we could see Isla Cano light to the north-east. We were about a hundred miles out from the Golfo de Nicoya. The days became hotter and the sailing more interesting. We passed plenty of shipping and were continually in sight of land or islands. On 16th we sailed in to the north-east shore of the Isla Montuosa. A beautiful green sailfish came out of the water close behind us and two porpoises accompanied us in to the shore. One of them had a sucker fish about two feet long attached to it under one fin and another small one by its tail. The sucker fish was an unhealthy blue and the porpoise's body was scarred round the point of attachment. At one time, as the porpoise jumped, the fish became detached, but was back and clinging in the same position in a moment.

We took the dinghy ashore; the island was like all tropical islands, the sand white, the sea a clear pale blue above it. On the eastward side some small reefs over which we rowed scarred the white sands below us, but to the westward, where the wind came and the seas rolled in, the reef stretched stark and bare some way from the shore. The Island was covered with palm trees which reached over the edge of the sand, where it was soft and hot between the toes, but just beyond their shadows the beach, washed by the ripples, was hard, marked only by the tracks of the hermit crabs as they moved their houses from one coral pool to another. We left before the tide went down and imprisoned us and the dinghy within the reef that we had crossed in comfort when it was high. Perhaps it was just as well for no sooner were we on board than we heard an angry shout, and saw a small party of uniformed men staggering up the beach under great loads of coconuts. Behind them marched a single guard armed with a long machete driving them up the beach. They were prison labour from the nearby Penal Settlement who had been collecting coconuts and as we left we saw their boat at the southern end of the island.

In the evening we sailed past Isla Jicaron and during the night we cleared Cabo Mala and the wind came suddenly fresh from the north-east. It was the trade wind blowing out of the gulf. We hauled in our sheets and set out across it for the Colombian shore. Throughout the 19th of February we sailed across the Gulf but could not win up beyond the seventh parallel. By the afternoon of the next day we were in tide rips and were surrounded by small fish about the size of herrings that kept flopping out of the water all round us. I felt certain that we were in a new current and that night took down the sails, sure that we would be set to the north.

It was a strange night of little wind, but of thunder and lightning and great black clouds which burst above us, sending the rain crashing on to our decks and pouring out of the scuppers. In the morning we found a fresh wind blowing from the north-west. We set sail to the north and soon saw the high Colombian coast. We sailed east of the Islas Perlas and anchored for the night by the Isla Pelado on the north shore of the Gulf. It was a change from the slow progress against the current for we had made 120 miles since we hoisted our sails. Next day we were at anchor off the Balboa Yacht Club, and the first half of our voyage was done.

12 Up the East Coast

When I went to the Canal offices to arrange for our passage they asked me if my ship had been through before.

'Yes,' I answered, 'in December 1950.'

'That's right,' said the clerk, looking it up in a file. 'We don't have to measure you then. That'll be ten dollars forty.'

'Good heavens,' I said, astounded, 'hasn't it gone up?'

'No. Same price. No change.' It was all done in about five minutes. I paid a deposit to cover this and some other small charges, and got the balance back a few months later.

Tzu Hang has been through the Panama Canal three times, twice under her own power and once on the deck of a freighter. The first time our pilot brought his wife and lunch for all, and this time the pilot brought a learner pilot and his wife and lunch for all.

She was a tall good-looking girl from 'the Badlands' in North Dakota, who the evening before had sleek brown hair, but now had it wrapped around curlers. They came on board long before daylight and we left while it was still dark. As daylight came a tall cargo vessel, her lights shining brightly in the twilight, stalked past us and preceded us into the first lock. From then on we had a race against closing lock gates. The pilots, one of whom wanted to get back to Balboa, and who, with his newly curled wife, wanted to go to a party in Cristobal, kept calling for more speed. *Tzu Hang*'s engine did its best, and through the Gatun Lakes, with a fresh trade wind blowing, we set all sail as well. We just reached the lock which leads out of the lakes in time and, as the gates closed, saw the land fall away below us and there was the Atlantic—our Atlantic—hazy and grey and wind-wrinkled, stretching out ahead. We were in Cristobal by five in the evening, and put our pilots and the girl

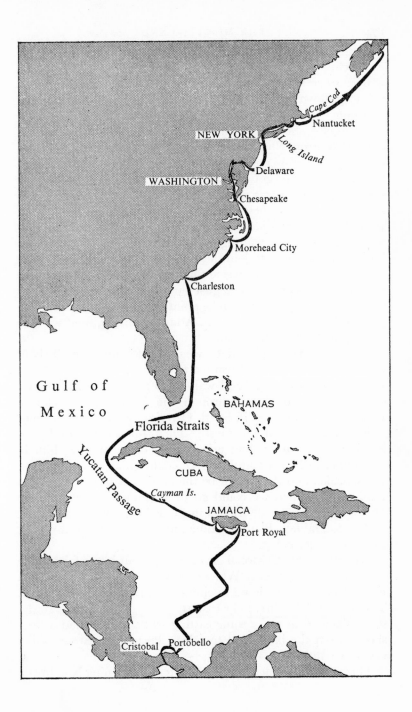

Cape Cod

Nantucket

NEW YORK

Long Island

Delaware

WASHINGTON

Chesapeake

Morehead City

Charleston

Gulf of

Mexico

BAHAMAS

Florida Straits

CUBA

Yucatan Passage

Cayman Is.

JAMAICA

Port Royal

Cristobal Portobello

from the Badlands with her hair still in curlers, ashore on the yacht club pier.

Ever since we had met Henry Dupont in San Francisco, on our way down, and he had suggested that we should join the Cruising Club of America, on their cruise to the Bras d'Or Lakes in Nova Scotia, we had kept this possibility at the back of our minds. From Nova Scotia we could go to Newfoundland and Iceland, the Faroes and Hebrides, on our way back to England. So far we had not got involved in any details of planning but now the planning was taken out of our hands. Henry, used to organizing vast business concerns, organized *Tzu Hang* almost without thinking. A large bundle of charts, orders, instructions, and invitations was waiting for us. We were to come and see him at Wilmington, to join the cruise at Halifax N.S. on about August 12th, and he suggested that we should leave them in the Bras d'Or lakes on about August 23rd, from where we only had a short sail to Sydney, which he pointed out would be a suitable port of departure for our North Atlantic crossing, and we'd be there just the right time too.

With these dates as key dates we thought in more detail about the voyage ahead of us. I wanted to go to Jamaica where I had started my soldiering. Beryl wanted to go to Cuba, and if we could not go to Cuba, through the Yucatan and Florida Passages to Charleston in South Carolina, which she had once visited, and wanted me to see. Then John Lewis of Lewis, Addison, and Steele, had asked us to come and see him in Farmville, in North Carolina. We could go and see him from Chesapeake, and that might be the best place to find a yard to haul out in. Then we could go to Wilmington and down to Delaware. Then to see friends in Long Island and Nantucket, and so to Halifax. Plenty of time and a lot to see, and we felt the urge to get going.

We sailed from Cristobal on March 5th out into a fresh trade wind and a rough sea. Whichever way one sails to Jamaica from Panama there is no avoiding a hard slog to windward. The winds tend at first to be easterly rather than north-easterly, so we decided to make some easting while we still had a little shelter from the land, and to sail to Portobello, twenty miles east of Cristobal.

The Spanish fortified Portobello after abandoning Nombre de

Dios, and it was used as a port for the transhipment of Peruvian treasure. Admiral Vernon sacked it in 1739 when he sailed in between the reef and the north shore and anchored under the guns of the fortress called the 'Iron Castle', which he destroyed. The Spaniards, demoralized and humiliated, fled round the head of the bay to the town of Portobello, where their poor morale so affected the defenders of Fort San Jeronimo and Gloria Castle, and the ships in the bay, that all surrendered without further fighting. They were allowed to march out, but Admiral Vernon destroyed the forts, and such was the skill of the builders that it took much longer, and far more energy and gunpowder to destroy the forts, than it had taken to beat the defenders.

When *Tzu Hang* sailed in between the reef and the jungle-covered north shore we could see no trace of the Iron Castle, but we could see the ruins of San Jeronimo and Gloria Castle and the corrugated iron roofs of the village of Portobello in the south-west end of the bay. We anchored in sheltered water. The jungle-covered hills enclosed us. All was still, silent, and deserted, except for three pelicans on a drifting log, and an old man who paddled past in a dugout canoe with three dogs inside. It was hard to imagine the six ships anchoring, the guns thundering, and the bay filled with the smoke of battle, as the landing parties rowed in, cheering, to the shore close off which we were now anchored. We marvelled how men could bring in great sailing ships, square riggers, under fire and with inadequate charts, while we find it difficult enough to enter in peacetime, with a handy craft, and a detailed chart on the table.

Ashore on the north side of the bay we found massive blocks of masonry below where the Iron Castle had once stood. They were portions of the demolished lower battery, whose crews had been put out of action by men firing from the fighting tops of Vernon's ships. The jungle was so dense and thorny and the heat so oppressive that we did not spend much time in exploring.

We discovered the remains of the causeway along which those who fled from the Iron Castle had run to San Jeronimo, and within the walls of Gloria Castle and San Jeronimo guns still lay on the terraces, where they had been dismantled by Vernon's men. Between the forts and under the shadows of the ruins of the church and the Governor's house stand the corrugated-iron-roofed shacks of the present inhabitants. There also stand the ruins of the great three-storied Aduana which once received the gold and silver from Peru, that the pack trains brought across the isthmus. From the style of the ruins it is obvious that the old overlords lived in great style. Would that we could see them now, walking in the evening in their elegance, the ships anchored in the bay with flags and pennants flying, and slaves working in the gardens and terraces that the jungle has long ago devoured.

Perhaps the present inhabitants, who are friendly yet reserved and all of Negro descent, spring directly from those slaves. However hard their ancestors may have worked, the villagers take life in a leisurely manner. There are one or two stores and a few dugouts fishing in the bay. There was a carpenter and his assistant hollowing out a log for a canoe, but apart from this no other signs of how they won a living. The shops were stocked with bananas and bread and a few tins, and there was a long wooden pier, but the only boat that came to it while we were there was an open motor-boat that brought the mail.

We sailed on March 12th and were soon reefed and bashing into a rough sea. For four days, choosing the most favourable tack as the wind shifted, we fought our way northward until on the 16th March the wind dropped to Force 4 and we unrolled the reef in the main and set the working jib. An afternoon sight put us happily farther to the eastward than I had expected. We had a strong trade again on the 20th and we entered Port Royal after dark on the 22nd, ten days out and 1,000 miles on the log.

Long ago, in 1926, I had sailed out of Port Royal in a dugout canoe with a Jamaican Negro called Prawl, at night, to go fishing on the California Banks, ten miles away. We sailed on the land breeze and came back next day on the sea breeze, sunburnt and seasick, but we had caught some barracuda and kingfish. In those days we used to pay a great deal of respect to shark and no underwater swimmer had become familiar with them. I still keep the same respect that I had then and I had just read a book all about sharks. From this I felt assured of two things: first that you can never be certain exactly what a shark is going to do, and secondly that he prefers to feed at night.

As we approached the entrance to Port Royal we hove-to while we checked our position, and drifted astern so that the logline caught on the propeller. The wind was down so we stowed our sails and started the engine, only to find that the logline was wrapped round the shaft. Beryl started to get undressed.

'What are you doing?' I asked.

'I'm going to try and clear it.'

'No you're bloody well not, give me that knife,' I said. 'That woman'—I thought as I hacked at the line packed round the propeller shaft—'she never bloody well thinks of sharks.' I worked feverishly holding my breath as my legs grew longer and longer, dangling and luminous, far below the keel. I came up with a splash of phosphorescence, and after getting my breath dived down again. 'And what's worse she doesn't even think that I'm frightened of the things. You'd think she'd never read that book.' Eventually it was done and I scrambled up the ladder, still intact.

'Well done,' said Beryl, as I handed her the spinner, 'you didn't lose the line you cut, did you?'

'Blast the bloody line,' I said, and wanted to add, 'Isn't it sufficient that I'm back on board?'

'But where else would you be?' I imagined her asking.

We went in under power against a light land breeze blowing over the Palisadoes, passing between small cays and islets covered with mangroves. Across the big bay the lights of Kingston seemed to spread far wider and higher than they did when I first knew them. We anchored opposite Morgan's Harbour, once the garrison swimming-pool, and now a beach club and hotel. Where we anchored I had fished for tarpon and a short way behind us I could make out the mangroves where I had waited for the evening flight of whistling teal.

Next morning we went ashore, and in the afternoon to Kingston. There was nothing, absolutely nothing there that I could see that had changed for the good. It could hardly have done so since I had first seen it when I was nineteen.

> When all the world is young, lad,
> And all the trees are green,
> And every goose a swan, lad,
> And every lass a queen.

Here I had owned my first polo pony and my first dog, here I had first made love, and here the excitement and delight at being alive had sometimes burst out of me, so that when riding or scrambling up a hill by myself I had sometimes to stop and bend my head and thank God for so much bounty. But now Kingston had spread and eaten up the surrounding country and all seemed to be dirty suburbs and everywhere there was the sight and smell of too many people. I found it almost impossible to recognize any place that I had known.

Warner Bolton, once a hard-riding No. 1 of the Kingston Polo Club, drove us to his house for lunch, and when he took us back to catch the Port Royal ferry, found himself held up in a narrow lane by the refuse truck. He waited patiently while the minutes ticked by and the lorry stopped in the middle of the road to empty the dustbins of successive houses.

'Ease me, Dadda, please ease me,' this eminent lawyer pleaded in the sing-song Jamaican accent with the athletic dustman, less than half his age. 'Please ease me, Dadda. My friends going to miss their boat for sure'.

'Why don't you give him a blast on your horn?' I asked.

'Good heavens, man. You can't do that. He'd never let me through.'

Presently the dustman strolled over to our car, and after Warner had formally introduced us, inquired after his health, and told him that he was a fine-looking fellow, we were allowed to pass. 'Got to handle them these days,' said Warner.

Port Royal was not so disappointing. The old barracks, except for those taken over by the Police Training School, were falling to pieces and empty, but there was no great change since my day. The fort came within the police area and was well cared for. I was able to get a photo of a police recruit standing in front of the plaque that reminds readers that Lord Nelson also stood there. The village was unchanged, but the small dugouts no longer sailed to California Banks; larger and more seaworthy motor fishing boats went instead. Prawl was dead but half the population of the village was related to him. Morgan's Harbour under its urbane and knightly host was a gay place with water skiers skimming between the anchored yachts and then gliding free towards the end of the swimming bath, until they suddenly collapsed like a moth that has flown through a candle.

In the little church at Port Royal, amongst the many memorials to soldiers and sailors who had lost their lives on service there, I saw one to two midshipmen drowned at Blewfield's anchorage, near Sav' La Mar, once used by Nelson's ships, where we were going.

I remembered Church Parade at Port Royal. The men sitting stiff backed with the sweat patches showing through their khaki drill tunics, belt buckles shining. Officers wearing swords and their wives smartly dressed and hardly a glance at the memorials. 'Qui Procul hinc, the legend's writ,' and we took it all for granted. Now with a small Negro population and a Negro priest, they meant even less to those who sat beneath them, but I found them infinitely more moving. Life was much simpler in those days. Then we did not question our right to govern, nor were we subjected to the insidious tyranny of the Welfare State, and its so often misguided idealism.

We sailed on March 31st, although for a long time it looked as if we would have to leave our anchor behind us. It was caught in some underwater snag, perhaps part of the old port sunk years ago by an earthquake, which divers were now investigating. There was a light wind and a calm sea as we sailed close past Bare Bush Cay, a strip of white sand topped by green bushes. The mountains above Kingston were buried in cloud, but the sun shone on Port Royal. Some motor fishing boats, painted red and blue, came past us with their crews, in spite of the heat, wearing yellow oilskins.

We anchored for a quiet night in Jackson Bay and continued down the south coast next morning. I was able to recapture some of the romance of my early days. There was Goat Island, where Mike Seymour, a Sapper, and I had tried to capture an iguana, and Black River where we had shot baldpate pigeon, and Alligator Pond where we had mistakenly blown out the end pile of a wooden pier, while trying to stun small fish for live bait, Now there were great dusty red scars on the hills above, where bauxite is mined. We anchored in Starvegut Bay, and there to our surprise we were hailed from the shore and taken off to a good dinner.

At Blewfield's which we reached next morning we went ashore and met a large and gentle police sergeant in blue trousers and grey shirt and with a red band round his cap, from whom, in search of a bath, we inquired the way to the hotel.

'It'll be a full mile, and mighty hot going,' he said as he showed us the way. In fact it was only a quarter of a mile and by the time that we had walked a mile up the hill we realized that we had passed the entrance. As we turned a small boy came padding barefoot after us to show us the right way. We crossed a clear stream where a blue heron was standing. There were yellow finches in the bushes and scarlet flowers, and brick platforms for pimento to dry, but the hotel was shut. The policeman arranged for us to have a bath in the cottage of a friend. It was very clean, looked after by an old maidservant, but we never met the owner. We had heard in Kingston that crime was so bad in parts of Jamaica that the police were unable to cope with it, but in the country, the sergeant told us, there was no trouble. The area round Sav' La Mar seemed quite unchanged and the people friendly.

Beryl got a lift into Sav' La Mar where a tall grey-headed woman, also shopping, who had discovered her name, came up to her.

'I heard that your name is Smeeton,' she said, 'and I do apologize for coming up like this, but are you by any chance related to a young soldier who used to be here?'

'Oh yes', Beryl replied, 'he's on our ship, *Tzu Hang*, at Blewfield's,' and they arranged that she should come later to the beach and that one of us would bring her out to tea. 'I met one of your old girl friends,' Beryl said to me when she got back. 'She will be on the beach at four and you have to go and pick her up.'

'What is her name?'

'I don't think I got it. Welly something.'

'What does she look like?'

'Tall, good-looking, grey hair.'

I searched my memory for a Welly but couldn't find one; however, she presently appeared on the beach. As I rowed in I kept looking over my shoulder trying to recognize her so that I would not be at too much of a disadvantage. It is very hard to meet an old girl friend satisfactorily from a small dinghy with an onshore breeze. In my anxiety to beach the dinghy and leap lightly and youthfully to my feet to greet her with warmth and recognition I mistimed the breakers and found myself prostrate before her in the wet sand, with the dinghy on its side and half full of water. It may not have been the first time. Welly summoned guests by telegram to a party at her lovely home next day. While we awaited their arrival she showed me some old photographs, including one of us both at a picnic.

'I hear that you are an old friend of Welly's,' said one of the guests later.

'Yes,' I said, 'we went on a picnic.'

'Miles,' said Welly indignantly, 'there was much more in it than that.'

How much more? I wondered, and wondered also what my memory had cheated me out of and how ungallant a man can be. Whatever it was some knock on the head must have driven it far away—undoubtedly to my loss.

April 8th and a light wind from the east as we left Sav' La Mar, but soon after we had cleared Negril Point the trade wind, no longer inhibited by the island, came fresh from the north. By nine next morning we had a hundred miles on the log and we were able to set the twins with the wind in the east again. Grey skies and a grey restless sea and the wind undecided so that we were soon back to fore and aft rig and within an hour back to twins again. Then flitting over the sea towards Cuba, a hundred and fifty miles away, came a swallow, and above it in careless unpremeditated flight, a night hawk, the white goat-sucker mark showing clearly on its wing. We wished him a safe arrival.

Beryl was feeling off colour and as the current appeared to have set us south of our course, we allowed *Tzu Hang* to jill quietly to the north under her main during the night. We set sail again in the morning and a fix showed that we were now slightly north of our course to Grand Cayman. At about midday, with 188 miles on the log, we sighted it to the south-west. We gave two wrecks on the reef at the east end of the island a wide berth, after thinking at first that they were ships at anchor, and then sailed close up the south coast in still water, past mangroves and low wooded shores, past sandy beaches and occasional cottages until we rounded the south-west corner and anchored off Georgetown.

Next morning we moved in closer to the shore and chose a sandy patch between coral on which to drop our anchor, where we could see it clearly in the sand at five fathoms. Georgetown is a flat little town, sun-bathed and quiet. There is a perpetual murmur of waves on the beach and the whisper of bare feet shuffling along the hot road. The islanders that we passed greeted us in a soft singsong voice and with a friendly smile. The holiday season, which brings a flock of migrating Canadians in search of the sun, was over. We found an old sailmaker who did some repairs for us, and when the sail was ready we left for the Yucatan Passage. We had telegraphed Havana, through the Cuban Consul in Kingston, asking permission to enter there. It was a most expensive cable to which we had no reply, and since we had discovered the day after leaving Sav' La Mar that the engine battery was down and we could not use the engine, we decided to give Cuba a miss and set sail instead for Charleston in South Carolina, about twelve hundred miles away.

For the first two days we made good progress with a favourable current to help us. On the second day I saw a solitary cattle egret labouring to the north, head back and legs trailing, on his lonely trial of endurance. He looked a most unlikely passagemaker, but these birds are great colonizers. They come from the old world by the way of South America and when I was first in Jamaica there were none there. Now Jamaica is full of them and the first arrivals in the southern United States were reported in 1952, where they are now well established. They have even been arriving in Hawaii. They are welcome immigrants, doing no harm, and living off the insects and ticks that bother cattle in hot countries.

On the same day, while Beryl and I were changing the jibs on the foredeck, we looked round to see a carrier pigeon marching about behind us and pecking at the salt-water splashes.

'He must be thirsty,' said Beryl, hurrying below and returning with a mug of fresh water. The pigeon drank greedily, not raising his bill to let the drops trickle down his throat, but plunging it deep into the water and sucking away like a horse. I picked him up easily and he was allotted the 'head' as his quarters. After a rest he was ready for food and from then on thrived on a Canadian breakfast food called Red River Cereal. On the second day he cooed, an event noted in the log, and thereafter he could be heard cooing every day, as he contemplated his lucky escape from the sea, or perhaps another issue of

20. Under temporary arrest at San Salvador

21. Hollowing out a dugout at Portobello

22. *Tzu Hang* anchored off Gloria Castle, Portobello

Red River Cereal. From the J.P.C. band on his leg we learnt
that he came from Jamaica, but he was four hundred miles
from his loft when he came on board.

On April 17th we were well into the Yucatan Passage, but
there we ran out of wind and in the next four days only made
137 miles. At one time we found ourselves in a counter current
and were set close in to the Cabo Antonio lighthouse, and finally
I gave up trying to make any easting and we worked our way
to the north. No sooner was this decision made than the
wind came from the east and we set off in search of the Gulf
Stream.

During the next few days we beat through the Florida Straits,
being checked every day by the U.S. Coastguard aircraft, who
keep a constant patrol there. The wind was light and dropped at
night, but we had the current now, and on the 25th it was
boiling along with us, and we saw many sports fishermen from
the Florida Cays trolling along the edge of the rips. These were
good days in spite of the calms and head winds, for we always
felt the slow movement of the great current. There was plenty
of interest too. We had many bird migrants on board, and in
spite of all precautions the cat managed to kill a savannah
sparrow, a swallow, and a yellow-throat. Then there were tugs
and tows, the sight of islands and cays fishermen and aircraft to
keep us interested. One day I saw a small arrow drawing a line
across the sky at a tremendous speed. 'That fellow must be
going faster than sound,' I said to Beryl, and almost immediately
there came a loud double thump followed by the noise of his
engine, but he was already gone. Wherever we went along
either coast of the United States we were reminded of its
enormous military power and there was a sense of armed
alertness, of watch above and watch below, for we saw several
submarines coming and going from their bases.

While abreast of Grand Bahama after a long calm spell when
we began to worry about being carried on to the Banks, the
wind came fresh from the north-west. The log for the next two
pages is smudged with wet, the only two pages in the whole
passage from Japan that have suffered. It was fast, wet sailing in
an awkward sea caused by the wind against the stream and at
one time we had our cockpit full of water, which was a rare
occurrence for *Tzu Hang*.

N

On one of these days we saw two cattle egrets labouring hopelessly into the wind. The sea was a dark grey with many breaking tops, and a black cloud spread right across the horizon. All was dark and ominous and against this darkness the plumage of the two birds shone starkly white, whiter than the breaking crests, as they struggled past our stern, so close that we could see the yellow on their heads and their black eyes. As they passed they were tossed, one up one down, one down one up, in a solemn ritual dance as they drove despairingly to sea.

We anchored off the breakwaters at the entrance to Charleston Harbour to await the tide, thirteen days after leaving Georgetown. While we waited a great dredger, operated by the U.S. Army Corps of Engineers, with the accommodation of a small liner, ploughed magnificently up the channel, up and down and out to sea to spill her load. With the change of the tide a fresh wind got up blowing out of the harbour. We tacked up between the breakwaters past Fort Sumter where the first shots of the Civil War were fired, and up the river to anchor outside the new City Marina. Here a Customs officer came to see us, and then sent a coastguard launch to tow us in. We hadn't been in long before I had a telephone message asking if I would see someone on the local newspaper.

'Yes,' I replied, 'I'd be delighted provided you bring me someone who is keen on racing pigeons. We have one on board for whom we wish to find a home.'

Presently a reporter arrived and with him a member of the Charleston Pigeon Fanciers Association. The pigeon fancier looked very like a racing pigeon himself. He wore a powder-blue windproof, had pale blue eyes, and a grey top to his head. He took our pigeon and put it in a box, turning his head in sharp jerky movement from one side to the other as he told us about pigeons. Next day he was back with an official message from his club. 'They wish to thank you,' he told us, for the kindness that you have shown to a racing pigeon. As he has not returned to his own loft he cannot again be used for racing, but he is a fine bird and he will be put to stud.'

I imagined the pigeon cooing happily to himself when he heard the news, and no doubt becoming a desperate bore in his old age, repeating like myself the same old story:

Two voices are there: One is of the deep,
And one is of an old half-witted sheep
That bleats articulate monotony.

Charleston, with its narrow streets and old-fashioned houses,
its long waterfront and its memorials and forts, seemed full of
history and very English after the west coast towns. There was
a constant coming and going of yachts through the Marina,
on their way up and down the inland waterways. There we
were introduced to an Army officer who told us about an old
couple that he had met in Japan. 'He was a retired soldier,' he
said, 'and they had both spent a lot of time in India. She was
about the same age—just creaking along all by themselves. I
wondered if you knew them?'

'Yes,' said Beryl, 'we do actually. You see, we're them.'

'Oh good Lord,' he said, wondering how deep he had put his
foot in, 'but the boat was white. It was a white boat,' he said.
He was wearing the braided lanyard of a General's aide and
was probably very good at remembering people. It wasn't
really fair to have changed *Tzu Hang*'s colour.

There was also a woman we met who had been at Pearl
Harbour. When she heard the bombing and the gunfire and
looked out and saw the smoke, she said, she ran in to tell her
husband that Pearl Harbour was being attacked. 'But it's
impossible,' he said, 'we've got nothing scheduled for today.'
It reminded me of another friend of Beryl's—an Englishwoman
married to an American. When her husband heard of Pearl
Harbour he burst into her room, saying, 'You bloody English.
You've done it again. You've attacked Pearl Harbour.' Shades
of the *Lusitania*.

We did not want to go up the waterways as we were not too
happy about the engine, and anyway thought that it would be
quicker to keep outside.

We set off on May 5th but since there was a weather report of
twenty-knot head winds, anchored for breakfast while we were
still within the harbour. After breakfast, feeling more ready to
face head winds against the Gulf Stream, we got up our sail
again and left. Round the outer buoy we were close hauled and
while we were in the shallow coastal waters found a short rough
sea. In the afternoon we met two submarines on the surface,

one with its diesel engines thumping loudly as it passed us, while the other, a nuclear submarine, slid silently by, looking like some huge killer whale.

By the evening the wind was freshening from the south-west and the glass dropping. We rounded the lighthouse on Frying Pan Shoals doing a good six knots which *Tzu Hang* kept up all night. By ten the next morning we were running at eight knots in a heavy sea and I began to worry about the shallow water in the channel leading into Morehead City. The wind was dead astern and Force 7 to 8. We hove-to on the starboard tack under reefed mizzen and backed storm jib. *Tzu Hang* made slowly to windward. It was now blowing a steady Force 8 and at one time I looked out to see a big trawler or coastal cargo vessel also nosing into the sea like us. She had a strange foreign look about her, looking neither wholly the one nor wholly the other, and perhaps because her bridge was red, we decided that she was a Russian snooper.

Next day the wind had eased and we raced in to Morehead City, followed by a motor fishing vessel. A month later we met the captain of this vessel in the Chesapeake. 'I think I've seen you before,' he said. 'We followed you into Morehead City and you looked much more comfortable than we were.' Fortunately his ship went off to another part of the harbour and he did not see us run aground on the edge of the channel. The quays were being extended and I discovered that my chart at a critical moment bore little relation to the shore. At this moment we were confronted by a new type of beacon, in general use in the waterways but one that I had not seen before. I started to pass on the starboard side, but was too far away and the water began to shoal.

I then attempted to pass to port and found the water shoaling again. Realizing that the channel was very narrow here I went in close to the beacon, but chose the wrong side. Poor Beryl was much worried by all the frantic instructions to go here and go there. Fortunately the tide was low. We laid a kedge in the channel, winched the line up tight and went below for tea. While we were having it *Tzu Hang* floated off and almost immediately a coastguard vessel came up and rebuked us mildly for anchoring in the channel. We persuaded them to show us to a berth. The wind was still blowing hard and we drew too much for the Marina, so tied to a quay which we pounded unhappily all night.

There were two good things about our visit to Morehead City. The first was Bill Stone, a yachtsman from the Chesapeake who was on his way back from the Bahamas by the inland waters. We had seen him but not spoken to him in Charleston. Now he passed us in the street and, although he was a complete stranger, I could feel the aura of culture and kindliness that surrounds him. Later he spoke to us and invited us aboard his yacht in the Marina. He told us that we could have his mooring opposite his house in Annapolis and gave us information about the Chesapeake. We could have found no better person than he for he is co-author of *Blanchard's Cruising Guide to the Chesapeake*. The other thing that we enjoyed was 'The Sanitary Fish Market and Restaurant', not so much for its cleanliness but for its name. It featured prominently on one of the coloured postcards of 'Morehead City's Fabulous Waterfront', a dull channel where sports fishing craft were moored.

Next day we left for Hatteras and the Chesapeake. All yachts are glad when they are safely round the Hatteras and there was a good weather forecast for the next day. As we crossed the Cape Lookout shoals we could see the blue Gulf Stream ahead, and were soon in it with its floating weed. A small sandpiper, quite exhausted, came on board. We put him in the 'head' but he did not live long. We passed the Diamond Shoal light by midnight, having made good time, but now we were under the influence of strong tides and sometimes made great progress and sometimes seemed to crawl along although we were sailing well. We stayed close inshore so that we might see what was to be seen, but it was mostly nothing, only a long low ridge of sand and pebbles. There was fog during the night and with a following wind we neither saw nor heard the Chesapeake Light vessel, nor Cape Henry, but at 6 a.m., taking our cue from a tug that came out, we turned in for the Bay.

The Chesapeake is a great bay, one hundred and forty miles long, its western shore divided by those great rivers that figured so prominently in the American Civil War—the James, the York, the Rappahannock, and the Potomac—and it is crossed near its entrance by a fifteen-mile-long bridge, with two gaps for shipping. At one the road dives suddenly under and at the other it climbs above the passing ships. The wind blew down the bay as it did all the time that we were there so that we beat with a favourable tide and anchored when the tide turned against us. We anchored for the first night amongst fish traps in the shelter of New Point Comfort, and on the second afternoon came into Fishing Bay on the north shore of the Piankatank river. This is a very well sheltered and beautiful bay amongst woods and pastures, with a yacht club at the head and a Marine Ways. Mr Deagle, the owner of the yard, when we ran him to ground, changed his mind about slipping us. He had enough work, he said, and no time to adjust his carriage to *Tzu Hang*'s shape.

There we left *Tzu Hang* at anchor while we went ashore on an excursion to Farmville to see John Lewis, of Lewis, Addison, and Steele, who had now left the Navy and was practising with his father's law firm. He had married a lovely southern girl called Kelly and to celebrate our arrival had spread a huge white ensign—a courtesy flag, which had been used by an American aircraft carrier in the Far East and which he had managed to get hold of—over half his house, while the other half was covered by the Stars and Stripes.

The country, North Carolina, was dull and flat cotton land but in the small towns the wide shaded roads, the red-brick white-porched houses, and the gardens all gave a feeling of prosperity, and well-settled comfort. Around Farmville there were more Lewises than there are in Llandudno, and if a Lewis wanted to make a will, have a suit cleaned, or buy some eggs, there were Lewises to look after him. Their hospitality was unbounded and Beryl and I felt as if we were the guests of a hundred Lewises.

We could not leave the cat on the boat so she had to come with us, but livestock are not allowed on buses. Pwe was put in a cardboard box and while we sat waiting for the bus to start I began to wonder whether she was not being smothered, since the airholes were small. I enlarged one with my finger whereat Pwe began to bellow at the top of her voice and tear the cardboard apart at the holes. I have never heard her make such a noise, nor have I ever seen Beryl so angry.

'You always have to meddle,' she hissed at me as she pulled Pwe out of the box and wrapped her in a jersey.

The driver had already been approached and all he had said was, 'Don't let the dispatcher see.' Now he ignored the noise and started off as quickly as possible. We had to change our bus before reaching Farmville, and Beryl smuggled the cat on board wrapped again in her jersey. As she passed two Negroes on her way to her seat one of them turned to the other and said, 'Look at that. Legs hanging down all over.'

After Farmville we went to Sabot to a friend of Welly— Welly of Sav' La Mar. He lived in a large country house in the lovely Virginia countryside, all hills and woods and pastures, and it was hard to realize that we were not in England. Our host was once commodore of the yacht club in front of which we were anchored and he was also until recently master of a pack of foxhounds. We went to see them in kennels; some of them were English, some bred from pure English stock, some were American and some half and half. There was a great difference between them, the Americans tending to have long ears and high domed heads, lighter bone and longer feet. The English hounds bred in Virginia were lighter than the English-bred hounds. There was no doubt which the English huntsman preferred. 'The only hounds you can tolerate,' he said, 'are the English hounds, or first-generation English bred out here.'

We had managed to arrange a haul out in a dry dock at Reedville farther up the bay. It was a busy dock much occupied by fishing boats and run by a man of great energy and few words who treated us as if we were foreigners who spoke a language that he had no hope of understanding. We waited at Fleeton Marina until there was an opportunity to go up, where he presently arrived in a motor-boat, threw us a line, and towed us away. From then until we were back at the Marina hardly a word was spoken of more than two syllables nor a sentence of more than three, but he did an efficient, fast job, and not too expensive, although we would have liked another day on the slip to let the paint harden.

Another two days beating up the bay until we arrived at Crab Creek just before Annapolis and tied to Bill Stone's mooring. It was in a little side creek, lined with trees, with here and there a landing stage and a yacht moored below a country house. There was just room for *Tzu Hang* to swing at the mooring and Bill's landing stage and his yacht only a few oar strokes away. The trees overhung us and only after dark were the birds quiet. As well as these idyllic surroundings we had the use of his house and his bath and his books, a hundred yards above the landing stage. We could hardly bring ourselves to leave and if he had asked us once more to stay longer I think we would be there still, with Bill in the Bahamas, wondering when he could again have his house to himself.

From Crab Creek, through Annapolis with its red-brick houses and white porches and the grey Naval Academy, which Bill described as 'Late Prison Architecture', to the Chesapeake–Delaware Canal, where we tied up on the inside of a long wooden pier on the north side of the entrance, at Schaeffer's Store. That was the end of the Chesapeake and for us it had been a beat all the way until the last few miles to Annapolis and on from Annapolis to the Canal entrance. A yachtsman could spend a year or two in the Chesapeake, which has so many little bays that he might always find a secluded anchorage. It reminded us of the Eisel Meer, with its short sharp seas when the wind blew, and the lowland on the horizon. It was like another street in our village, for while we were staying with Bill Stone we came across Mel Smith whom we had met when he had a big three-masted ship, the *Annya*, at Cadiz; John Miles whom we had met when he was the American Consul in Malta, and again when he had been economic adviser in Johannesburg; also Admiral Sir Nigel Henderson, who had lived in a yacht in front of us when he was with N.A.T.O. in Paris, and with whom we were able to spend a few days at Washington, and Captain Bartol of the U.S. Navy, now I'm sure an Admiral, who had been so kind to us in Adak in the Aleutian Islands.

Henry Dupont sent his car to pick us up and we drove to his house, away in the country, in grass parkland, with big trees.

A Negro butler met us and rang a bell to let Emily Dupont know that guests had arrived. Presently she came driving up over a curving lawn in a golf cart with two English collies running beside her, so that with the beautiful country behind her, she looked like a modern 'Diana of the Uplands'. The house is full of brass cannon, the collection of which is one of Henry's hobbies, and later, when he arrived, he hauled out a mass of charts so that we were soon charted up as far as Long

Island Sound, and our heads buzzing with further instructions
of where and when and how we were to join the Cruising Club
of America on their northern cruise, and what we were to do
in between.

Before entering the Chesapeake–Delaware Canal, we were
hailed by the patrol boat of the Corps of Engineers, to whom we
had to report our mast height. It is as well to add something to
the height as otherwise, when the bridges raise to allow the
yacht to go under, they will only raise sufficiently to give a few
feet clearance, which causes great anxiety to those on deck as
the ship rushes under the bridges on the tide. The currents run
from $1\frac{1}{2}$ to $2\frac{1}{2}$ knots and it is worth waiting for a favourable
tide. Boats going through with the current have right of way
over those coming against it.

When we came out of the Canal and into the Delaware
River we had no chart but managed well enough without,
since the Channel was well buoyed. We anchored before the
tide changed north of Cross Ledge. There was a nasty choppy
sea and *Tzu Hang* kept cracking her anchor chain so that it
jarred in the hawse hole. We lowered another anchor on the
same chain to act as a weight and the jarring stopped immediately. After a very good night we sailed for Sandy Hook
and made a fine passage, rounding the light the following
afternoon and anchoring off the yacht harbour. I had never
been to New York and looked forward to our trip through the
East River and into Long Island Sound with great excitement.

Early the following morning while Beryl and I were still
only thinking of rolling out of our bunks, we heard a hail and
the sound of a yacht's motor. We put our heads out of the
hatch to see Thurston and Ruth Smith passing on their way to
East River and their home on Oyster Bay. We had met them in
Charleston, on their way north by the Inland Waterways,
and they had asked us to come to the Seawanaka County
Yacht Club, where they had promised us a mooring.

It was a perfect still morning, with a light mist lying in the
water until the sun chased it away. We carried the tide with us
all the way through the Narrows and under Throg's Neck
Bridge. Manhattan seen from the East River on a summer's
morning was an unforgettable sight. It looked still and deserted
—a model or a cardboard cut-out. Such high and narrow

buildings could not be real. It was Sunday so that the traffic on the river was not excessive, but Long Island Sound was full of yachts and pleasure craft. Huge triple-decker motor-boats charged past under their automatic pilots, skippers with hands in their pockets and cigars in their mouths. There were great glistening yachts and little family sail boats.

We slipped down with the wind right aft. As we approached a black buoy I decided to pass between it and the small marker buoy, outside the channel proper. Then I had a feeling that there was something behind me, and looking over my shoulder saw the racing yacht *Palawan* approaching, close-hauled on the starboard tack. Behind her a long row of tall sails showed that she was leading a race. I saw also that she would slice past our stern with a yard or two to spare, so continued on my way. What I failed to appreciate was that she also was going to round the buoy and that I was going to be plumb in front of her as she did so. It really didn't matter as she only had to carry on the width of my beam before turning, but racing men do not like giving up inches, certainly not the crew on the fore-deck. They opened their mouths like a lot of sea lions on a rock and bellowed instructions, disapproval, and invective. As they passed my stern I saw the skipper signal them to be quiet, but I had already lost my nerve and put the helm still farther over so that we had to jib all standing in order to come inside the buoy and out of their way. Just as the skipper of the *Palawan* was abreast of our stern I heard him say quietly 'Spinnaker, please,' which stopped their howling and put them to work. His unruffled authority, the friendly smile of a pretty girl in stern, and the shout of 'Sorry' from another of his crew compensated for the ill-mannered sea wolves in the bow, all of whom I wished might fall into the Sound.

In Oyster Bay there was a forest of masts outside the yacht club, but I can usually recognize a yacht that I have seen once, as I can a horse, and I picked out Thurston Smith's ship at its moorings. A moment later we saw him waving from his lawn, and the yacht club boat coming out to show us to our moorings.

We left *Tzu Hang* for two weeks at the Seawanaka Yacht Club while we stayed with friends on Long Island, living in such comfort and in such beautiful surroundings that if it had not been for the morning and evening flight of aircraft coming

in and leaving for Europe, we might have been almost reluctant to set out once more to sea. Like a small migrating duck
who dallies by some secluded pool, yet hears each day the call
of geese flying northward, the sound of their engines reminded
us that we too should be gone.

Early one morning I blew 'Going Home' on my hunting
horn, our foghorn, to let Thurston Smith in his house above
know that we were going. An angry and tousled head bounced
out of the hatch of the yacht lying next to us, to tell us that there
was no boat service till eight o'clock.

It was a fine day as we continued our sail down Long Island
Sound in warm hazy weather. The Sound was calm and
occasional yacht sails appeared like lighthouses as we slid
slowly on, bound for Mystic on the Mystic River. We anchored
for the night by Duck Island and continued next day in foggy
weather up a narrow but well-buoyed channel to the museum
port. In the days of sail it was a village seaport where ships
were built, and some of the buildings, the shipyard that main-
tains the ships, and the blacksmith's forge are original from
the old days. With typical American enthusiasm others have
been brought in complete from other places, including one of
the old outstations of the New York Yacht Club.

Tzu Hang found herself in famous company. There was an
old whaling ship, the *Charles W. Morgan*, built in 1841; there
was the *Bowdoin* built for the Arctic exploration who made 26
expeditions; the *Gundel*, built in Denmark, in which 29 men
and women escaped from Communist rule in Latvia and sailed
to Boston; and there was the small full rigged ship, the *Joseph
Conrad*. The *Joseph Conrad*, only a hundred feet long, was built
in Denmark as a cadet training ship, where she helped to train
over 4,000 cadets. She was run down in a fog in 1905 and sank
with the loss of 22 lives, but was recovered. Later she was
bought and sailed round the world by Alan Villiers, who sold
her to an American, George Hartford. He kept her as a yacht
for three years and in the end gave her to Mystic. There she
will no doubt live to a prodigious age in unfailing beauty,
bringing something of the romance of the days of sail to those
who walk her decks. Also there was the old yacht *Brilliant*,
who still does regular cruises from Mystic in a sail training
scheme; and there are various fishermen, including one old

'Banks' schooner, the *L. A. Dunton* from Boston, complete with
dories and long lines, right out of *Captains Courageous*, who looks
as if she is just about ready to see the 'Virgin' spout again.

On our first afternoon we were tired and went to the plane-
tarium where we both fell asleep, lulled by the spinning
heavens and knocked out by the recorded talk. Next day,
refreshed by a night at the dockside, we tackled Mystic anew,
and saw most of it. We also received, on account of *Tzu Hang's*
record and Henry Dupont's recommendation, much undeserved
attention from Waldo Johnstone, the busy director of this
museum seaport with the beautiful Indian name.

From Mystic we had an uneventful sail down Fisher Island
Sound, and then a most exciting beat against a fresh head wind
through the centre passage in the shallows which join the
island to the northern shore. Soon afterwards the fog shut us
in, thick all-encompassing fog. There was still a fresh wind,
as we beat to the west, hoping to make the refuge harbour at
Point Judith, but presently we decided to anchor, groped our
way inshore, and dropped the hook on stony ground in an
uncomfortable sea. Soon after dark the fog cleared away and
we could see the lights of Point Judith a few miles away, but
the wind was going down also and we decided to stay where
we were.

Next day was a little better and we managed to make Vineyard Sound with only one tack, and anchored in the most
beautiful surroundings in Tarpaulin Bay. There was one small
yacht anchored at the head of the bay, and when they left we
had it all to ourselves. I had never been to the east coast of
America and now found myself constantly amazed by the
amount of unspoiled country that we saw. Even only a short
drive out of New York, up the Hudson River, we found ourselves deep in the country, and here there wasn't a house to be
seen.

From Tarpaulin Bay we continued through Vineyard Sound,
past Woods Hole where there is the big marine biological
station, past Vineyard Haven, and on to Nantucket. Foggy
weather again, but whereas yesterday we had seen hardly
a yacht all day, today being Saturday the sea was full of them.
It was soon obvious that many were bound for Nantucket also,
so we were relieved of all major problems of navigation. In

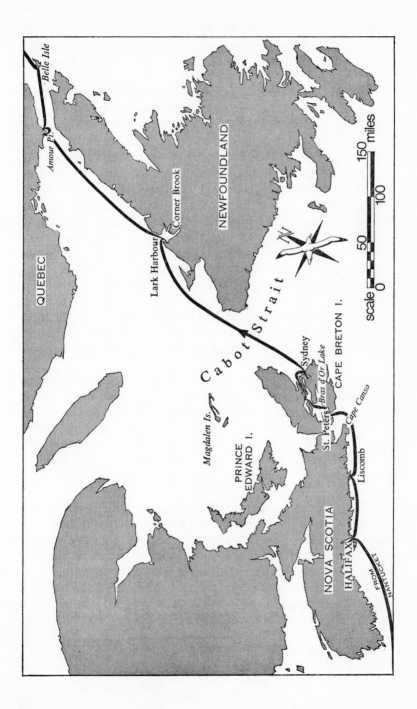

Nantucket we anchored in what little room was left in the harbour. On Nantucket Island also were our friends Ardale and Anna Golding whom we had last seen in Paris when their ship was berthed at the same quay, below the Palais de Chaillot. Nantucket was full of weekend tourists when they came to collect us next morning. They drove us across what they and the locals call the moors, but which might be better described as heath, to Siasconset. Their house was on the cliff west of Siasconset near a lighthouse which moaned sadly all the time that we were there. Their pack of corgis, which used to run barking up the quay in Paris and sometimes pursued Pwe, were just as ready to hunt her as before. From time to time a file of hikers, finding their way along the cliff, passed between the window and its edge, making a grey frieze of marching figures against the swirling fog beyond. It was a particularly foggy month in Nantucket, and when after a few days we left for Halifax, we drifted in fog or thick summer haze all the way.

The yacht club at Halifax had everything in wonderful order for the Marblehead–Halifax race which was due to arrive in a day or two. There were rows of red buoys for the new arrivals to moor to, and a splendid boat service manned by young men on holiday from the university to bring the crews ashore. We were not racing and we were also Canadian, so we felt a bit guilty about arriving just at this time, but the members of the club were all ready to practise their hospitality on any arrival, and it needed a strong head to withstand it. There were all kinds of entertainments planned and since it was Centennial year they were planned on a large scale with nothing less than a whole ox to be roasted on the breakwater.

They were still going on when we set off for Liscomb, the second stage in the Cruising Club Rally. The American Cruising Club ships were mostly ocean racers, or at least fast enough to compete in an ocean race, so Beryl and I had to hit only the alternate anchorages so that we might keep up with them. *Cyane*, Henry Dupont's lovely ocean racer, left in front of us under power, since there was no wind, and we soon saw her tall mast and the tracery of her rigging disappear into the fog. We picked up our buoys all right but never saw the shore. From then on we became well accustomed to the sound of an overtaking yacht as they came past us, and disappeared as

quickly into the murk. None of them seemed to be at all
deterred by the fog and I don't think that they knew where they
were any more than we did. We found our way into the long
sound that leads in to Liscomb because there was a big
diaphone at the entrance and once we had heard that we were
all right. Once inside, the fog cleared and we found ourselves
sailing up a long, narrow and completely uninhabited sound,
with low pine-covered shores. The sun was shining and there
was a warm, peaty look about the water. We were the first in
as we had travelled through the night and the Sound was so
deserted that we felt almost as if we were exploring it. We tried
to imagine what it would be like in winter, the water all frozen,
the trunks of the pines black under the snow on the branches,
the silence. I long to spend a winter in this sort of surroundings.

Our passage to the entrance of the Bras d'Or Lakes, across
Cape Canso, was just as foggy, in fact more so as the fog had
even penetrated into Liscomb Sound and we had to anchor
for a time before we could see our way at all. Since we carried
on through the night while the others stopped we were again
almost the first into the lock at St Peters, after groping our
way between the two whistle buoys that mark the limits of the
bay.

Beryl and I, since up to now we were the only representatives
of the Royal Cruising Club, were anxious not to put up a black
in front of the Cruising Club of America. We had already got
the reputation of being the slowest boat in the fleet, although
we were about level with *Integrity*, the lovely Maine schooner,
built by Waldo Howland; but this was compensated for by
Tzu Hang's long cruises in out-of-the-way places. Because of
this also we were supposed to be adequate navigators, and up
to now, when tackled by an overtaking ship as to our exact
position, I had been able to give an answer with completely
unjustified assurance. Leaving the lock at St Peters we made
too large a turn round a beacon and stuck on the mud. Never
was a dinghy over the side and a ship kedged off in quicker time.
It had the horrible speed of long practise, but we were seen.
Perhaps it was because we were visitors that they were kind to
us, for no one mentioned it except to say that no one can say he
has cruised in the Bras d'Or until he has been aground.

It would be hard to be over-enthusiastic about the Bras d'Or

Lakes for a cruising ground in July. It was marvellous weather. We had some good sailing breezes, the country wild and beautiful and the water warm, and two races, during one of which *Tzu Hang* tussled with *Integrity* for last place, and I believe that there was one other, a Colin Archer design, behind us. We would have done better if we had not split our genoa. But it was all good fun with lavish hospitality and the pipes playing at Beinn Bhreagh, Melville Grosvenor's house at Baddeck. While we were anchored off Beinn Bhreagh I heard an anchor chain rattle down and said to Beryl, 'That's an English ship, the Americans never use chain like that.' I put my head out and there was Rory O'Hanlon in his yacht from Dublin, an eminent surgeon who looks like mine host from some coaching inn of last century, with Douglas Heard and his wife, also an old friend, as his crew. It was yet another street in our village.

It was time for us to leave. All the others were racing as we beat round the point of Beinn Bhreagh; we turned, with a stiff following breeze and a following tide, for once sailing nearly as fast as they were, but heading north for the northern entrance to the Bras d'Or. It was a marvellous sail, the steep pine-clad slopes sliding past on each side of us until we shot out on a boiling tide through the narrow gates of Great d'Or and into the Cabot Strait. Then round to Sydney and since we had had a fair wind and a following tide to leave the Bras d'Or we had a head wind and foul tide to enter Sydney, so that we had a hard flog and it was almost dark by the time we anchored off the yacht club.

Here we were at last, at our stepping-off place for our journey home to England, almost within spitting distance— under two thousand to the Fastnet by the shortest route, any- way. It didn't seem so very far now; it was July 23rd, plenty of time to go round by Iceland and the Faroes, if we wished. Of course we wished to do so. It was unlikely that we'd have another chance of seeing them. We were not going to be so short-handed either. Anna Golding's son, Charles, who had been staying with her in Nantucket, was looking for a passage. He was an intelligent and an amusing companion, an American who had been educated in England, and who spoke German, French, and Arabic, although none of them was going to be

3. Sailing north from Reykjavik

4. Isafjordjap in northern Iceland

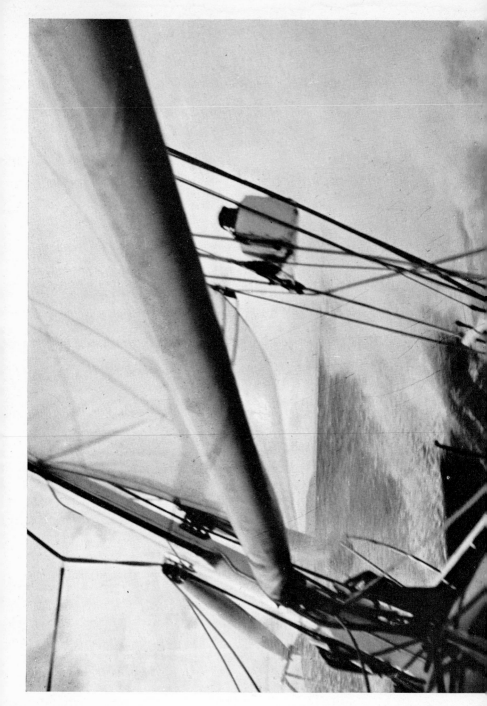

25. Landfall on the Butt of Lewis

much use to him on the journey. Although Charles had done quite a bit of sailing with his father I do not think that he could be described as a dedicated yachtsman, but at the moment he was dedicated to a cheap passage to England and did not mind about the time.

13 Across the North Atlantic

We left Sydney on July 30th well provisioned except for diesel for our voyage. It was a Sunday. We took *Tzu Hang* round to Nickerson's wharf and found that no fuel was available on a Sunday. Pwe got under the house in search of fish heads and other stinking debris left by the tide under the pilings on which it was built, and we had a difficult job in recovering her. We were glad to leave Sydney. It was one of the dreariest towns that we had ever visited, and except for Captain Parker, who writes about Nova Scotian sailing vessels, and his family, the people are the most reserved. Sydney reminded me of Granton, the port near Edinburgh, on the Sabbath.

We celebrated our departure and Charles' birthday with a bumper dinner of warmed-up stew, overripe strawberries, and a bottle of Heidsieck, while *Tzu Hang* idled across the Canso Strait. The Straits of Belle Isle were reported free of ice at the northern entrance, but the Pilot says that there is always ice at the entrance to the Straits at this time of year, the only question being how far in or how far out—dependent on wind and tide—the ice may be found.

For the first two days we had the fog that we were beginning to take for granted in this part of the world, and little wind. On the third day, with a light wind and the sun shining, the wild Newfoundland coast clear to starboard, we had perfect sailing with the anticipation of reaching Lark Harbour on the Newfoundland coast that night. We made it, but we lost the wind before dark and had to motor twenty miles with the water pump leaking badly. We motored up a narrow sound by moonlight, with rugged cliffs close on each side, and anchored at about one o'clock in still water, a short way from the wharf. We were up early in the morning to bring *Tzu Hang* alongside.

The houses were little bright painted boxes down a single street. It was a fishing village and everyone was catching cod, netting them deep down. They were gutted and split, and dried on small racks which the children carried out and in to the storerooms, as the sun came out or the mist came down.

The whole atmosphere of this village was as different from Sydney as could be, so that I began to imagine Beryl and myself settling here and keeping a lobster boat. Here there was laughter and enthusiasm and friendliness. Fishermen waved as they passed us on their way to the bay. Two young people in a small car stopped and asked us if they could drive us anywhere to show us the country. They took us to Petit Port, a tiny cliff-locked bay with a shingle beach, and some fishing boats lying at their moorings.

'Could *Tzu Hang* lie here in the winter?'

'Oh no,' they said, 'we pull up all the boats in the winter.'

They were called Sheppard. 'It's very difficult,' said the girl, who had shining dark hair and blue eyes, 'we're all Sheppards here. There are six Johns and seven Alices just round here.'

The main object of putting into Lark Harbour had been to get some diesel fuel, but now we found that there was none in the village, and that we would have to go to Corner Brook, a large port where ocean-going ships come for timber and oil. It was a long way up the sound so we hired a truck instead and brought a forty-five-gallon drum back in it and saw a bit of the country as well. Steep, rocky, pine-covered slopes dropping down to the sound, with here and there a small farm. Just as we had expected Newfoundland to be, the trees more stunted, the climate colder, and the hills less grand than our own British Columbia. We were much better off in Lark Harbour than we would have been in Corner Brook, even if the post office was 'just a nice walk away', which turned out to be at least a mile and a half.

We left Lark Harbour on August 4th, and when we got out into the bay, found a big swell and little wind. We sailed close to the rocky shore of Guernsey Island, the main flapping as we rolled in its lee, under grey overcast with visibility about five miles so that we soon lost sight of the land. In the evening the coast appeared again, and by eight o'clock in the morning we were running towards the Straits in thick fog, with the wind blowing 6 to 7 behind us.

'What do you think?' I asked Beryl. 'I don't want to run through the Straits in this fog. We'll be out before daylight and the Pilot says that there is always ice somewhere in the entrance. We could put in to Forteau Bay.'

'Well, let's put in there,' she said. 'I'm all against running through in this weather.'

The tide was now strongly with us, so I laid a course to hit well upstream of Forteau Bay, on the coast of Labrador. Before doing so I got a good fix on Flowers Ledges beacon on the Newfoundland coast, and on Amour Point beacon, the north-east entrance point of Forteau Bay. Our new course brought the wind on to our quarter and *Tzu Hang* began to sail faster, but the bearing of Amour Point beacon did not change. Soon we had lost Flowers Ledges beacon, but Amour Point on the starboard bow, still bearing the same, grew louder.

We were running fast heading for the coast, but visibility was down to about 300 yards. Still there was deep water well within this range. All I had to do was to spot the coast in time to turn down it, then follow it until it gave me a weather shore in Forteau Bay. I checked the beacon again. Still no change in its bearing.

'Damn it,' I cried to Beryl, 'we'd better head up some more. That beacon is getting mighty loud.'

The wind was now abeam and so was the beacon and we were racing along, heading dead in for the coast.

'We'll hand the main,' I said, 'so that we're not going so bloody fast.' Charles and I stowed it and *Tzu Hang* carried on at a less relentless speed—straight, I thought, for the shore about a mile above the south-west entrance point of Forteau Bay. I flitted anxiously between the bow and the radio set. The noise of the beacon grew steadily louder but the bearing remained the same. I found that I could no longer get a null point. It was a new set that Charles had brought with him and I had had no opportunity to test it properly. Now I began to suspect that there was something wrong with it.

'I see some land,' Beryl called. Although she has good eyesight she never sees land unless it is fairly obvious. I jumped on deck looking towards the bow. 'No, there,' she cried pointing to starboard. No doubt about it. Land close to starboard under the foot of the fog. For a moment I thought that I must be still farther up the coast than I had expected, heading into a slight re-entrance, but now some white, mist-shrouded cottages appeared, and at the same time the swell began to hump as if it wished to break. With a jump at the heart I realized that we were just off the north-eastern entrance point and within Forteau Bay, and that although we were sailing parallel to the shore we were being swept on to the beach by the swirling tide.

'About,' I shouted to Beryl. 'Put her about.'

Tzu Hang came round under her mizzen and jib, but she came round sluggishly and seemed to heave herself slowly over the cresting swell. 'Up with the main,' I called to Charles, kicking myself that we'd ever brought it down, and dreading that at any moment I'd hear the stern thump on the sand. Up it went with both of us working at it, and as it began to draw I was able to take another look behind us at the white cottages. They were no nearer but this time I saw behind them the base of a white tower and at the same moment heard for the first time the blatt and thump of the diaphone on Amour Point lighthouse. If I had kept up the main we would still have had plenty of time to put *Tzu Hang* about, and we would have had the power to haul out of danger immediately, but I should have trusted to my radio and then I would not have got into any danger at all. I think it was one of our narrowest squeaks, for there is a shallow point running out from the lighthouse over which the tide sets strongly, and we were much too near it.

As soon as we were well clear we turned and ran down to Anse du Loup, another bay five miles farther down the coast. We turned in and beat up to Schooner Cove, finding our way between various fish nets. The wind whirled the fog over the promontory that sheltered us, and *Tzu Hang*, with her anchor down in good sand, swung this way and that under its assault. It was as if we were back in the Aleutian Islands, for there wasn't a tree in sight. If Charles had realized how glad Beryl and I were to be there he might have changed his mind about coming with us.

Next day was clear, with a light following wind. A perfect summer's day. We heard fishermen talking on the radio.

'It blew right strong yesterday,' said one. 'We couldn't

get in at all.' 'It was a son of a bitch yesterday,' said another.

Anyway today was all right. At the head of the bay little white houses showed like tombstones in a cemetery. We sailed down the centre of the Straits, away 'down north' as the Newfoundlanders say, the great green and red cliffs of the Labrador coast to port, and the blue hills and black rocky headlands of Newfoundland to starboard. Belle Isle, all steep cliffs with green grass above, looked uninhabited except for the lighthouses at each end. We sailed close to the west coast, looking for an anchorage. Green Cove, a third of the way up, was narrow and exposed to the south-west swell, but behind Lark Island there were several fishing schooners at anchor. By the time that we were there the wind had piped up and we decided to continue towards Iceland. Next morning there were only the gliding fulmars and shearwaters, the skuas, and kittiwakes to be seen.

Later on we saw several ships as we were still near the trade route through Belle Isle, including a fishing vessel from Fécamp, whose crew in true French style gave Beryl a series of wolf whistles as they passed.

'Of course it's just ridiculous,' she said, 'because they can't possibly see me at that range,' but nevertheless she enjoyed it. Of ice we saw not a trace.

It is about 1,400 miles from Anse du Loup to Reykjavik and it took us fifteen days. On two of these we had strong winds and on each did over 140 miles, under mizzen and storm jib for part of the time, but the others were on the whole foggy and windless. It was an uneventful voyage, marked chiefly by variations in the barometer that seemed to promise or rather threaten us with much worse gales than they eventually brought. On Sunday August 13th the barometer dropped fifteen millibars between 6.30 p.m. and 10 p.m., and rose twenty millibars before 7 next morning. On this day we celebrated Pwe's fourteenth birthday by giving her an extra helping from a tin of her favourite food, made from the best kidney and liver, and fit for the cats of millionaires. We also celebrated her birthday with an extra rum sour in the evening, and our last bottle of Beaujolais.

When I relieved Beryl on the morning of August 21st at four, and gave her cold cheek a kiss before she went below for her best sleep of the night, daylight was already coming. The wind

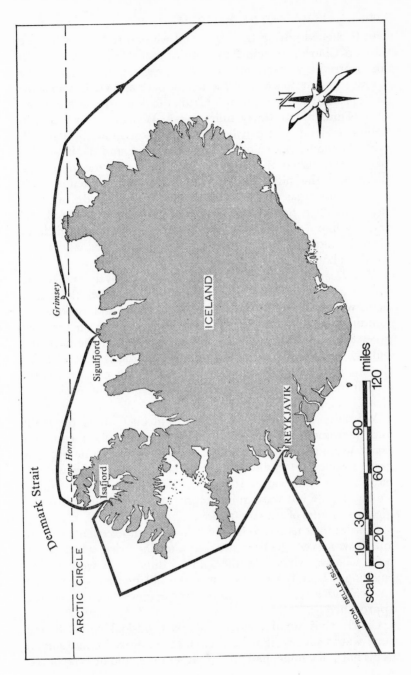

had freshened during the night and we had rolled down a big reef on Charles' watch. Now, under reefed mizzen and main and storm jib we were making good progress. At half-past four I saw a mountain away to the north, bare and cold, with snow at its peak. It was the Snaefellsjokull, the westernmost mountain of Iceland, about thirty miles away. Whichever way a ship comes, Iceland, if it can be seen, is a most romantic landfall, with the mountains standing high and bleak and the blue cliffs below. We rushed on seeing first the skerries off the south-west point and the high land north of Reykjanes, then the air station and tanks at Keflavik, which drew us south, until we saw Gardskagi light, apparently unconnected with the shore, sticking like a finger out of the sea. We headed up a little to clear it and the long, low promontory appeared above the troubled horizon, and the white line of breakers below.

Tzu Hang was rollicking along, making a lovely end to the passage, with the lighthouses coming up one after the other. Soon we could see Grota light at Reykjavik, and various tall buildings, and finally the little yellow lighthouse on the low, green island of Engey, where ships turn down for the harbour, but the best line for the entrance is the southern edge of Esja, the mountain just north of Reykjavik which can be clearly seen from the sea before passing Gardskagi, if the weather is clear.

We sailed in towards the harbour entrance under the main and then anchored outside. There a Customs officer came on board us and stayed on board to show us where to tie up, to a green wooden vessel alongside the wharf, so that we would not have to tend our warps. It was just as well, for the next night we had a gale but were quite secure, and well sheltered by the high green sides of our companion.

Charles took us out to dinner ashore in an excellent restaurant. It was a very good dinner, but a terrific price, which made poor Charles wince. At the end of dinner we were sitting enjoying a brandy—it was before the bill had arrived—when an Icelander, rather the worse for having dined too well, approached us.

Charles has small features and is good-looking, although none would suggest that he is effeminate. Since he had joined us his hair, like mine, had grown rather long, and he is favoured by the most remarkable eyelashes that his sister might well envy. The Icelander bent over him with what he no doubt thought was a captivating smile and asked him if he might have the pleasure of a dance. This suggestion so shocked Charles that for a moment he was unable to answer except in an incoherent mumble, which the Icelander took for a modest assent. He placed his hands on Charles' chair, ready to remove it as he stood up. This was too much for me. 'Of course he doesn't want to dance with you,' I said, and then becoming a little confused myself, I added, 'If you wanted him to dance with you, you should have asked my permission first.' By this time Charles had recovered and told the Icelander, in a clear male voice, that he never danced with men he had not met before. The Icelander withdrew, apologizing, but chiefly to me, for his blunder.

Doctor Bjarnason, an athletic and studious man, who is head of the Icelandic Forestry Department, came on board. He is waging a ceaseless war against the despoliation of Icelandic soil by erosion. Half Iceland is already a barren, volcanic desert and Doctor Bjarnason's arch enemy, the Icelandic sheep, is striving to complete the job. Although the grass that we saw never seemed to be overstocked, it was always crisscrossed by sheep paths. In heavy rains and during the run off from the snow the water follows these tracks, until it washes the earth away and makes stony barren watercourses. Iceland has only two main industries, fishing and agriculture, and the sheep are one of the props of Icelandic agriculture.

Doctor Bjarnason is in continuous search for a quick-growing tree which can withstand the climate. Once Iceland was covered with forest, which perhaps reached its maturity in milder times. Forests protect their growth, but once the trees have gone there is nothing to shelter the saplings. If only the Doctor could persuade trees to grow once more, and the farmers to cut down on their stock of sheep, the erosion could be checked.

Iceland is trying to attract tourists and it has lots to show them, but at the moment it is handicapped by the bad roads and the lack of suitable hotels. There is excellent salmon fishing, but at a great price. There are camping tours that can be made on the sturdy Icelandic pony. Nothing is more attractive in the pony world than a piebald Icelandic pony. There are ponies of many colours, but I can only say what they look like as we had no intimate dealings with them.

In Iceland also there are the most beautiful girls, with unforgettable eyes that they did not hesitate to use on Charles. You may walk into an office in Reykjavik and forget immediately what you have come for, bewitched by some black-headed blue-eyed Celt behind the counter, or by a golden girl of unmistakably Scandinavian origin. Perhaps it is the long dark winter that gives them such a wonderful complexion. If there is another life on this earth I should like to spend a long dark winter with one of them, but it seemed to me that Charles could have spent the coming winter with some of them if he had wished.

We were driven by Baldo Thorstanson, one of the Doctor's men, to see the geysers and the Thingvellir, a green valley where the first parliament of all was held. He drove a Russian car over corrugated dirt roads at such speed that it seemed to us that he was carrying out an endurance test, both on us and on the car.

'No,' he told us, 'you have to drive them this speed to stop the vibration. Only the Russian cars will stand up to it.' The car looked like a Russian, a member of the Politburo, square not very attractive, but very durable.

From Reykjavik we had a really splendid sail, the wind freshening all the time. Malarrif lighthouse appeared suddenly, looking very near and menacing out of the fog. By then it was blowing Force 8 and we cut down to storm jib only, sailing north-west to give Bjargtanger a wide berth and in order to keep the headsail filled. During my watch I had a sudden feeling of danger and looking over my shoulder saw a cross sea hump up on our beam. It hit us a solid thump, making *Tzu Hang* heel far over, so that I was standing on the side of the cockpit. There was a crash from below and I heard Beryl calling to ask if I was all right. Little water came on board but it was one of those irregular seas, running across the general pattern, which can put any small yacht in danger, especially when the waves are several times magnified as they are sometimes in the Southern Ocean. *Tzu Hang* whipped up again and was soon running on as before.

Next day we continued on the same course, with the wind easing, and in the evening set the mizzen and staysail and let

Tzu Hang sail quietly towards the mouth of Isafjordjup. At daylight it was ahead of us, with great tall cliffs on each side sawn off flat at their tops. The sea was soon oily calm and we motored in, passing several fishing vessels on their way out. The harbour of Isafjord is behind a long spit and is reached through a twisting channel. On the end of the spit there was a stranded British trawler, stranded on Christmas Day the year before.

An Icelander we met in Isafjord told us his account of the unfortunate accident, but I did not believe him, as he told us also that there was a Force 12 gale at the time, and anyone could put a ship on the spit in a Force 12, with snow flurries obscuring the marks on shore and covering the bridge windows with ice. The alternative is to stay out in the fjord as they did last year when two were lost, one aground and one capsized, hove down perhaps by just such a sudden cross sea as the one that belted *Tzu Hang*, but on a larger scale. Perhaps radar reflectors on the channel buoys might help a trawler to come in, for there is good shelter once a ship is in the harbour.

We tied to an Icelandic ship which was immediately invaded by a crowd of tow-headed children, so that they might have a better look at us and the cat. In pleasant contrast to Japanese students they made no attempt to invade us. Isafjord is a lovely place. The great fjord and the mountains behind; the streets clean, the houses good, and the shops neat and well filled, the children so blond and merry, the jerseys so colourful, and the people friendly.

Standing outside one shop we saw a boy from a British trawler. He was about seventeen and was wearing blue jeans, white woollen stockings turned down over short sea boots, a Faroe jersey, and a white woollen cap over his blond hair that reached to his shoulder. Inside the shop was his mate, similarly dressed but with no cap on his unkempt dark hair, which was considerably shorter than his friend's. He had just succeeded in selling a box of Hull chocolates at black-market prices to the girl behind the counter. Now he came out to his friend who was also hugging a parcel.

'Goo on, lad,' he said, 'she'll tak 'em. Give the' a good price intiet' bargain.'

'Noah,' said woollen cap.

'Well, give 'em ter me then. Ah'll fix un for the'.'

Woollen cap handed over his parcel and received in due course the good price. We asked them both on board. One was quite at home, talking to Beryl with assurance, but woollen cap, when asked below, said 'Noah'.

I went up again and sat in the cockpit and asked him about his job. In a short time all his oppressive shyness had gone as he told me about trawling. About gales, about their eighteen-hour day, about the frantic fight against ice in bad conditions and about good captains and bad captains, good catches and poor. I was soon thinking that it isn't short hair that makes the man.

From Isafjord we sailed round Cape Horn, the lovely north-western point of Iceland, which does look like Cape Horn. Now we were in Denmark Strait, where the *Bismark* was shadowed by two British cruisers, H.M.S. *Norfolk* and H.M.S. *Suffolk*, and where I had often wished to go. I tried to imagine them on the edge of the fog as we sailed north until we were sure that we had crossed the Arctic Circle, and then down to Sigulfjord. We arrived, rather late in the evening, when the still mountains on each side of the entrance were lit with a golden light. There is never a harsh colour in Iceland, all green and blues, brown and gold, all mellowed and blended as if by age, all preserved by cold and washed by rain, all often lightly veiled in mist or bracketed by rainbows.

At Sigulfjord next morning we tied up to a wharf where there were rows of red-painted tables for off-loading and washing fish, and rows and rows of wooden barrels for salted herrings. The harbourmaster came on board and invited us to a lunch of fresh fried trout and a bath at his home. Then he drove us round in his car, also a Russian one. He took us to a fish-canning factory where girls worked during the season for twelve hours—two shifts each of six hours, although the extra time was voluntary. They were busy as bees, fingers flying, and some so pretty that they looked as if they should not be working at all. He also took us to a fish-meal factory where herrings were brought on conveyor belts straight from the ship to huge cisterns where they decomposed. When a certain stage had been reached they were spun so that the oil and the flesh for fish meal were separated. The smell was so awful that we only got as far as the first cistern in our pursuit of knowledge, and then fled, handkerchiefs to our mouths and noses and much to the delight of two old Icelanders, who were stirring the hell broth.

The harbourmaster drove us up a new road that was being constructed along the coast. There we saw some of the black and white sheep, with wool like the Shetland wool, which are typical of the country. During the winter, he told us, they used to be sheltered in turf houses near the sea, so that they might eat seaweed. Now I think that they have more sophisticated fare.

From Sigulfjord we sailed to Grimsey, an island that we had already seen from the hill above the harbour, but which took us until next day to reach, as at first we had no wind at all and later we had plenty of wind right on the nose. It is a green island on the Arctic Circle. Its western face is low with jagged rocky points and basalt pillars enclosing shingle beaches, but its eastern face is high and perpendicular. The island is about three miles long and a mile wide at its widest point and has a small port and a fishing village.

There were three English trawlers there, over a hundred years old, and now owned by Faroe Islanders, who had put in for the weekend. The cook was a young man who spoke English fluently. He came on board with the captain, his father-in-law, and whilst they drank a glass of rum they showed us where to go in the Faroes.

In the afternoon we walked to the lighthouse at the southern end. The basalt columns, like bundles of pencils, reminded us of the Giant's Causeway in Northern Ireland. The village policeman, wearing a fur cap, was cutting the cheeks from codheads, from a catch brought in that morning, and the harbour was full of kittiwakes, so bloated with offal from the cod that they could hardly fly. The island was the haunt of hundreds of thousands of Arctic tern, which favoured the rocks on the lower southern and eastern shores. Everywhere dead tern were lying, but only because of the normal mortality amongst the vast numbers that were there, which took to wing in plaintive hordes as we walked along the beach. The high cliffs of the eastern coast belonged to the fulmars. They were nesting there. The turf overhung the cliff in places like snow cornices, but in places we could approach the very edge, and look down almost a thousand feet to the sea below. There fulmars held their position almost stationary in the wind and only a few feet from us, or turned and slid past, turning their heads to look at us, bodies and wings immobile on the updraught from the cliffs.

Back on *Tzu Hang*, Stanley, the cook from the trawler, gave us some of the fish cakes fried in batter that he had cooked for the crew. He had two baby puffins that they had taken from the cliffs and were carrying back to the islands. At least they weren't short of a fishy diet, and seemed quite at home on his arm. The trawlers left next day but their place was taken by some Icelandic trawlers, with whom we exchanged visits. They drank our rum and brought us *styr* (a cottage cheese), bread, and smoked mutton as gifts. We went back to them for coffee. Grimsey is a very worthwhile place to visit but the harbour is shallow and the breakwater offers little protection if the wind blows up from the south-west. Then it is time to seek the protection of the other side of the island.

We left on September 5th, but just managed to creep away under sail, for we were now in the centre of a slow-moving high, which remained almost stationary over Iceland for the next few days, keeping us with it. It was cold in the cabin, down to 34 degrees, and it was not until the 9th that we got any wind. Next day we were wrapped in wet mist and it was only on September 11th that we sighted Kadluir light on Kalso. It turned out to be the stern light of a fisherman, but I guessed that he would be fishing just outside the ten-mile limit, and soon after we spotted a light again. This one was definitely flashing every ten seconds and not dipping behind the waves.

It was my watch again. Daylight was coming and yet I could not see the land. The light blinked paler now, and well above the horizon. Then gradually, like hands spread out to welcome the day, mountains and fjords took shape before me. A landfall of superb beauty. A land for fairies, gremlins, and trolls; a land of rock castles and caves and flying buttresses; all in the golden light of a rain-washed sky.

As we closed them and picked out Kalso Fjord, which leads down to Klagsvik, the mountains grew taller and the sides of the fjords more austere. In front of us there was a trawler dwarfed by the cliffs, which butted their heads into the clouds above. The wind had gone light and we wallowed slowly on until it suddenly blew fresh and squally out of the fjord. We tacked backwards and forwards across the entrance in short tacks, and once we were fairly in and the water calm, took down our sails and motored up the fjord towards Klagsvik. At times the cliffs fell sheer to the water, at times there was a narrow stretch of sloping or terraced grass field below the black rocks. Here the hay was drying on wire stretched between posts. Where the cliffs relented and allowed some small fields to appear, there was a hamlet. The red roofs of well-built wooden houses clustered near the water, and below the houses there was a wooden boat ramp, where boats were pulled up into a communal boathouse. Houses, boats, and boathouse, terraced fields and cows all looked like toys beneath the cliffs that propped up the grey ceiling on each side of the fjord.

The Faroes, like Iceland, rely almost entirely on the fishing industry for their wealth, but the standard of living looks high. The wooden houses are large and well kept, painted in many colours as in Iceland. The boats are all of a Scandinavian type with a high double sheer, and even the smallest have a Viking look about them. In the new church in Klagsvik one has been hoisted to the ceiling to remind all comers that the men of the Faroes seek their living on the sea. There were one or two houses that had turf roofs, but the majority were shingled.

Again we were treated with the utmost friendliness. We had two tours of the town—one with the harbourmaster and one with the family who ran the laundry. By now we were getting quite experts in the fish-canning plants and here we saw the most modern, which skinned, headed, tailed, and boned the fish on a conveyor belt. We carried away with us a large assortment of delicious pickled herring in the most elegant tins. We left Klagsvik on September 14th with only two hundred and fifty miles to go to Stornoway in the Hebrides, but just as when we left Iceland we were dogged by frustrating calms and head winds, and it was not until the 19th when Charles had run out of cigarettes, that we saw the Butt of Lewis.

As we saw the cape, the wind came fresh at last and we stormed down to it close hauled, with *Tzu Hang* flinging a short sea all over the place. We passed the lighthouse in the afternoon and the wind dropped again in the evening, so that we motored through the northern Minch and came in the morning to Stornoway, where we had been eight years before.

It was in fact the end of a passage east about round the world, although we had never set out to make a circumnavigation, nor thought of our voyage as an attempt to make one. We had gone where we listed and had finally come to a port that we had visited at the beginning. Ahead was the same berth, the only berth available, under the public lavatory, that we had used before. *Tzu Hang* was flying her quarantine flag, and as she edged up to the quay she passed a converted trawler, now making summer cruises with passengers about the islands. On her deck was a stalwart woman in a blue jersey and wearing a beret, a veritable Britannia, with who knows what desire to have travelled far in her own ship.

'Look,' we heard her say to her companion, 'they've come from abroad,' and as we passed she hailed us in a voice that might have reached a royal yard.

'Well done,' she cried, 'Well done.'

We took it that she was addressing *Tzu Hang*. Good, loyal, sometimes abused but ever loved, *Tzu Hang*.

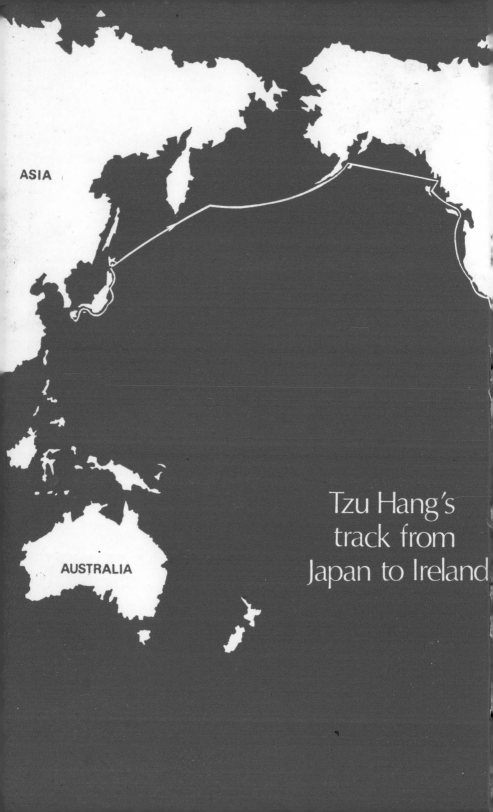

ASIA

AUSTRALIA

Tzu Hang's
track from
Japan to Ireland